Measuring National Income in the Centrally Planned Economies

In 1991 "communism" collapsed. The cold war was over and the West had won. Whole cities, Moscow, St. Petersburg, Warsaw, Beijing, Budapest and Bucharest – indeed, whole countries – were privatised for nothing or next to nothing. This was probably the greatest expansion of the world market in history. And yet, according to national income measurements of the Central Intelligence Agency, the Organisation for Economic Co-operation and Development, the World Bank and the International Monetary Fund, this gigantic expansion of market production, led to a decline in market production in the very countries where it was introduced. How to explain this paradox?

This book traces the origin of the West's national income measurements, from their origin in the *Balance* of 1923/4 developed in the USSR to the United States in the early 1930s via two Soviet exiles, Simon Kuznets and Wassily Leontief, and then back to the USSR again, after a vigorous debate, through a protégé of Kuznets, Abram Bergson. Bergson developed an Adjusted Factor Cost (AFC) imputed national incomes to a centrally planned economy, based on physical not income measurements. This book provides a detailed assessment of the failure of the AFC method to measure the real growth of actual market production during the transition period.

This book provides a detailed account of the application of national income measurements to the centrally planned economies. It assesses all of the major contributors to this debate, including Colin Clark, Naum Jasny, Alexander Gerschenkron, G.Warren Nutter and Abram Bergson. It provides a new, much higher estimate of the expansion of market production during the transition period, based on an estimate of the actual growth of real market production. It discusses the very significant implications of this re-estimate for contemporary theories of globalisation.

William Jefferies has a PhD from Manchester Metropolitan University, UK.

Routledge Studies in the Modern World Economy

Measuring National Income in the Centrally Planned Economies

Why the West underestimated the transition to capitalism

William Jefferies

Routledge
Taylor & Francis Group

LONDON AND NEW YORK

First published 2015
by Routledge

2 Park Square, Milton Park, Abingdon, Oxfordshire OX14 4RN
711 Third Avenue, New York, NY 10017

Routledge is an imprint of the Taylor & Francis Group, an informa business

First issued in paperback 2018

British Library Cataloguing-in-Publication Data
A catalogue record for this book is available from the British Library

Library of Congress Cataloging-in-Publication Data

Jefferies, William, 1965–
  Measuring national income in the centrally planned economies : why the West underestimated the transition to capitalism / William Jefferies.
    pages cm. — (Routledge studies in the modern world economy)
  Includes bibliographical references and index.
  1. National income—Former communist countries.   2. Capitalism—Former communist countries.   3. Former communist countries—Economic conditions.   I. Title.
  HC244.Z9I5173   2014
  339.3'2091717—dc23
  2014024841

ISBN: 978-1-138-81832-3 (hbk)
ISBN: 978-1-138-38387-6 (pbk)

Typeset in Times New Roman
by Apex CoVantage, LLC

To my brother Rob.

Contents

Figures

Tables

Acknowledgements

Thanks to Tony Hines and Paul Brook for their support, encouragement and criticism; to Viv Davies and Hillel Fridman for their helpful comments throughout; to Dave Gaye for his proofing; and to Eleanor Davies for her constancy and love.

Throughout the volume, material has been excerpted from "On the Alleged Stagnation of Capitalism," a forthcoming paper in the *Review of Radical Political Economics*. Permission to print this material is granted by The Union for Radical Political Economics.

Glossary

AFC	Adjusted Factor Cost
BP	British Petroleum
CCA	Capital Consumption Allowance
CCP	Chinese Communist Party
CEE	Central and Eastern Europe
CES	Conference of European Statisticians
CIA	Central Intelligence Agency
CIS	Commonwealth of Independent States
CMEA	Comecon (the Council for Mutual Economic Assistance)
CPE	Centrally Planned Economy
CPSU	Communist Party Soviet Union
EBRD	European Bank of Reconstruction and Development
FDI	Foreign Direct Investment
FSU	Former Soviet Union
G7	Group of Seven: the US, Japan, France, Germany, Italy, UK and Canada
GDP	Gross Domestic Product
GGDC	Groningen Growth and Development Centre
GK	Geary Khamis
GNP	Gross National Product
GSP	Global Social Product
HPE	Historical Planned Economies
IMF	International Monetary Fund
IVA	Inventory Valuation Adjustment
JEC	Joint Economic Council
MIC	Military Industrial Complex
MPS	Material Product System
NBER	National Bureau of Economic Research
NDP	Net Domestic Product
NEP	New Economic Policy
NMP	Net Material Product
NNP	Net National Product
OCC	Organic Composition of Capital

OECD	Organisation of Economic Co-Operation and Development
OICA	International Organization of Motor Vehicle Manufacturers
OSS	Office of Strategic Services
PPP	Purchasing Power Parity
Project RAND	US Air Force Project Research and Development
SEZ	Special Economic Zone
SNA	System of National Accounts
SNIP	Abram Bergson's *The Real National Income of Soviet Russia Since 1928*
SSB	Chinese State Statistical Bureau
tmt	thousand metric Tons
TSSI	Temporal Single System Interpretation
twh	terawatt-hours
UN	United Nations
UNCTAD	United Nations Conference Trade and Development
USGS	United States Geological Survey
USSR	United Soviet Socialist Republics
WSA	World Steel Association
WTO	World Trade Organization

1 Introduction

In 1991 "communism" collapsed with the triumph of the capitalist market. The cold war was over and the West had won. The entire accumulated output of formerly centrally planned economies including entire cities such as Warsaw, Moscow, Beijing, Prague, Leningrad, Sofia, Shanghai, Kiev, Bucharest and Budapest, along with all of the associated infrastructure of a modern society, from hydro schemes to railways, electrical transmission systems, roads, ports and airports were passed to the world's capitalists for nothing or next to nothing. An area encompassing a third of the world's surface and half its population was subject to the rule of capital. For the first time in at least seven decades, a truly global market embraced the entire world.

The old capitalists of the West or the new capitalist classes fashioned from the old state apparatus or trained at the behest of the Central Intelligence Agency (CIA) created a capitalist system that, in the words of the International Monetary Fund (IMF), "destroyed" the old economy (Koen & Marrese 1995, p.1). It was as Yegor Gaidar, the prime minister of Russia and architect of shock therapy, dryly noted "repulsive, thievish and socially unjust" (Spulber 2003, p.314). In the former USSR output collapsed. In Central and Eastern Europe (CEE) the largest falls in production everywhere coincided with the introduction of market prices. The life expectancy of Russian males fell by 10 years (Murrell 1996). East German industries were sold off for a dollar, while the entire privatisation receipts for the total Soviet economy amounted to a meagre US$7.5 billion (Dornbusch & Wolf 1994). The Chinese social security system or "iron rice bowl" was dismantled (Maddison 2006). The old world was destroyed, even if the new world had yet to be built.

The impact of this one-off shock stretched far beyond the transitional economies themselves. The dissolution of the bipolar world meant that the balance of power, however relative, between the old Warsaw bloc and the North Atlantic Treaty Organization (NATO) was replaced by the hegemonic rule of the United States. The neo-liberal counter-reform programme, begun by Thatcher and Reagan, was consolidated across the West, as entire heavy industries were closed and shipped to the so-called emerging markets in this newly created global market. The nationalised industries of dependent, formerly third-world nations were

privatised. Trade barriers were dismantled, tariffs fell and foreign direct investment soared. This was arguably the greatest expansion of the world market in
history.

If national income is a measure of the value of economic production within the
market area, it must have increased as the real market grew. Yet the official statistics turned the world on its head. All of the official agencies responsible for the
measurement of the world economy, the IMF, the World Bank, the Organisation
for Economic Co-operation and Development (OECD), the Commonwealth of
Independent States (CIS) Statistical Commission, the European Bank for Reconstruction and Development (EBRD) and so on measured the expansion of this
new market production, this new national income, as its contraction.

This base-level error was the result of the authorities' method of estimating
"national income" in the centrally planned economies. This method called the
Adjusted Factor Cost (AFC) was developed in the aftermath of the Second World
War. It meant that the categories of the US System of National Accounts (SNA)
were superimposed on, what was acknowledged to be, a non-capitalist economy.
This method imputed national incomes where these incomes did not exist, and so,
as the centrally planned economies collapsed, the creation of national income –
production within a real market boundary – was measured as the collapse of it. In
hock to an ideological method of the AFC, according to these agencies, the expansion of capitalism across a third of the world actually led to its contraction, and
their figures defied the truth.

Measuring National Income refutes this idea. By disaggregating the collapse
of the central plan from the growth of real market production it develops, for the
first time, estimates of the growth of real national income with the growth of real
market production in the transition economies.

Far from the 1990s being a decade of capitalist stagnation, world capitalist
aluminium production increased 60.3%; hydraulic cement, 96%; steel, 56%; electricity, 61%; automobiles, 27%; and gross domestic product (GDP Geary Khamis
[GK] PPP), 52%. By the 2001, when the process of capitalist restoration was
complete, the transition economies accounted for 37% of world capitalist employment, 31% of its aluminium, 44% of its hydraulic cement, 24% of steel, 16%
of electricity, 8.5% of cars and passenger vehicles and 17% of GDP (GK PPP).
The official agencies underestimated the growth of the Chinese economy during
the transition from central planning to capitalism by 20%. They underestimated
the growth of the united German economy, through the incorporation of East Germany into it, by 16%. They underestimated the growth of the market economies in
CEE and the CIS by more than $2.1 trillion (GDP GK PPP). They underestimated
world growth in the 1990s by half.

So how could the official measurements be so wrong? What was the root of this
monumental blunder? How to explain this total failure of official economic theory
in its application to the centrally planned economies?

Measuring National Income shows how all modern systems of national income
measurement were derived from the original *Balance* developed by Soviet theoreticians in 1923 and 1924. The *Balance* was an application of Marx's schemas

of reproduction, published by Engels in 1885, in *Capital Volume II*. The *Balance* measured the value of the material product sector in the commodity economy during the 1921–28 New Economic Policy (NEP). This limitation was criticised at the time, for the exclusion of services and the government sector meant it was unnecessarily narrow. However, the basic application of the method, despite these limitations, formed the template for all subsequent SNAs.

This explains why in every SNA value is created in production and then realised in exchange. A distinction is drawn between property income (the total of rents, interest and profits) or surplus value, in Marx's original schema, and wages or variable capital. It explains why the different sides of national income, whether viewed from the production, demand or income side *balance*. To this day, even though the SNAs mention the labour theory of value nowhere, the growth of national income measures the change in labour hours, plus or minus the change in productivity (an aggregate of changes in the intensity and quality of labour and the organic composition of capital). Leaving aside the essential identity between the *Balance* and the modern SNA, there is an even more compelling reason for appreciating the origin of capitalist national accounts in Marx's *Capital*.

The US SNA was developed by Simon Kuznets, a former member of the Jewish Marxist Bund group and a follower of Georgi Plekhanov, the founder of Russian Marxism and Wassily Leontief, the creator (or rather imitator) of input–output accounting, who had participated in the original Soviet *Balance* debate. Kuznets and Leontief explained that as physical things are incommensurate as use values, or in other words, because there is no fixed correlation between what one physical quantity and another exchanges for on a market, then the physical qualities of things cannot explain their exchange value or price. Consequently there must be some other *value* that determines price. But what was this value? Neither Kuznets nor Leontief ever defined it. They preferred to conceal Marx's definition, the socially necessary labour time required for the production of a commodity, even if they never abandoned its use. This is understandable. They were after all working in the United States, at the behest of the "intelligence community". The choice between Stalin's gulag and America's Ivy League was no choice at all. While in Britain J.M. Keynes, who oversaw the development of the UK national accounts in the late 1930s, referred to Marx's schemes of circulation in his notes to prepare the General Theory, but excluded any reference to them in the published edition. As a result there is no definition of value in the national accounts, other than the assertion that value is the total sum of different values, which is rather like defining *banana* as the sum of bananas.[1]

Measuring National Income shows how the determination of Kuznets and Leontief to have value without value theory, to separate value from its location in exchange value, and more specifically the socially necessary labour time required for the production of a commodity and measured in exchange, was mirrored in the Soviet Union during the plan period. From 1930, Stalinist theoreticians abandoned the historical nature of Marx's categories, rooted in the actual social relations of production. Instead, they asserted that although there was no exchange at market prices in the centrally planned economy of the

USSR, commodities, that is the things produced for sale on a market existed, even though nothing was produced for sale on a market or indeed sold at market prices. The "sale" of labour was no real sale at all. The quantity of labour and the quantity and quality of consumer goods were established in physical terms by planners in advance. A conscious disproportion between the physical quantity of consumer goods supplied and the amount that could be theoretically purchased was established. This shortage affected neither the quantity supplied nor the "price" of supply. Rather, it ensured that all consumer goods were consumed, hence the queues.

Stalin resolved this irresolvable contradiction by insisting that that the law of value, the law that regulates production in a capitalist economy, existed in the centrally planned economy, only not as a regulator of production. The retention of the notion of *value* in the planned economy assisted the Stalinist apparatus in concealing its exploitation of the working class. This meant the accurate accounting of real socially necessary labour times was impossible, given that criticism of such inaccuracy, and therefore wastefulness, was likely to be met with a bullet to the back of the head or an ice pick in Trotsky's case.

This logic chopping was reflected in the *Materialy*, a planning document drawn up for the first years of the plan period in 1930. It created a new measure of "national income" in the centrally planned economy, based on aggregates of concrete but not on social labour hours. There was no mechanism to transform individual labour into social labour in the USSR, as there was neither exchange though a market nor any workers' democracy or control whatsoever. This was no communist society as understood by Marx and Engels but a "communist" society in which a parasitical apparatus extracted surplus labour from the workers and farmers. The direct producers could not compare the fruits of their labours because the dictatorship denied any democracy in society. Wages were driven down to provide resources for investment, with the terror of state execution or of the gulag inflicted on the population to ensure producers' compliance. There was exploitation, but the mechanism of surplus extraction was not a market one. This was no capitalist society.

The use of concrete labour hours to create some notion of value – where none actually existed – was reflected in an unresolved debate around the validity of Soviet statistics in the Western intelligence and academic community. It was eventually concluded that the statistics of the plan apparatus measured quantities of real things, whether in tons of steel, pairs of shoes, square metres of housing or labour hours expended, but although these figures were "true" – more or less as rough measures of inputs and outputs in the central plan – they were untrue as measures of value, of socially necessary labour time. There could be no value without exchange value and no national income without a wage market that responded to supply and demand, without profits to capitalists, interest to bankers or rent to landlords.

Measuring National Income shows how it was nonetheless, a modified form of these official statistics that provided the basis for all the subsequent Western estimates of Soviet "national income". Abram Bergson, a student of Kuznets and

Leontief and from the war on the head of first, the Office of Strategic Services (OSS) Russian division and, then, the US Air Force's Project Research and Development (Project RAND), developed an AFC to measure the central plan according to the categories of the Western SNA. The AFC eliminated the turnover tax, subsidies and profits that were used by the apparatus as components of various aggregates when valued at prevailing prices and then added notional amounts for returns to fixed and working capital and land. The AFC ultimately provided the foundation for all official Western estimates of Soviet "national income", and although Bergson acknowledged the limits of his method, he used quotation marks whenever referring to the "national income" of the Soviet centrally planned economy. As the years went by, these limits were forgotten and the quotation marks disappeared.

The attempts of Western theorists to measure Soviet "national income" saw much innovation in comparative techniques. In 1939 Colin Clark, a colleague of Keynes and one of the first statisticians to apply gross national product (GNP) measurements to the British economy, developed the first-ever application of purchasing power parity (PPP). Unconvinced about the reality of Soviet apparatus prices, Clark priced estimates of twelve key Soviet physical outputs in UK pounds to develop estimates of the "value" of Soviet output. Clark also extended the coverage of his national income estimates to include the services sector and pointed out how the different calculation of depreciation in the central plan, based on a nominal installation or "historic" cost, meant that Soviet depreciation was underestimated and the output of its economy, therefore, overestimated. The issues of coverage and depreciation became two of the defining features of alternative Western measurements over the years.

Alexander Gerschenkron followed Clark in using a type of PPP estimate, although in his version based on the output of machinery. Gerschenkron's major innovation was to point to the importance of index year relativity in influencing the estimate of the growth of national income. All national income estimates aim to measure the change in real output, the actual value added in a given period, through the aggregation of the actual price that commodities exchange for on a market. But they need to differentiate between the real growth in value production from inflation, a change in price without any change in value. This is particularly difficult in a period when the economy is going through an industrial revolution, such as the USSR experienced in the 1930s. Manufactured goods were "priced", not sold, based on an administrative estimate of the average installation cost during the first three years of production. As productivity increased the amount of physical outputs relative to the amount of physical inputs, the amount of concrete labour hours required to produce a given output, was reduced and so the administrative "price" fell. As a result, estimates of national income based on the base year – the Paasche index – would be higher than those based on the later given year – the Laspreyes index – as the installation "price" of machinery was higher in the base year than in the given year. There is no reason in principle for preferring either the base or the given year. They show different rates of growth, illustrating both the physical increase in output and the change in the structure of production.

The Soviet apparatus preferred the base year, to provide the best possible measurement of the growth in output, whereas the West preferred the given year, to provide the worst.

Naum Jasny, another Menshevik exile now working the United States, developed the final major contribution to the debate on measuring Soviet output. Jasny accepted Clark's general estimates, but rather than measuring the output of the Soviet centrally planned economy by comparing it to the prices of output in a capitalist market economy, Jasny used detailed Soviet price manuals to "correct" national income estimates for the subjectivity of the apparatus. This method was much criticised by supporters of Bergson as being subjective itself. This issue was essentially irresolvable as the absence of market prices meant that there was no objective standard against which to judge the subjective estimates. There could be no definitive answer by definition.

Measuring National Income shows how Bergson's building-block method was generalised across the new centrally planned economies of central and eastern Europe and then into China. Objections from economists as varied as Alec Nove, the noted historian of Soviet history; G. Warren Nutter, Milton Friedman's first graduate student, who was commissioned by the National Bureau of Economic Research (NBER) to produce alternative estimates for the Eisenhower administration; and P.J.D. Wiles, a neoclassical economist based at the London School of Economics (LSE), were brushed aside. Instead, the CIA and then the United Nations (UN) established a commission to reconcile the Material Product System (MPS), the centrally planned accounting system and the SNA. No difference of principle was considered to exist between the two alternative accounting systems. In spite of the intensity of the cold war, the economic differences between "communism" and capitalism were reduced to the "manipulation of accounting items in different ways".

The application of the figures to China was overseen by Simon Kuznets, who, working on behalf of Abram Bergson, oversaw a number of studies that applied the AFC to China's central plan. Their work was hindered by the Great Leap Forward (1958–61) and then the Cultural Revolution (1966–71), which abolished the state statistical section. The official data that provided the basis for Western estimates of Soviet national output were simply wiped out. It was only fully restored with the advent of the pro-market reform programme begun by Deng Xiaoping in 1978. Over the next decade and a half, the step-by-step reintroduction of market prices in China transformed the economy from a centrally planned one into a form of state capitalism. The state retained ownership of the largest 1,000 enterprises, but market prices now determined the proportions in which goods exchanged in the vast bulk of the economy. Various Western estimates were made of China's national income during the transition period by economists such as Angus Maddison, Ren Rouen, Thomas Rawski, Carlsten Holz and Harry X. Wu. They all sought to correct the distorted prices of the planned period and replace them with truer, if not "true", prices of their own. In so doing they conveniently obliterated the distinction between the central plan and market economies and replaced the real market boundary with an imputed one of their own that imagined what things would have been like if the central plan did not exist.

Measuring National Income provides the first detailed critique of the application of these Western measures to the transition of the central plan to a market economy. It considers the means by which official agencies were able to escape their ideological predisposition to underestimate the size of the original planned economy and to revise down the fall that occurred with capitalist restoration. In an extreme expression of this tendency, the neoconservative adviser to the Yeltsin administration, Anders Aslund, concluded that the entire idea of an output collapse in the former USSR and CEE with the end of the central plan in the 1990s was a "myth". This study shows that the collapse of planned production was no myth. There was a real and phenomenally deep economic crisis there, with the aggregate of physical output falling even faster than after the Nazi invasion of 1941. The point that the Western and now the Eastern commentariat entirely failed to notice was that this was not a fall in national income but, rather, a consequence of its growth. National income – output within the market boundary – massively expanded, and as a result the total physical output of the centrally planned economy slumped. Even in China where there was an exponential increase in production following the introduction of market reforms, the growth of real national income was underestimated by a striking $765,376 (GDP GK PPP), or 19.8% (see Table 4.18). By failing to measure the real growth of real national income in the real market boundary, or in other words, by failing to measure the very thing the SNA was designed for, the imputed figures of the Western agencies demonstrated their real redundancy in practice.

Measuring National Income develops the first estimates of the growth of real national income in the real market boundary during the transition period. By disaggregating the output of the central plan from that of the market, it is able to trace the collapse of planned production in CEE and the CIS and its gradual replacement by market output in China. This method applies deflators drawn from official estimates of the growth of the market to various key physical outputs, steel, hydraulic cement, aluminium, electricity and automobiles, to reflect the transition of key sectors of the real economy. It also deflates GDP (GK PPP) from the Groningen Growth and Development Centre (GGDC) to separate the growth of the market from the decline of the plan. The striking results of this new method prove that the growth of output within the market boundary was indeed a growth of capitalist national income. The growth of the market was a consequence of the decline of the plan. The results of this new method, illustrated in Table 1.1, transform our understanding of the empirical growth of the world market. Its significance can scarcely be overstated.

Measuring National Income reviews the post-transition debate among neoclassical theorists. The collapse of production with the introduction of the market had been no more anticipated by these theoreticians than had been the end of the plan itself. In 1980 Bergson hosted a conference that produced estimates of Soviet output until the new millennium. On one side of the argument Stephen Rosefielde

Table 1.1 World total, capitalist and centrally planned production various physical indicators and GDP percentage change

	1990–99	1999–2010	1990–2010
Electricity			
Total	24	45	80
Capitalist	44	52	120
CPE	–68	–100	–100
Aluminium			
Total	24	73	115
Capitalist	45	86	169
CPE	–56	–100	–100
Hydraulic Cement			
Total	30	107	185
Capitalist	60	123	275
CPE	–62	–100	–100
Steel			
Total	2.3	81	85
Capitalist	39	96	163
CPE	–78	–100	–100
Automobiles			
Total	16	39	61
Capitalist	21	41	71
CPE	–63	–100	–100
GDP			
Total	30	56	112
Capitalist	42	61	129
CPE	–63	–100	–100

Sources: British Petroleum (BP; 2012), US Geological Survey (USGS; 1989–2011), World Steel Association (WSA; 1989–2011), International Organization of Motor Vehicle Manufacturers (OICA; 1990–2010), and GGDC (2012).

Note: GDP in millions of 1990 US$ GK PPP, 1991–99.

pointed out that because output was never sold in this non-market economy, how could the functioning of the market be imputed to it? He concluded that as nothing was sold and as sales are a measure of use in the neoclassical model, so nothing useful was produced either. On the other side, Mark Harrison defended the CIA and Bergson. Harrison pointed that that useful stuff had been produced and that as use is a measure for value in the neo-classical model, so value must have been produced too. Neither side was able to appreciate that this was a non-market economy that produced use values but not exchange values. The limits of the neoclassical method were starkly illustrated by the failings of both sides.

Measuring National Income discusses how its new disaggregated method for the measurement of national income during the transition period has an impact on various contemporary theories of globalisation. It considers the ramifications of its new understanding on various other measurements of the economy such as productivity and profitability and discusses how the one-off expansion of the world market as a result of the transition of the centrally planned economies to capitalism led to the transformation of the world economy and created a new period of capitalist development or a long wave in it.

Note

1 Steve Keen criticises Keynes for this ambiguity and argues in favour of Marx's schemes of circulation as described in Volume II of *Capital* (Marx 1992). Keen (2011) provides a very thorough summary of the contradictions of contemporary neo-classical economics. Fundamentally, Keen argues these contradictions arise from a misconceived attempt to model an imaginary economy in terms of a harmonious static equilibrium. Keynes General Theory ([1936] 2008) has long since demonstrated that static equilibrium is a special case that never exists in the real world, hence Keynes's emphasis on the general case and, indeed, the title of his book. Keen makes some pointed comments around the attempts of modern day Marxians to "solve" Marx's transformation of values into prices, the transformation problem. Marx's transformation model describes how value shifts between capitals of different compositions in response to the competitive tendency to equalise profit rates. According to Keen this model fails to meet the conditions demanded by static equilibrium. This criticism was originally demonstrated by von Bortkiewicz (1907) and was repeated most effectively in recent times by Ian Steedman (1977). Keen points out that the attempts of latter day Marxians to solve this problem have failed. Their acceptance of the premise of static equilibrium precludes a solution. Keen also rejects Marx's solution for this violation of static equilibrium, that is the very thing for which he criticises neoclassical economics. Ironically, this is the very strength of Marx's solution; it demonstrates that the transition from values into prices is one of dynamic disequilibrium that is, and it accords with the actual dynamic of the market economy itself, as, indeed, von Bortkiewicz recognised right back at the beginning.

References

BP, 2012. *BP Statistical Review of World Energy 2012*. London: BP. Available at: http://www. bp.com/assets/bp_internet/globalbp/globalbp_uk_english/reports_and_publications/ statistical_energy_review_2011/STAGING/local_assets/pdf/ WSA, World Steel Association, Brussels. Available at: http://www.worldsteel.org/statistics/statistics-archive/ annual-steel-archive.html.statistical_review_of_world_energy_full_report_2012.pdf. USGS, United States Geographical Survey, Washington D.C. Available at: http://minerals. usgs.gov/minerals/pubs/commodity/myOICA, World automobile production statistics, Paris. Available at: http://oica.net/category/production-statistics/.b/.

Davies, Dornbusch, R., & Wolf, H., 1994. East German Economic Reconstruction. In O.J. Blanchard, K.A. Froot, & J.D. Sachs, eds., *The Transition in Eastern Europe*. Chicago: University of Chicago Press, 155–190.

Keen, S., 2011. *Debunking Economics*. Second revised & enlarged edition. London: Zed Books Ltd.

Keynes, J.M., (1936) 2008. *The General Theory of Employment, Interest and Money*. London: BN Publishing.

Koen, V., Marrese M., 1995. *Stabilization and Structural Change in Russia*. 1992–94. IMF Working Paper No. 95/13 New York: IMF.

Marx, K., 1992. *Capital Volume II*. Second edition. London: Penguin Classics.

Maddison, A. 2006. *The World Economic, a Millennial Perspective*. Paris: OECD.

Murrell, Peter. How Far Has Transition Progressed? *Journal of Economic Perspectives* 10(2): 25–44.

Spulber, N., 2003. *Russia's Economic Transformations: From Late Tsarism to the New Millennium*, Cambridge: Cambridge University Press.

Steedman, I., 1977. *Marx after Sraffa*. Oxford: NLB.

US Geological Survey, 1989–2011. *Minerals Yearbook Vol. I—Metals and Minerals*. Washington, DC: US Geological Survey. Available at: http://minerals.usgs.gov/minerals/pubs/commodity/myb/.

von Bortkiewicz, L., 1907. Wertrechnung und Preisrechnung im Marxschen System. *Archiv für Sozialwissenschaft und Sozialpolitik* 25: 10–51, 445–88. (Reprinted in Value and Price in the Marxian System, *International Economic Papers* 2 [1952]: 5–60.)

World Steel Association, 1989–2011. Annual Crude Steel Production Archive. Available at: www.worldsteel.org/statistics/statistics-archive/annual-steel-archive.html

2   The measurement of Soviet economic growth

2.1   The five-year plans

The Bolshevik Revolution of 1917 overthrew capitalism in the former czarist empire. Disappointed that the hoped for international revolution never arrived, the young Soviet Republic somehow survived a period of bitter civil war from 1918 through 1921, but at a tremendous price. Much of the economy was destroyed as everything was subordinated to the military struggle for survival, the intolerable burdens of which were only partially lifted with the defeat of the counter-revolutionary "White" armies in 1921, as the Bolshevik victory was combined with the ruthless destruction of democracy throughout society. The Kronstadt rebellion was crushed, internal party factions banned and the one party rule of the bureaucratic apparatus established. The NEP of 1921 used market measures to revive an economy destroyed by civil war. It combined a state capitalist nationalised industrial sector in which until 1927 enterprises were required to make profits with a rural free market economy (Baykov 1970, p.426). But the NEP was a system fraught with contradictions. The very market measures that had revived the economy revived the capitalist classes that had been overthrown in the 1917 revolution. This threatened the rule of the Soviet apparatus, so the NEP was abandoned in 1927/8 and from "socialism at a snail's pace" (Cohen 1980), the slogan coined by Nikolai Bukharin, the leader of the party's right, a programme of forced collectivisation and autarchic planning was introduced. In just four years the Soviet economy was transformed into a system of ultra-centralist top-down planning (Harrison 1994).

The market and market prices were abolished. The foundation on which the Western SNA was built was done away with. Instead, a bureaucratic apparatus determined all decisions of production and consumption for society as a whole, using a plan based on physical inputs and outputs (Nove 1977). Initially, Gosplan, the planning ministry, prepared "control figures". These formed tentative aggregate targets for a limited number of strategic outputs and inputs. Projected supplies of these inputs were supposed to correspond to nominal output targets. Agencies exercising operational control – the ministries, *glavnoe upravlenie* or *glavki* or "enterprises" – then elaborated the control figures into more detailed targets during negotiations with subordinate agencies.

After approval by the party and the government, the plan was submitted to the ministries as an operational directive. More detailed programmes were then worked out for subordinate agencies (Bergson 1964, pp.135–37). R.W. Davies[1] noted that

> [i]n such an economy the processes by which resources are allocated must evidently be different in kind from those of competitive economies. If there are to be prices, they cannot be market-determined, and must be fixed by the government or the planning authority: hence neither the level of investment nor its allocation between different uses can be determined through a self-adjusting price mechanism. (1958, p.140)

Each production unit or enterprise sought to minimise its targets, the quantity of output required of it, and to maximise its inputs, the amount of physical resources available to it. The hoarding of labour, machinery and raw materials was a constant feature of the plan. Managers used informal trade networks to supplement allocated inputs, albeit at state prices and through the state bank to meet plan targets (Berliner 1957). Naum Jasny commented "[t]hat the ultimate receivers pay the fixed price for the goods received by them is merely secondary. It does not impart to the transactions the character of a market" (1951a, p.10).

The nature of the central plan had important implications for the quality of statistical information available to Western analysts. The hierarchical centre required accurate information to plan the economy. At the same time, subordinates, from ministries to enterprise heads and workers on piece rates, were rewarded according to that same data. They received bonuses for meeting targets and suffered punishment for their failure to do so. The regime exaggerated its achievements to reinforce its legitimacy. There was no such thing as independent information. By 1960 there were an estimated 2.5 million persons directly employed in keeping and processing records. Even so, the data were selective, ambiguous and overstated. Slow-growing industries and the fast-growing military sector were both under-represented. Categories were blurred. Primary sources did not contain adequate definitions of industries in terms of the administrative and territorial coverage, the product coverage and the stage of fabrication at which output was being measured. There was a general overstatement of absolute levels of output but within limits defined by the material interests of the various participants (Grossman 1960).

R.W. Davies, a Stalinist economist who collaborated with E.H. Carr on a mammoth history of the foundations of the planned economy, published a summary of the official statistics in 1991. Davies's summary took advantage of the opening of the Soviet archive opened after Glasnost. Davies observed that Soviet statistics omitted data that presented unfavourable developments, used current prices without acknowledging the effect of inflation/deflation, modified definitions to "improve" performance and reduced the range of material through the 1930s, but he concluded that "in spite of all these deficiencies, nearly all

Western economists and economic historians agree that on many matters Soviet statistics can be rendered reliable if they are carefully scrutinized and adjusted" (Davies et al., 1991, p.2). The system of top-down command planning remained essentially unaltered, despite the various reform initiatives until 1985 when Gorbachev became the general secretary of the Communist Party of the Soviet Union (CPSU). He oversaw the abolition of the central plan by the end of the 1980s (Gregory 2004, p.245).

Plan prices were passive inasmuch as they were used at all. The value of the stock of means of production and housing was based on its physical characteristics (Kaplan, 1963; Moorsteen 1962). Depreciation of the means of production was measured on the basis of wear and tear rather than obsolescence (Jasny 1951a, p.89). A controlled "market" had a limited role in the distribution of consumer goods in periods when direct rationing did not operate, but changes in demand did not affect the quantity, quality or type of consumer goods supplied or their price. They did not increase or diminish the size of the employed workforce. There was no profit, no interest and no rent. An accounting form of profit did appear during the 1960s, as the apparatus sought to use quasi-market measures to stimulate the plan. They hoped that by enabling enterprises to retain a portion of the social surplus, they could increase incentives to raise productivity. This initiative conflicted with the taut planning of the centre, increased disproportionalities and added to the plan crisis. Even so this was not profit as understood in the capitalist West. It was not a surplus value realised on sale. In the capitalist West national income is based on an actual record of sales at actual prices in the here and now; in contrast, Soviet "national income" measurements were produced *post factum* (Davies 1985 p.44). Physical deliveries were not matched with their financial equivalent (Gregory 2004, p.241). They reflected but did not affect planning decisions. Private ownership of the means of production and capital accumulation were outlawed, peasant farming based on individual plots abolished, and working class consumption subordinated to investment. Abram Bergson, the director of the Soviet section of the US wartime OSS, explained:

> The characteristics which have led the writer to call the present investigation a study in socialist economics are several: first, the ownership and administration of the bulk of the community's industrial resources by the government: second, the direction and integration of this sector, though it is true with varying effectiveness, by a system of planning: and finally, the differential wage system. . . . the last characteristic, it will appear, distinguishes the Soviet economy from the ideal, communism, rather than from competing systems. (1944, p.6)

This system of bureaucratic central planning raised the question of whether "value" was produced in this non-market economy. Marx's categories applied to a historically specific and limited form of economy, a capitalist one based on generalised commodity production:

The product of labour is an object of utility in all states of society: but it is only a historically specific epoch of development which presents the labour expended in the production of a useful article as an objective property of that article: i.e., as its value. It is only then that the product of labour becomes transformed into a commodity. (Marx 1982, p.153)

Marx's categories were historical; they were developed from and were specific to the capitalist mode of production: "Marx consistently denied the law of value would operate after the end of commodity production" (Meek 1956, p.259). The centrality of commodity exchange for value measures was supported by Ludwig von Mises, the key proponent of Austrian marginalism. Von Mises (1975) considered that because socialist production was never exchanged, it was impossible to establish its price or value. This point, at first sight, a semantic argument of little importance, goes to the heart of the dispute around the relevance of national income measures to the centrally planned economy.

2.2   The social content of value

In a capitalist economy it is not the total number of hours worked that determines the value of production but the total of the socially necessary hours worked. Two identical commodities, which have taken unequal amounts of individual labour, will embody a larger or smaller share of the labour of society or labour in general. Competition establishes the proportion of this general labour for any individual commodity; it is nothing more than the process whereby individual labour times are merged into one, the average for that commodity or the socially necessary labour time required for its production. This price will be modified by the movement of value between sectors to equalise profit rates, but all things being equal, only this single average price, when multiplied by the quantity of commodities sold, can equal the total labour time taken to produce these various commodity producers: "[i]ndividual labour contains general human labour only in so far as it is socially necessary" (Engels 1975, p.372). This distinction between the physical quantity of labour hours worked and the proportion of them that is socially necessary was developed by David Ricardo and formed a key part of Marx's later theory. If value is measured by the concrete quantity of physical labour expended then less efficient labour will have a higher value than more efficient labour will: "if the value of a commodity is determined by the quantity of labour spent on it, the more idle and unskilful the labourer, the more valuable would his commodity be" (Engels 1975, p.372). Market competition ensures that "it is the quantity of labour required for its production, not the realized form of that labour, by which the amount of the value of a commodity is determined" (Marx, 1982, p.677). However, in the centrally planned economy, Naum Jasny, a Soviet exile who developed estimates of plan output in the 1940s and 1950s, noted that "disregard of cost and all kinds of waste are among the principal weaknesses of the Soviet system" (1951a, p.9). As a result,

[t]here is no such close correlation in the Soviet economy between production costs and selling prices (the latter being understood as minus turnover taxes resting on the finished goods: turnover taxes on raw materials are part of the costs) as is observed in a private economy. Such a normal procedure as adding an appropriate profit to the production costs and accepting the total as the approximate selling price is inapplicable to the Soviet economy. (Jasny, 1951a p.84)

Workers could be cajoled into work through a combination of direct repression and piece rates, but if production units were allocated a larger quantity of inputs to produce a smaller quantity of outputs, they received a higher payment. They were rewarded for their inefficiency.

In a capitalist mode of production concrete labour times incorporate both necessary labour time, the amount of labour required to reproduce the labourer, and surplus labour time, the amount of labour above that minimum. The act of exchange expresses their sum and provides the objective basis for the measurement of national income. In the centrally planned economies no such mechanism existed. The apparatus did not separate necessary from surplus labour. Such transparency would have rendered the position of the dictatorial apparatus at the head of a nominally socialist and even communist "state" impossible. The financial aggregates of the central plan obscured the real relations of production. Planned prices were arbitrary and subjective. Enterprises received different quantities of inputs and therefore, different quantities of their nominal rouble unit of account to produce different quantities of outputs, "valued" at different amounts. These amounts did not correspond even approximately to the surplus product. Some surplus labour time was incorporated in the various taxes and margins, but it was impossible to cost these labour times, even in the aggregate, accurately. Much labour was socially unnecessary, duplicated, remedial or hoarded. If transposed to a market economy this wasted labour did not add to total output. Thus, the aggregation of concrete labour hours in order to convert them to notional market values overstated "national income" in the USSR.

Forced labour robbed the worker of the self-discipline needed to harmonise labour times in the absence of competition. There could be no universal standard of labour to replace money as the universal equivalent. In a capitalist system, money forces labour times towards the average and eliminates the inefficient as enterprises make losses and go bust. In the USSR there was no such mechanism: "Technically the procedure is that the losses of individual enterprises are offset by profits, if any, of the same 'glavnoe upravlenie' (glavki) or trust (immediate subdivisions of the commissariats)" (Jasny 1951a, p.84). This increased the total aggregated concrete labour time in a way that was incompatible with a market economy. Capitalist accountancy and the Western system of national accounts could not be applied to it.

Richard Moorsteen, a collaborator of Bergson and part of the US Air Force's Project RAND, discussed whether Soviet machinery prices were "meaningful" in the sense of accurate indicators of factor costs or market prices (1962 p.8). Moorsteen claimed that there was "no definitive solution" to this question, although he considered that as Soviet prices did not include charges for rent, entrepreneurial profit or interest, it was "impossible to value the marginal product of any factor correctly" (Moorsteen 1962, p.13). "Impossible" seems fairly definitive, but Moorsteen continued, stating that as the price books compiled by planners showed some consistency and inasmuch as industrialisation reduced the administrative "price" for assorted outputs, there was some comparison between the movement of market prices and administrative ones. He concluded that although it was impossible for Soviet prices to be meaningful, this did "not refute the hypothesis that Soviet machinery prices are 'meaningful'" (Moorsteen, 1962, p.13). Even though these points were "inadequate to confirm" they were "meaningful" (Moorsteen 1962, p.13). It was impossible for planned prices to be "meaningful", but this impossibility did not refute their meaningfulness. Mark Harrison, a contemporary defender of Bergson, argues that despite their deficiencies, Soviet data of production, prices, outlays and employment were not arbitrary fabrications:

> they are meaningful (although the meaning was rarely to be found on the surface), are capable of interpretation, and if interpreted correctly, provide a sufficient foundation for statistical aggregation and economic evaluation. Soviet GDP can be measured. (1996 p.170)

Moorsteen and Harrison miss the point. Soviet aggregates were meaningful. They represented a real thing, the physical quantity of concrete labour time required to produce a given output, but they were not meaningful as market prices, as the foundation for measures of national income.

Alec Nove considered that Soviet prices reflected "Soviet realities" and that "the Soviet price system was not an arbitrary creation of the government" (1955, p.257). Soviet planners used prices, the accounting totals attributed to production units, as a measuring rod. Enterprises had to meet costs, the accounting total of physical quantities of inputs allocated to them from income. These accounting prices were interrelated and so assisted the production of the required assortment of goods. When policy required they could be adjusted for the use of relatively scarce and costly productive resources. Consumer goods were under-priced relative to effective demand to ensure the disposal of goods, while agricultural prices needed to provide adequate incentives for the farmers. Nove considered that the limitation of Soviet national income measures to material goods was in the tradition of Adam Smith, but Nove failed to differentiate between the subjective value estimates of the planners and the objective value facts of the market.

Paul Studenski, alongside Julius Wyler, developed some of the earliest Western estimates of Soviet national income. He noted that after 1931 Soviet,

> estimates in constant prices lost their contact with reality. The estimates became completely divorced from all current financial transactions of society, all of which are expressed in current prices. They could no longer be

related to the national budget, the unified financial economic plan, and the five year plan, or any parts thereof. . . . National income estimates became a mere index of the growth of material production and a very imperfect and abstract index at that. (Studenski 1958, p.352)

Studenski's emphasis on the significance of current prices repeated a point made by Leontief (1943). But the real issue with Soviet prices was more fundamental; without exchange, prices were never reduced to an objective abstract standard. They were accounting totals only. The aggregation of physical labour hours was not an alternative way of measuring the value production of the centrally planned economy: it was a different way of measuring a different economy. It meant that in Soviet accounting, measures of the efficiency of output did not determine production decisions (Campbell 1960). Soviet economists were aware of this, but ignored its significance (Lapidus & Ostrovitianov 1929). The central plan lacked both the democracy of the producers and the act of exchange. Trotsky, the 1925 head of the state electro-technical board, remarked that

[i]f there existed the universal mind described in the scientific fantasy of Laplace – a mind which might simultaneously register all the processes of nature and society, measure the dynamic of their movement and forecast the results of their interactions – then, of course, such a mind could *a priori* draw up a faultless and exhaustive economic plan, beginning with the number of hectares of wheat and ending with the buttons on a waistcoat. True, it often appears to the bureaucracy that it possesses just such a mind: and that is why it so easily emancipates itself from control by the market and by soviet democracy. The reality is that the bureaucracy is cruelly mistaken in its appraisal of its own spiritual resources. (Day 1988, p.29)

On one hand, false accounting obscured the parasitic social role of the apparatus: on the other, it was the inevitable response of every layer of society to the tyranny of Stalinist centralisation. To the extent that planned prices did accurately represent the production of real things, they were no truer from the point of view of a capitalist market economy. Soviet planned prices were not meaningful as market prices even if they were meaningful as physical plan quantities. Nevertheless, it was these planned "prices" and the physical quantities of production that underpinned them, which provided the basis for the subsequent attempts to develop a Western "real" national income for the USSR.

2.3   The *Balance* of 1923/4

In 1923–24, P.I. Popov and L.N. Litoshenko produced the first balance of a national economy published anywhere (Spulber 1964). Its first 350 pages described its methodology and analysis; its second 275 pages presented its statistical materials. Zoltan Kennessy, in his overview of the history of national accounts, noted that the "early efforts regarding the establishment of national economic balance of

Russia in 1923/4 should be recognised" (1994, p.11). The *Balance* was based on a development of Marx's *Capital II* schemes of reproduction. G.A. Fel'dman, a contemporary of Popov who worked on the *Balance*, considered that Marx's work was "applicable to any social formation since it represents in its most abstract form, the process of production and exchange apart from its historical specificity", provided it was understood that this application differed according to the "historical content" of the categories. Marx's categories corresponded "to the requirements of analysis of market relations"(Fel'dman in Spulber 1965, p.4). They had to be modified for use in a planned economy in order to disclose the connections between income, consumption, accumulation, capital formation, the effectiveness of capital utilization and productivity. These were the connections between "the economic categories which determined the possibility of realizing the basic conditions of our development". Popov observed that although Marx's schemes of reproduction were developed to analyse a capitalist economy, to the extent that capitalism was a form of social economy they could have a wider application. There were questions as to whether they applied to an economy "constructed on socialist foundations, but there is no question at all that his schemes do apply to an analysis of the productive relations of Soviet society, which is a transitional form as society moves from a capitalist to a socialist economy" (Popov in Spulber 1965, p.13). L.N. Litoshko, the co-author of the *Balance*, observed that the physical balance did not enable the comparison of one branch to another, it could not measure how changes in price affected demand and supply, for this a common value measure based on market exchange was "indispensible" (Litoshko in Spulber 1965, pp.45–46). V.G. Groman pointed out that the *Balance* needed to consider the social form of production, whether it be socialist, state capitalist, private capitalist, small scale commodity or semi natural (Groman in Spulber 1965, p.97).

The young Wassily Leontief provided a useful summary and critique of the *Balance*. Leontief noted that on the income side, the balance presented the value of the separate large-scale branches of the economy – industry, agriculture and construction according to their functional relationship to the process of production: (1) individual consumption, (2) raw and other materials, (3) fuels and (4) tools of production. Values were broken down into their component parts, local production prices, transportation expenditures and trade mark-ups. The income side showed how values were distributed and used. It generally followed the expenditure side (Leontief in Spulber 1965, pp.88–89).

Leontief pointed out the *Balance* only accounted for "objectivised" material goods. As such it produced an unnecessarily narrow picture of the total income of the economy because it excluded services such as state expenditure or passenger transport. Although it revealed the internal organic structure of the economy, following Marx, Leontief explained that national income was a measure of the total product that resulted from the process of production. This issue of coverage was taken up thirty years later by Western economists when developing their own independent estimates of Soviet national income.

National income was the sum of newly created values and of the value of the goods expended and worn out in its creation. The distinction between new value and old value was that new value – the net product – could appear no more than once in the process of production whereas cost expenditures could repeatedly pass from one stage of production to another. Costs amounted to less than the sum of the individual total products. The net product of several branches of production was always equal to the sum of the individual net products. Every statistical sum should show that the relationship among the values of its component parts corresponded to the actual relationships of individual data. Leontief concluded that "such a method provides a possibility of comparing the economic weight of all the areas of production with one another, leaving aside their technical peculiarities". Leontief was explicit that "the total amount of goods can be computed only with reference to a commodity economy" (Leontief in Spulber 1965, pp.91–92).

Leontief left the USSR in 1925 and undertook a doctorate in Germany *Die Wirtschaft als Kreislauf (The Economy as a Circular Flow)*, under the direction of Werner Sombart and Ladislaus Von Bortkiewicz, notable for his critique of Marx's solution to the transformation question. Sombart was a very prominent economic historian who had corresponded with Engels. Sombart's history of capitalism stressed the role that double entry booking had played in the origin and development of capitalism from Italian traders based in Renaissance city states. Sombart viewed Marx's value categories as a logical device without a real existence in the capitalist economy (Murray 1993). This may in part explain Leontief's later willingness to apply these measures to the central plan. By 1931 Leontief was exiled in the United States as a research associate for the National Bureau of Economic Research (NBER). There he applied the input–output and national income methodologies developed during the Soviet *Balance* debate to the United States economy at the very same time that Kuznets had been commissioned to produce the US SNA. Before the 1917 revolution Kuznets supported the Jewish Marxist Bund in Ukraine and studied the works of Plekhanov, the founder of Russian Marxism. Kuznets briefly worked in the Ukrainian state statistics department after the defeat of the Whites before fleeing to the United States around 1921. This theoretical legacy shaped his subsequent work: "[i]t was the process of this loss of faith in the tenets of Plekhanov Menshevikism which coloured all of his later work" (Kapuria-Foreman & Pearlman 1995, p.1527).The influence on Kuznets of this early Marxist education on the US SNA developed by him in the early 1930s are clear to anyone acquainted with the various works.

Leontief (1951) was now nominally an adherent of Marshall's neoclassical theory, so he made no mention of Marx's schemes of reproduction at all in his theory; instead, he referenced Marx's inspiration, François Quesnay's *Tableau Economique*. But the nominal adherence to Marshall made no difference to the theory at all. All the essentials of Leontief's work remained the same: value was added in production; marginal productivity theory was rejected; property income, interest, rent and profits formed surplus value; the separation between use value or "product" and exchange value or "value" remained; a rise in productivity reduced the price of output; and so on. Only Leontief's debt to Marx was hidden (Clark 1984).

2.4   The Soviet value debate

The 1920s Soviet value debate overlapped with the more strategic discussion around the rate of investment in the industrial sector. Bukharin (Cohen 1980) and Preobrazhensky (1980), from the right and left wings of the industrialization debate within the CPSU, shared the same methodological approach to the use of Marx's concepts of political economy. Bukharin and Preobrazhensky contended that all Marx's categories of political economy were deduced from value and only meaningful in a commodity capitalist economy (Kaufman 1953, pp.251–52). Under the central plan to the extent that the actual social relations specific to a capitalist mode of production such as money, prices, wages, interest, rent and profits disappeared in reality, so too did the categories that described them (Spulber 1964, pp.29–30). In their place direct material accounting analysed the direct material allocation and production of inputs and outputs. Preobrazhensky explained:

> Here the category of price is purely formal in character, it is merely the title to receive from the common fund of the state economy a certain sum of means for further production and for a certain level of expanded reproduction. (1965, p.164)

In the early 1920s I.I. Stepanov-Skvortsov and A.A. Bogdanov led the "Mechanist" school to challenge this orthodoxy. Stepanov asserted that Marx's political economy abstracted from both "laws specific to each particular stage in the development of production and exchange" and developed a number of "general laws concerning production and exchange in general". A.A. Bogdanov asserted that it was nonsense to claim that under socialism "commodities, prices, wages, etc., exist and do not exist" (Stepanov & Bogdanov in Spulber 1964, p.31). Value categories existed under socialism and would exist under communism. Planning must be based on the "knowledge of the value of the product" of accumulation and of consumption. For the Mechanists the essence of abstract labour was psychophysiological. It was a natural category independent of the social forms of the productive system. Value as produced by abstract labour continued to exist in a socialist society, as did the law of value albeit in a modified form.

Bukharin, Preobrazensky and Obolenskii-Ossinskii argued, against Stepanov, that with the development of planning in the Soviet Union "the vestiges of commodity-producing economy were in process of disappearance" (Obolenskii-Ossinskii in Spulber 1964, p.32). To the extent that it was replaced by planned production so value would disappear too, Preobrazensky summarised this view in 1925:

> For surplus value to exist it is necessary that value in general should exist, that is, that the product of man's labour should be a commodity. And this means that we are here concerned with a historical category characteristic only of commodity production. (1965, p.183)

During 1926 to 1927, the discussion resurfaced around the "Idealist" group that adhered to the ideas developed by I.I. Rubin (1990) in his 1923 *Essays on Value*. Rubin asserted that the abstract form of labour is characteristic of, and specific to, the capitalist division of labour and social relations, based on a market economy, production for sale. This determined that the productive resources of society were distributed according to a capitalist accumulation process driven by profit. In the planned economy, labour was not alienated but directly social, concrete not abstract. Marx's categories of political economy disappeared in theory to the extent that they disappeared in real life (Kaufman 1953).

In 1930 the Central Committee of the CPSU rejected Rubin's "Idealist" view as part of a general purge of Marxist economic opinion. Rubin was arrested and denounced as a member of a "Menshevik conspiracy". He was condemned as a "wrecker" and "enemy of the people" (Jasny 1972; Kaufman 1953, p256). He was tortured and disappeared. Although the Mechanists were criticised too, the Central Committee adopted the essence of their view in what became the new orthodoxy of the Stalinist Marxism. Bukharin, Stalin's chief theoretician until the adoption of central planning in 1928, wrote that "Stalin is an unprincipled intriguer who subordinates everything to the preservation of his power. He changes theory to suit the needs of the moment" (1982, p.298). The new orthodoxy was expressed by Lapidus and Ostrovitianov:

> The law of value still regulates productive relations to a certain extent: and therefore we cannot reckon the goods produced in terms of labour hours, but are compelled to adhere to value calculations, although behind the value form there is hidden planned regulation. (1929, pp.473–74)

In 1930 L.M. Gatovsky summed up the new Stalinist consensus that market, price and money expressions remain valid in a centrally planned economy (Kaufman 1953, p.265). According to the Stalinists, "[c]ost accounting[] is based on the conscious use of the law of value" (Meek 1956, p.272), because "[t]he law of value acts in socialism, but acts in a transformed manner" (Miller 1953, p.423). In 1951 Stalin considered whether the law of value existed and operated under the socialist system. He answered, "Yes, it does exist and does operate. Wherever commodities and commodity production exist, there the law of value must also exist" (Stalin 1972). Seemingly unaware that market production had been abolished by the central plan he introduced, Stalin continued, stating that although the law of value existed and operated it did not regulate, "[i]n brief, there can be no doubt that under our present socialist conditions of production, the law of value cannot be a 'regulator of the proportions' of labour distributed among the various branches of production". The law of value that regulated the distribution of production existed, but not as a regulator of production. This gobbledygook went alongside the denunciation of traditional accounting methods, which were denounced as "bourgeois" or "Trotskyist". Accounting became a form of data keeping. Profit ceased to be a major success criterion, and the survival of an enterprise no longer depended on its solvency

(Bailey 1990). Alexander Gerschenkron, a strong but shrewd, opponent of Marxism commented:

> It is my belief that the so-called "Marxian ideology" plays a very insignificant part, if any, as a determinant of Soviet decisions in the field of economic policy. The function of Marxian ideology in Soviet Russia has been essentially one of vindication of policies that have been adopted on the basis of quite different considerations. (in Gerschenkron 1953, p.26)

2.5   The *Materialy*

The *Materialy* was an internal planning document produced under the direction of N. Osinskii in 1931. It measured the material production produced under the early central plan between 1928 and 1930 (Davies & Wheatcroft 1994, p.28). It sought to establish the balance of the national economy during the first five-year plan. It expounded the newly established Stalinist understanding of "value" in a planned economy.

Marx (1976) noted in his *Critique of the Gotha Programme* that the abolition of exchange in a socialised economy meant that labour was no longer indirectly social. It was no longer mediated through the sale of commodities on a market but was directly social. In a socialist economy actual costs of production, the actual amount of labour time required to produce a given output, could be directly established through the direct democracy of the association of producers. But the terror of the USSR's secret police state was anything but democratic.

Without market exchange or socialist democracy, the apparatus had no mechanism for measuring the real social cost of production. The *Materialy* expressed the contradictions of this neither one thing or another economy. It explains the confused attempt of the central planners to demonstrate the correspondence of the physical output of the plan with a notional "national income". The planners were clear that "the crucial distinguishing feature of our expanded reproduction in comparison with capitalist reproduction is that it is not the reproduction of capital but the reproduction of use-values" (Pervukhin 1985, in Davies et al. 1985, p.121). The planners abstracted from the social preconditions for the existence of the value form, to assert that while surplus value did not exist in a planned economy, value production did:

> The value of a social product (a commodity) in capitalist society consists of the following three fundamental parts: 1. The embodied value of means of production consumed in production ("C"), 2. The value of labour power ("V") and 3. Surplus value ('M'). The last two elements (V+M) are the value newly created in the given cycle or the given year, and at the level of society as a whole they equal national income. Consequently, if we eliminate the surplus value form (which does not exist in socialist society) national income may be taken to be the sum of labour expended by society in production in the given year. (Pervukhin 1985, in Davies et al. 1985, p.106)

If there is no exchange value, then there is no value. If there is no value then there is no surplus value. Even so, the *Materialy* measured Soviet "national income" by separating the contribution of living labour to annual physical production. Soviet "national income" represented the "value" of the total labour expended in the given year and expressed in a form of subjective accounting unit or as its authors would have it, in monetary terms. It was "analogous to a commodity producing society, which expresses production and national income through money in value terms", inasmuch as it counted the "value" of the physical quantity of use values produced in a year that could be ascribed to living labour (Pervukhin 1985, in Davies et al. 1985, p.107). This "value" was no value at all, but a subjective and arbitrary fabrication of the planning agencies. In 1933 Trotsky commented:

> Cast iron can be measured in tons: electricity, in kilowatts: cloth, in meters. But it is impossible to create a universal plan without reducing all its branches to one and the same value denominator. If the denominator is itself fictitious, if it is the product of bureaucratic discretion, then it eliminates the possibility of testing and correcting the plan in the process of its implementation. Fixed prices that are not controlled by a stable currency open up unlimited room for bureaucratic subjectivism in the area of planning. (in Bukharin, 1982, p.300)

Capitalist prices are not determined post-factum, after the sale of the product, but in the here and now at the point of sale. Market prices oscillate around average socially necessary labour times, as capital seeks to maximise profit rates. In a capitalist economy the labour of the individual only becomes part of the labour of society on exchange. The profit motive is driven by unequal exchange, the divergence of prices from values, through the act of sale in a market. The profit motive and exchange cannot be separated. In those industries with higher than average levels of productivity, the weighted average of labour time exceeds the average and vice versa. Under normal market conditions, this weighted average informs the market price.

Competition reduces many prices to a single market price. That price when multiplied by the volume of sales of this similar product allows for the payment of the total social labour time expended in that industry. More productive firms will be able to sell their commodities at a price above their value. This does not alter the total profits produced, but redistributes them. The extra profit of the more productive firms comes straight out of the pocket of their less efficient rivals, because increases in productivity are immediately rewarded by higher profits. Money acts as the means of exchange, the universal equivalent and means of redistribution.

This movement of capital establishes, or tends to establish, the socially necessary labour time incorporated in the product at the moment of exchange, modified by the redistribution of capital to maximise profit rates. Prices are active. They change according to supply and demand and determine the distribution and redistribution of the productive resources. Bureaucratic subjective centrally planned prices are something else altogether, neither a regulator of nor regulated by, the market.

After the Second World War, Soviet and Polish economists reprised the value debate; they conceded a "guarded acceptance" of the existence of the law of value in a planned economy. The assorted economists could not demonstrate how concrete labour could be transformed into abstract social labour without exchange. Strumilin, a leading participant in the debate, tried to produce a "work time calculus", but "it was only by shrewdly dodging the intractable task of reducing concrete labor to abstract labor, and socially necessary expenditures to individual work-time expenditures, that he is able to make any headway in offering a solution to the pricing problem based on Marxian value concept" (Zauberman 1960, p.24).

The financial statistics produced by the Soviet authorities were not based on objective costs, because inputs were allocated in physical quantities, not paid for by firms, because there was no real money and no real firms. Outputs were not a measure of revenue but of physical amounts of production. Soviet accountants could count the number of labour hours expended and divide this by the quantity of goods produced. They could establish an average physical correlation between them, but this had no financial consequences for the aggregate plan targets, or the individual enterprise. Even if they decided that a unit of labour was worth a given amount, it had no material impact on what was produced, consumed or invested. It was an accounting numeraire used to reimburse the enterprise wage fund. This was not a value relationship. It meant that the use of Soviet financial statistics, even if modified, could not establish the true "value" of Soviet output, because this output had no genuine market value, because there was no genuine market.

From the early 1930s Western statisticians sought to develop independent estimates of Soviet growth. S.N. Prokopovich (1931), a Russian former Legal Marxist, then exiled in the United States, developed the first Western estimate of Soviet national income. He examined Soviet growth in the post-revolutionary period up to 1930, including the first two plan years. Prokopovich commented on the narrow basis of Soviet national income measurements, limited to material products only. He thought that Soviet value measures did not accurately reflect the growth of physical production, not for any reason of principle but because of failing to account for the deterioration in quality of production during the Soviet period. He attributed the growth of output in the first two plan years, to a forced reduction in consumption to fund investment in fixed and circulating capital. He very shrewdly noted that without competition between capitals there was no internal mechanism in the central plan to raise productivity. But his study was too early to consider the real impact of central planning. Prokopovich did not remark at all on the change from market to plan prices.

2.6   Colin Clark's *Critique of Russian Statistics*

In 1939 Colin Clark, a Cambridge statistician who pioneered the use of gross national product (GNP) as the measure of national income (Stone 1985, in Davies et al. 1985), produced an initial estimate of Soviet output in UK prices. Clark's (1939) *A Critique of Russian Statistics* attempted to apply the new national income measurements to the centrally planned economy of the USSR. It sought to "collate and test Russian statistics, by tests of internal consistency and by comparison with statistics of the external world" (Clark 1939, p.1); Clark employed the method of aggregation to determine the actual quantities of goods and services produced in Russia at certain recent dates "expressed at the market values of these goods and services prevailing in Great Britain during a base year (1934)" (1939, p.1). This was the first extensive Western use of purchasing power parity (PPP; Wiles 1964).

Clark explained that the procedure was necessary as "prices in Russia do not necessarily bear any determinate relation either to the cost of production of goods, or to the consumers' demand for them being fixed by the planning authorities in accordance with their own decisions" (Clark 1939, p.1). In the West national income and economic activity was limited to marketed output "Every pursuit whose products are either sold on the market or are largely directed toward it is treated as economic: no others are, although their yield in the way of satisfying wants may be substantial" (Kuznets 1975, p.124). In the USSR, where nothing was produced for sale on a market, measurements of national income based on market prices should not have applied:

> In a planned economy like the Soviet Union, the phrase National Income does not necessarily mean the same thing as it does elsewhere. In the Soviet Union certain goods and services are supplied at arbitrarily low prices, others at arbitrarily high prices, and to add together the values of outputs of all goods and services at these arbitrarily determined prices would not give us anything like a measurement of national income. (Clark 1939, p.3)

The very notion of Soviet national income based on non-existent market prices was a contradiction in terms. To establish what he considered a satisfactory measurement of the Russian national income necessitated reckoning the quantities of goods and services produced, either at the prices which prevailed before the planning regime started or at the prices prevailing in some other country. This required the establishment of a common coverage of economic measures. Soviet measures of material product included transport, wholesale and retail distribution and postal services but

> exclude the rents of dwellings . . . services performed by public authorities (which we have now included, in line with the definition of national income now used in other countries) and also other personal services, for which some allowance must be made, such as professional and medical services, domestic service, catering, barbering, cab-driving etc. (Clark 1939, p.5)

Clark estimated the value of such services from the proportion which they are found to bear to the national income in other capitalist countries with a similar development of the productive resources. There is no particular reason why a centrally planned economy, in which consumers preferences were established without reference to the consumers themselves, should share a similar distribution of output between production and services as a capitalist economy. Nonetheless, Clark was working with limited information and attempted to establish a thoughtful guesstimate.

Clark needed to establish a price-index number to correct for the differences in prices, but the existence of the turnover tax levied on consumer goods meant that "the price at which goods and services are sold will be very different form the incomes of their producers". Clark rejected one possible solution, the removal of turnover taxes from the calculation, noting "[w]e can hardly adopt the clumsy expedient of constructing price-index numbers in which all goods are reckoned at their untaxed prices" (Clark 1939, p.7).This "clumsy expedient" was to provide the later basis of Bergson's AFC. Instead, Clark aggregated physical units of output, to establish the real value of roubles versus British pounds sterling.

Clark started with food "because food production can be expressed in terms of a comparatively limited number of physical units" (1939, p.7). Clark's index was composed of twelve physical quantity series: cotton cloth, woollen cloth, trucks, passenger cars, locomotives, freight cars, aluminium, copper, lead, paper, cement and gold for the period from 1928 to 1937. Clark made no allowance for changes in the composition of output of trucks, locomotives and freight cars by size and type (Hodgman 1954, p.98). The quality of output affected costs of production and value and this made international comparisons of different physical products more difficult.

Clark noted that establishing the purchasing power of the rouble over other goods and services was a far harder problem, not least as planned prices meant that roubles had different values depending on what they were purchasing. Even in 1928, the final year of the NEP, the different purchasing powers of the rouble were very marked. For food 6.5 roubles purchased the equivalent of £1 of 1934 purchasing power; for other consumption goods and services, 18.5 roubles to £1; for investment goods, 24 roubles to £1:

> These discrepancies are of course the result of deliberate policy, and the principal instrument by which they are created is the turnover tax. In the 1934 budget, revenue from turnover tax and profits of State enterprises amounted to the enormous total of 43 milliards. Turnover tax and levies on profits fell comparatively lightly (again a matter of policy) on the heavy industries, and for this reason we can regard their ratio to purchasing power parity (29 roubles to £1) as fairly indicative of true costs of production in Russia. (Clark 1939, p.39)

These figures reflected the high costs of production in newly established industrial plants and the deliberate policy of the USSR government. The apparatus used the internal terms of trade to tax rural incomes to fund industrialisation. Clark's figures demonstrated how the collapse of agriculture in the period of forced collectivisation from 1928 to 1931 offset the growth in industrial production. The forced savings required for the rapid increase in investment directly resulted in a collapse of food consumption "the value of food consumption per head of the population was 18 per cent lower in 1934 than it had been six years earlier" (Clark 1939, p.22).

In capitalist economies the price of the fixed capital stock is determined by the rate of interest multiplied by service life less the cost of upkeep. This price fluctuates around the current replacement cost of the fixed capital. The principal element determining service life is expected obsolescence, which is the average period before technological progress renders the continued use of the machine more expensive than its replacement. A high rate of interest and low rate of obsolescence create a high value and vice versa.

In centrally planned economies investment in means of production took the form of an interest-free grant from the central authorities. Machines were allocated in physical quantities. The Soviet fixed-capital stock was a quantity of means of production that increased the physical amount of use values each unit of labour could produce. It did not provide revenue streams as in the West. It was not capital. There was no rate of interest, and machinery was not rendered obsolescent by technological advance. In a capitalist economy technological advance means that machinery is often scrapped long before its potential useful life. Not so in a centrally planned economy, where the original "value" of the machine was a purely nominal unit of account. This amount was depreciated according to the reduction of the machine's usefulness due to wear and tear, but repairs restored the nominal value of the machine (Campbell 1960). Clark considered that if the lower, Soviet depreciation rate were applied, it would have systematically underestimated depreciation and so overstated output in comparison with similar Western investments. The problem of measuring value of the fixed-capital stock, and the appropriate rate of depreciation, was a recurring theme of Western alternative measures of the central plan. Clark bypassed it by adopting Western rates.

According to Clark, as shown in Table 2.1, Soviet national income increased during the decade from 1928 to 1938 by 54% rather than by the official figure of 320%. Clark's estimates of real income per capita showed that by 1934 the USSR produced less per capita, as shown in Table 2.2, than before the First World War. Clark concluded that

> [t]hus the net return after the tremendous effort of the First Five-Year Plan seems therefore to have been an increase of 4 per cent in net income per head, which is now 2.5 per cent lower than it was in 1913. As will be shown below, there was a serious decline in agricultural productivity which offset the industrial gains. (1939, p.41)

It was only after the Soviet authorities retreated from the worst excesses of collectivisation in the mid-1930s and the newly proletarianised peasantry had become at least a little more attuned to the factory that the volume of industrial

Table 2.1 Real income at 1934 sterling prices and per head of population

	Aggregate Income, £m
1913	2,803
1928	2,840
1934	3,299

Source: Adapted from Clark (1939, p.41).

Table 2.2 Per capita income at 1934 sterling prices

	Per Head, £
1913	20.1
1928	18.8
1934	19.6

Source: Adapted from Clark (1939, p.41).

production started to grow rapidly. Between 1934 and 1937 it increased by "about 67 per cent" (Clark 1939, p.65), because the "[a]verage income per head of the working population taken as a whole [had] risen by as much as 42% between 1934 and 1937" (Clark 1939, p.69).

Clark's rejection of official Soviet financial statistics and prices reflected a difference amongst Western statisticians as to how to establish the nominal "real" output of the centrally planned economy. Clark's groundbreaking use of PPP to overcome the distinction between non-capitalist Soviet prices and capitalist market ones pointed to one solution to the problem. It abstracted from the social relations of the central plan and measured physical output in the prices of a comparable Western economy. His differentiation between rouble values in different sectors addressed the significance of the turnover tax and provided at least a tentative answer to the issue of coverage with alternative estimates of the quantity of services in the planned economy were not included in the Soviet NMP. Naum Jasny gave a critical but essentially positive appraisal of Clark's work:

> Clark applied the prices which he chose to data in physical terms, which themselves were very incomplete and in part arbitrarily estimated . . . the industrial goods considered by Clark were only a small part of the total industrial output. The increase in total industrial output of 209 per cent during 1928–38 implied in Clark's estimate nevertheless agrees well with the present writer's estimates. It seems however, that with an increase in industrial output of this size, national income could not possibly have risen by only 26.1 per cent during these years. (1951a, p.144)

Jasny concluded that "Clark's methods of estimating are perhaps somewhat courageous . . . and can stand improvement" (1951b, p.8), but as Jasny regarded the official statistics expressed in values "as a pack of lies", he concluded that "after years of study the writer came to accept Clark's general position, if not his decimal points" (1951b, p.9). The validity of Soviet statistics in general and the "value" of measurements used to estimate official Soviet national income was a key point of contention between the rival Western statisticians.

2.7   Leontief's *Russian National Income and Defense Expenditures*

During the Second World War, Western estimates of Soviet national income were transformed when the work of isolated individual economists was superseded by a systematic research programme. The major impetus was provided by the US OSS. Wassily Leontief and Simon Kuznets oversaw the appointment of Abram Bergson to the head of Soviet research. The US intelligence establishment wanted to establish whether the Soviet Union would survive the Nazi invasion in 1941, the potential effectiveness of military aid, the extent of war damage and how this might influence Soviet reparation demands, the speed at which the USSR would recover after the war and its military capacity during and after the war. Kuznets explained that they were guided by two essential purposes:

> The first may be defined as political, in that the interest stems from the possible impacts of differences in rate and structure of economic growth on the relations and balances among nations in a changing world setting. The tendency would then be to compare the economic growth of the USSR with that of other major countries on the world scene . . . the second may be defined as analytical, in that the interest in the comparison lies in testing some hypotheses concerning common and divergent characteristics of economic growth and of the factors behind them: and the content of these hypotheses would decide the choice of countries, aspects, and periods for comparison. (1963, p.372)

They needed accurate figures to justify military expenditure and they wanted to demonstrate the superiority of the free market system over planning. This meant that Western estimates were by no means the objective summaries of detached observers. On one hand they sought to downplay Soviet achievements so as to justify the superiority of the free market and on the other hand they sought to exaggerate them to justify the size of the US armed forces. In 1947 the OSS group established the US Air Force's Project RAND led by Bergson (Samuelson 2004). The work of this organisation was eventually subsumed within the CIA and was to form the hegemonic consensus for Western estimates of Soviet national income.

Wassily Leontief produced the OSS's first estimate of Soviet national income in a Research and Analysis paper in September 1943. In this short paper Leontief developed several themes that recurred in Western estimates over the next decades. Leontief used a Simon Kuznets definition of national income that did not mention the market boundary, buying and selling or economic and non-economic production. This was critically ambiguous when national income measurements were applied to the Soviet centrally planned economy. Leontief abandoned his earlier 1924 insistence that national income measures were predicated on commodity production, but in other respects, his assessment repeated his earlier critique of the *Balance*. He pointed out that the Soviet definition of national income only included the net output of the "commodity producing" or more accurately the tangible consumable goods produced by industry, agriculture, construction, transportation and trade. A commodity in this definition was any material use value.

The exclusion of the service sector and the use of constant 1926/27 prices made current comparisons with military expenditures impossible and added to the problem of international comparison. Leontief's initial estimate of Soviet national income was extrapolated from the proportion of wages in total money income. On

Table 2.3 Production of the most important commodities per capita of the population in the USSR and the United States

Commodity	US in 1937	USSR in 1942 planned	US output as % of USSR output
Coal (kg)	3,429	1,190	288
Oil (kg)	1,356	269	504
Steel (kg)	397	156	255
Cotton textiles in m²	61	20	301
Leather shoes pairs	2.6	1.4	182

Source: Adapted from Leontief (1943, p.10).

the assumption that this proportion was relatively stable, at 1940 67.2% of money income, if wages were 161 billion roubles, then GNP was 285 billion roubles. After adding investment and services and deducing direct taxes, government borrowing, savings and subsistence farming, the final figure was 338 billion roubles.

Direct translation of rouble amounts into dollars was impossible at the official exchange rate. Because the rouble was undervalued its use would result in "a major overstatement of the Russian position" (Leontief 1943, p.9). This was confirmed by a physical comparison of key sectors of Soviet output with the United States, as shown in Table 2.3.

As output in the USSR had collapsed after the Nazi invasion, while US output had expanded, Leontief thought this comparison overstated the strength of the USSR relative to the United States. Leontief drew no firm conclusions about the relative size of the Soviet economy compared with that of the United States but considered that the United States must be more than 2.47 times that of the USSR.

2.8   Julius Wyler's *The National Income of Soviet Russia*

Julius Wyler considered that it was necessary to "draw away the 'veil of money'" from estimates of Soviet output (1946, p.508). The use of multiple Soviet prices constant rather than current prices and the over pricing of new output not produced in the base year 1926–27 meant that Soviet financial statistics could not be relied upon. Instead, Wyler developed estimates of Soviet output based on the physical quantity and quality of goods and services measured in US prices. Wyler built on the work of Prokopovich, Clark and Leontief by measuring national income in current roubles and then converting the results into dollars in 1940 US dollars. This produced national income estimates for the years 1928, 1934 and 1937 (Wyler 1946, p.504).

In his study, Wyler was aware of but did not touch on the wider context of the "collective Soviet economy", from the social interpretation of this system, the source of value, the interplay of controlled prices and wages, to the more technical questions of the statistical translation of these peculiar features into capitalist terms, except insofar as they directly had an impact on the data. Wyler claimed that Marx's (1976) *Critique of the Gotha Programme* "demonstrated that surplus value is not abolished in the socialist society. But instead of being appropriated by the capitalist exploiters, it is relinquished to the state on behalf of the working class" (1946, p.505). Actually Marx said almost the exact opposite: "within the cooperative society based on common ownership of the means of production the producers do not exchange their products: similarly, the labour spent on the products no longer appears as the *value* of these products" (1976, p.345, emphasis in the original). Paul Studenski, the later author of a classic history of national accounts, who cooperated with Wyler at this time, claimed "since governmental services are not marketable, Marx did not consider them a part of production" (1958, p.184). This was not true either. Marx's definition of a commodity was economic, not ideological, for Marx a commodity was a useful thing that was sold. Things that were bought but not sold, exchanged against revenue but not capital, do not produce surplus value, but they are nevertheless a part of economic production. The misunderstanding of Marx's views by Soviet and Western theorists was a running theme over the next decades.

According to Wyler, Russian national income was the equivalent of net national product at market prices but not at factor costs. In the USSR differential prices meant that the same expenditure in the various sectors did not equal the same volume of goods. This perfectly illustrated the problem. Factor costs in a market economy are based on the market price for land, labour and capital, that is rent, wages and interest. In the central plan, without rent, wages or interest and with multiple prices for the same good, there was no reason why the two sides of the national accounts should balance. Wyler resolved this problem by substituting the American for the Russian price of the various output and services of a similar kind and quality.

Wyler concluded, as shown in Table 2.4, that in 1940 Soviet national income at market prices ranked second to that of the United States, but a per capita income of 258 dollars was only 38% of the American per capita average of 685 dollars. What was particularly striking was the drop in consumer expenditures from nearly 80% of the total national product in 1928 to 44% in 1940. Only between 1934 and 1937 did consumer expenditures per capita actually rise.

Table 2.4 National income or product of the Soviet Union, 1928–40, at market prices in terms of US prices in 1940

	1928	1937	1940
In billions of dollars	20.2	37.8	45.1
Index 1928 = 100	100	187	223
In dollars per capita	136	229	258
Population (in millions)	148.6	165.1	175

Source: Adapted from Wyler (1946, p.511).

2.9   Alexander Gerschenkron

Alexander Gerschenkron was part of the Project RAND team working alongside Abram Bergson. In a wide-ranging debate about the validity of official Soviet statistics, Gerschenkron (1947, p.217) noted that there was "considerable evidence to suggest . . . Russian indices of the physical volume of industrial output – the main gauge for measuring the rate of economic development have 'an upward bias'". Nonetheless, Gerschenkron assumed that Russian statistical data was "free from deliberate distortions. Serious students of the Russian economy agree that the Russian practice is to withhold certain statistical information rather than to falsify it" (1947, p.217). Gerschenkron considered that by far the most important reason for thinking that Soviet prices were inflated was the impact of the introduction of new technology, particularly in the fast growing machinery and electrical sectors, on the "so called constant prices of year 1926–27" (Gerschenkron 1947, p.219). The rapid transformation of the Soviet economy rendered the 1926–27 base-period pattern obsolete. These "unchanged" prices were originally intended to provide a mechanism for the hierarchical regulation of self-interested enterprises under public ownership (Harrison 1998). As the range of the commodities, or more accurately outputs, produced by industry widened, the selection of the appropriate price weights for new products presented a difficult statistical problem. New "commodities" were valued at the price current in the period when they were first produced on a large scale. This was the so-called Gerschenkron effect:

> In a country in the first stages of industrialization the spread between prices of industrial goods of a low degree of fabrication and prices of highly fabricated goods is relatively larger, than in a well-developed industrial country. This is often reflected in the structure of protective tariffs. As the country progressed on the road of industrialization, the spread tends to become narrower. At the same time, the share of relatively fabricated goods in total output increases. If prices of the first year of the period are used as weights, the increase in output over the whole period appears greater than it would if prices of the last year of the period are employed. It is quite likely, therefore, that if, e.g., prices of 1938 had been used in Russia, the index for the period 1928–38 would have shown a smaller rise than is the case on the basis of 1926–27 prices. (Gerschenkron 1947, p.221)

As the first year of production was relatively inefficient and therefore the cost of production relatively high, subsequent increases in output raised the index more than would be the case if prices of a later year of large scale production were used. Re-computing the index in prices of later years removed the specific inflationary bias caused by introduction of new commodities at prices higher than the general level of 1926–27. It eliminated the hybrid character of the index. This re-computation formed a key part of both Jasny's and Bergson's later recalculation of the growth of Soviet national income. Gerschenkron suggested that a possible method for checking the "suspected error" in the indices of aggregate output was through comparison with figures on the output of basic industrial products and freights transportation, all expressed in physical units (Davies & Wheatcroft 1994, p.32).

This problem of index year relativity was expressed in the use of two alternative indexes, the Laspreyres and the Paasche. The Laspeyres index number measures the change in output from the level and pattern of consumption of the base year. The Paasche index number measures the change in cost of living from the level and pattern of consumption of the given year (Chapman 1963, p.29). Growth transforms the relative prices or value added per unit of product. The faster the rate of growth, the greater the structural shifts in the economy, the sharper the change in value relationships and the more pronounced the difference between measures weighted at the beginning or the end of the period. As rising productivity causes unit prices to fall, weighting by "post-industrialisation" prices will yield lower rates of growth than weighting by "pre-industrialisation" prices (Grossman 1953, p.3). Alec Nove pointed out that because no set of price relationships are more "true" in any absolute sense than another, no statistician can legitimately describe the Soviet series as "wrong" merely because of the peculiarities of the 1926–27 price structure. Nove argued that the pre-industrialization weights could be a more accurate basis on which to assess the sacrifices made during the first period of central planning, as the fall in the price of industrial goods relative to primary produce was a consequence of the process of industrialisation itself (1957, p.118). For Jasny the use of base-year weights by Soviet statisticians was ideological. Keen to demonstrate the growth of the economy under planning they used this effect to exaggerate the growth of output:

> The more the pre-plan price pattern changed, the less favourable the new price pattern became for demonstrating achievement. Thus it happened that, although the economic pattern of the country had fundamentally changed and the 1926–27 price pattern had been outmoded for a long time, the Soviets stuck to the prices of that year for use in the most important economic indexes. (Jasny 1951a, p.5)

Alexander Gerschenkron's (1951) own estimates of Soviet output were based on a dollar index of Soviet Machinery output, which compared physical quantities of Soviet machinery with American equivalents, between 1927/28 and 1937. Gerschenkron acknowledged the essential choice in developing these comparisons was between the use of Soviet or non-Soviet data as weights in the index. Jasny as well as Donald Hodgman (1954), Gerschenkron's doctoral student, had already demonstrated how current rouble prices could be deflated to account for the change in industrial structure and inflation. The advantage of this method was that it possibly allowed a closer representation of the actual structure of Soviet output or their "scarcity relations".

Its disadvantage derived from "the difficulty in appraising correctly the degree of meaning and consistency inherent in any set of Soviet values". These were, after all, non-market planned prices. Gerschenkron praised Hodgman (1954) for avoiding the use of weights pertaining to a non-Soviet economy in developing his national income estimates that, of course, formed the very basis for Gerschenkron's own work.

Gerschenkron (1951) followed Colin Clark and Julius Wyler and repriced physical units of Soviet output at US dollar prices. This sidestepped the issue of the pricing of new Soviet machinery output that accounted for 72.8% of machinery output in 1933. Soviet data on quantities of machinery were gathered for as many items as possible. Eventually 128 items were found.

These items were then compared with American equivalents. Soviet output multiplied by US prices yielded the dollar values. The gross value of these 128 Soviet machinery items increased from 100 in the 1927–28 base year to 525 by 1937, or from $203 million in 1927–28 to $1,065 million in 1937. Official Soviet indices were around three times higher by 1937. Gerschenkron's index implied an average growth of 13.9% from 1929–30 to 1937 compared to the official 32.4%.

Gerschenkron's use of US prices for Soviet output established a clear point of comparison between the two economic systems. He did not try to create an ideal capitalist market within the USSR. He was relatively clear about the limits of his method, but this was more by intuition than any clear theoretical distinction about the nature of value in the two rival systems. In fact none of the participants in the debate pointed to the real distinction between the objective and subjective nature of value in a market and a centrally planned economy. This included the Marxists Paul Baran (1947), another Russian exile and a former employee of the OSS, and Maurice Dobb (1948). Although Dobb explained that the capitalist factors of production did not exist in the USSR, he used a measure of national income based on the very same non-existent income flows (Dobb 1966). Dobb's contribution essentially consisted of an uncritical defence of whatever statistics were produced by the Soviet authorities (Dobb 1948; Jasny 1950).

2.10   Naum Jasny

In three books published in 1951 and 1952, *The Soviet Economy During the Plan Era* (1951b), *The Soviet Price System* (1951a) and *Soviet Prices of Producers' Goods* (1952), later summarised in *Soviet Industrialization 1928–1952* (1960), Naum Jasny sought to provide a systematic estimate of Soviet national income "to yield a reasonably trustworthy and reasonably comprehensive picture of the results of Soviet plans" (Jasny, 1951b, p.3). Jasny was at pains to explain that his motivation for an accurate assessment of Soviet growth was very personal:

> All too frequently it is assumed that those who do not accept Soviet statistics underestimate Soviet attainments, and, more recently, that they underestimate the Soviet threat. This may be true of some, but not of the present writer. He is afraid of the Bolsheviki. He considers them a menace not to be underrated as long as they are able to channel perhaps half of the national income into new investment in the armed forces, and especially atomic-bomb development,

even though such channelling implies extremely low consumption levels for the population. (1951b, p.6)

Jasny's distrust of official Soviet data was a major point of difference between his analyses and those of the Bergson school. Jasny wanted to establish "the rate of exaggeration of the official national income estimates" (1951b, pp.12–13):

As soon as price and cost indexes are applied to such data, one of the principal mainstays of Soviet propaganda disappears. But the price and cost indexes are essential. Without them the data in current prices are almost useless. The reduced consumption levels can be easily ascertained also by analysis of consumption in physical terms. (1951b, p.57)

Jasny needed to account for the effect of the rapid inflation, particularly in consumer goods, during the first decade of the plan. The inflation of consumer goods provided a mechanism through which planners could indirectly reduce consumption to provide material inputs for investment in means of production. The 1928 plan allowed both nominally rising urban living standards and massively increased industrial development investment. This was impossible. A key debate during the 1920s was how to fund long-term investments in hydroelectric schemes, electrification, steel works and the like, which required massive quantities of inputs but only delivered output after several years. This problem was not abolished simply by wishing it away. Rather, the Stalinists drove down consumption to provide resources for investment in means of production.

Jasny estimated net national product according to the Soviet concept from the production end. This corresponded to national income at market cost (Jasny 1951a, p.132; 1951b, p.12). The four principal items in net national product, net investment, military expenditures, private consumption and expenditures on education and health services, were established by an estimate of the gross outputs of agriculture, industry, construction, freight transportation and communications insofar as they served production and trade. Outlays such as depreciation were then deducted and the balance added up. All other services were disregarded (Jasny 1951b, p.11).

Clark had already shown roubles had different values depending on which sector of the economy they were used to measure. Material inputs were priced differently according to whether they were allocated to consumption or investment. Jasny estimated that at wholesale prices the 1926–27 rouble was "worth 70 U.S. cents in terms of farm products, 50 cents in terms of consumers' goods, 30 cents in terms of producers' goods, some 25 cents in terms of industrial constructions, and so on" (1951b, p.26). Jasny showed that by 1937 the prices of all producers' goods measured on a tax free basis were about 75% above the 1926–27 level, whereas the prices of all consumers' goods had increased more than eightfold and wages not quite fivefold (1951a, p.37). Consumer goods paid huge taxes, typically from about 30% up to 88% of the price. A turnover tax of 88% of the retail price would have raised that price by as much as 733% (Jasny 1951a, p.74). This tax amounted to about 60% of the retail prices of consumer goods in 1937. In 1948 state subsidies to the national economy were equivalent to "perhaps 70 billion roubles: on certain important goods, such as lumber and steel, the subsidies were at least equal to their prices" (Jasny 1951b, p.40).

Jasny repriced the principal budgetary items "converting each item of expenditure to values at real 1926–27 prices" (1951b, p.40). Separate conversion factors were worked out for the principal items of national income. In what was to be an important difference with Bergson, this procedure excluded the necessity of adjusting for either turnover taxes or subsidies. Jasny's price indexes aimed "to make estimates of national income in current prices useful by applying price indexes to the various items of which it is composed" (1951a, p.148). Jasny criticised the alternative procedure to "adjust the data for the various factors which distort the picture" (1951a, p.148). Like Gerschenkron, Jasny noted that

> [t]he difficulties of statistical analysis arise in part from the fact that, because of great changes in the economic setup and important accompanying circumstances, even correct indexes of national income and production are poor yardsticks for measuring changes in the Soviet economy during the plan era. (1951b, p.6)

Jasny repriced these goods to remove this effect: "new commodities and new models of old commodities brought into line by the writer with those of commodities and models which existed in 1926–27" (1951b, p.10). As the "unchangeable 1926–27 prices" were actually falling, outputs expressed in those prices regularly showed much greater increases than the outputs in physical terms (Jasny 1951b, p.19). As a result "huge disparities" can be observed between increases in industrial output computed at "unchangeable 1926–27 prices" and increases in output of the principal raw materials measured in physical terms (Jasny 1951a, pp.11, 108).

Jasny recalculated outputs with the result that the economic significance of the industrial output and especially of producers' goods and construction relative to agricultural production in the beginning of the Plan era was "considerably lessened" (1951b, p.26). Jasny's index was based partly on output series weighted by his Soviet "real 1926/27 prices" and partly on adjustments of various official Soviet aggregates. Hodgman, a proponent of Bergson's use of current Soviet prices, thought it was doubtful if Jasny's price indices covered a sufficiently varied and broad selection of products to be truly representative. Hodgman thought that by not separating subsidies and profits from the price indices Jasny's estimates had a downward bias for the period between 1928 and 1937 (Hodgman 1954, pp.101–03).

In spite of the great rise of nominal wages, the share of wages in the total production costs of industry declined "rapidly all through the peaceful years of the Plan era" (Jasny 1951a, p.22). Direct rationing from 1928 to 1937 was only briefly relaxed in the late 1930s, before being reimposed after the Nazi invasion in 1941. After the end of the war, and once they were able to re-establish central control, Soviet planners preferred nominally low prices for consumer goods combined with nominally high wages. As demand did not affect either the price of goods or their supply, this was effectively a form of forced saving. It ensured that the entire available quantity of consumer goods was purchased but meant that a proportion of wages could not be spent. This provided the illusion of prosperity while forcing workers to save their surplus roubles (Chapman 1963).

State enterprises competed for labour, and this ensured that planned increases in nominal wages were fulfilled, but for a simultaneous increase in consumption to take place, then productivity growth would have needed to exceed the rate of increase in the urban population. Jasny credited Bergson for demonstrating that Soviet data for the number of wage earners, the average wage and the total wage fund did not coincide (1951a, p.26). The emphasis of Stalin's plan was an aggregate increase in output, not the efficient use of inputs to achieve it. Productivity growth targets were not generally met.

Nominal outlays on labour per given product rose, while living standards fell. Inflation was the inevitable result. This was compounded by the catastrophic fall in agricultural production in the early years of the plan. In this period low real wages corresponded to relatively very high prices of consumers' goods (Jasny 1951a, pp.15–18). Jasny pointed out the misleading way in which the Russian series on crop production changed in 1934, from the actual yield (barn yield) to the gross yield including harvesting losses (biological yield; Jasny 1950, p.94).

Jasny criticised Bergson for accepting too uncritically the official Soviet figures. Bergson's (1944) study of Soviet wages differentials in the 1930s made no reference to the overall reduction in real wage levels in the first phase of the plan, even while it pointed out the stratification of Soviet society. But Bergson was able to demonstrate that Jasny's figures for Soviet consumption arrived at very similar measures of increase after 1933, such that by 1937 consumption had at least reached if not exceeded its 1928 per capita levels (Bergson 1953, p.11).

Gerschenkron complained that Jasny should have informed the reader that "information on the change of methods is derived from Soviet sources" (1950, p.250). In Jasny's opinion it was the differences in wage levels that meant it was impossible to say that "the national income of the USSR is so many per cent of that of the United States" (Jasny 1951b, p.13). Jasny explained:

> In calculating the real expenses on investment and "defense", the rouble expenditures shown by Soviet data either must be recalculated to entirely different prices (foreign, or Soviet pre-Plan prices), or they must at least be adjusted for turnover taxes and deficits or profits. In these adjustments not only the direct subsidies to given industries, but the indirect ones to industries using subsidized investment goods, raw materials, and transportation facilities have to be considered. (1951a, p.145)

Bergson (1953) showed that Jasny's calculations for 1928 to 1937 were in fact at current prices, a form of Laspeyres not Paasche index. Jasny described his volume measures as "real" 1926/27 prices when they were actually current price weights (Harrison 1999). As a result Jasny's estimates of Soviet national income were remarkably similar to Bergson's (Davies & Wheatcroft 1994, p.35). Bergson thought that

> Jasny sets himself the interesting task of calculating Soviet national income in terms of the same standard as is used in the official statistics, i.e., 1926–27 prices, but with a valid valuation of new commodities. I believe there is a good deal of foundation for the assumption implied throughout that the rouble price system was more meaningful on the eve of the five year plans than it was later . . . I shall point out . . . however, some limitations in the dollar standard of Clark and Wyler that arise because of the differences between Soviet and American preferences and technology. Considering the vast economic transformation in the USSR under the five year plans, the reader will readily see that the procedure used by Dr. Jasny must encounter entirely comparable difficulties. (1953, p.6)

2.11   Kaplan, Hodgman and Shimkin

Norman Kaplan (1952) led a team of Project RAND economists to develop an input–output table from a captured 1941 Soviet plan (Turgeon 1952). Kaplan used planned not actual economic data. Kaplan's table was limited by the absence of the defence industry and the restriction of plan coverage to the production of material outputs. This forced him to guesstimate the output of many sectors. Foreign trade was not included, and there was no reconciliation between the production and expenditure sides. Mark Harrison (1996) later attempted to complete the table with actual data from the newly opened Soviet archive. Harrison applied Bergson's (1961) methods; he repriced, rebalanced and estimated missing elements to complete Kaplan's work, but could not avoid bold suppositions to render Kaplan's tentative results less tentative.

Hodgman considered that Bergson (1944) had proved that Soviet and capitalist wages were conceptually similar. Hodgman (1954) developed estimates for Soviet industrial production that used salaries and pay rolls, including pay roll taxes to represent value added in a given industry. Hodgman's weights used 1934 Soviet wage-bill data adjusted to include payroll taxes of various types. Differences in wage levels represented differences in value added. He applied factor costs to value Soviet output. Hodgman's estimates covered large-scale industry in 1928 expanding to total industry by around 1933 and thereafter. The limited sample of data available fell off during and after the war. In 1937, 137 products were covered; in 1940, 22 products; and in 1950, 18 products.

Dimitri Shimkin (1953) undertook a comprehensive and detailed assessment of the USSR's production of six key mineral and metal groups. These had the advantage of being relatively homogenous. They were traded openly on world markets at known prices. They provided a relatively unambiguous quantitative measure for international comparisons. Official Soviet statistics of imports and exports could be tested against Western sources. The distribution of mineral deposits, smelters, refineries and mills had a significant influence on economic and military power.

The efficiency of the USSR's planned production could be directly compared with the West in terms of the consumption of inputs and its reprocessing of waste outputs. The growth of the economy of the USSR could be compared with that of the United States during its period of industrialisation from the 1890s as reflected in its use of minerals. The Shimkin index uses a modified version of Hodgman's weights and included estimates for military production. Shimkin found that the relative economic growth in the USSR was nearly twice as fast as in the United States during its fastest period of growth from 1902 to 1917. For the entire period in the USSR from 1926 to 1950 and from 1902 to 1947, its growth was three times faster even when including the Second World War (Shimkin 1953, p.312). The limited character of this study was both its strength and weakness; it allowed ready comparisons with obvious weaknesses to be made but did not provide a comprehensive statement of value comparisons between the two economies.

2.12 Abram Bergson

Abram Bergson became the "authoritative" figure in the field of Western estimates of Soviet national income (Powell & Moorsteen 1966). Whereas Jasny's work was acknowledged as that of a "pioneer", it was dismissed as too personal (Davies & Wheatcroft 1994, p.35). It was claimed that Jasny's price index data were derived from data of "uncertain meaning" and computed without reference to "any specified system of weighting", his index was "virtually impossible to interpret" (Moorsteen 1962, p.2). In contrast Bergson and his team at the Project RAND were admired for their "careful accuracy", "detail" and citations from Soviet sources (Davies & Wheatcroft 1994, p.35). Bergson's methods used official Soviet statistics, but changed the base year and developed an AFC, which redistributed official Soviet estimates of value among the factors of production according to neo-classical marginal value theory (Bergson 1953, 1961; Bergson et al. 1954). They were generalised across the "communist" centrally planned economies (CPEs) and became the standard procedure for the measurement of the "real" output of these economies (Gregory 1981). In 1985 the World Bank's Paul Marer explained that Bergson's AFC

> appears to be a practically feasible alternative to prevailing prices in CPEs. In brief, the adjustment involves eliminating the turnover tax, subsidies, and profits that are components of various aggregates when valued at prevailing prices and adding notional amounts for returns to fixed and working capital and land. (Marer 1985, p.172)

In 1961 Bergson published *The Real National Income of Soviet Russia since 1928* (SNIP). This was the final product of his attempt during the Second World War to measure the output of the USSR initially for a single year, 1937. Bergson used inverted commas in referencing his "real" measures throughout the SNIP. From the outset Bergson's project was more definitely ideological than either Clark's or Jasny's. Bergson wanted to establish whether "the economic principles taught in the West really are susceptible of general application" (Begson 1964, p.vii).

Neo-classical economics taught that the only form of rational economic activity was market production. Non-capitalist centrally planned production and indeed socialism were necessarily irrational. But did their irrationality mean they were immeasurable? Stephen Rosefielde, a later theorist from the Bergson school, labelled Bergson's system the "theory-normed valuative method". Rosefielde believed its strength derived from the fact that it was an *a priori* non-empirical, non-realist method. Its presumptions "cannot be falsified" (1981, p.21):

> Theory acts as the norm for assessing the meaning of observed economic behaviour. The truth of the theory is presupposed, not tested. As a consequence, the theory-normed valuative method is *not* an *empirical method* in the classical meaning of the concept. It is an interpretative technique, a hypotheti-codeductive device for drawing inferences from a priori theory rather than a method empirically verifying causal relationships. (1981, p.11, emphasis in the original)

It was neither a "positive nor [] a realist methodology. Its filial connections lie elsewhere, with the Cartesian tradition, with a priori rationalism" (Rosefielde 1981, p.11). This idealist hypothetico-deductive method, or, more accurately, hypothetical-deductive method perhaps, directly echoed that of Carl Menger, one of the founders of Austrian marginalism who created an analytically or abstractly conceived world to describe the market economy (Clarke 1982, p.198). The behaviour of Soviet planners did not correspond to the welfare standard of neo-classical economics, but for Bergson's theory this was beside the point. The truth of his method was presupposed. It was not subject to empirical verification. It was not a realist method. Following the collapse of the USSR, Rosefielde (2004) was to reconsider his support for Bergson.

Bergson sought to reconcile the irrational behaviour of reality with the rational behaviour of the *a priori* abstraction. Bergson's "principles represent an application to socialist resource use of a particular value theory. This is the marginal value theory accepted in the West" (Bergson 1964, p.13). But marginal value theory is no objective theory at all. It defines value by the sum of value produced by the three factors of production. This tautology defines value by itself. What counts in a capitalist economy is effective demand, not demand. If the value of the money commodity were determined subjectively, like the subjective determination of every other commodity, then nothing would have a price. Every consumer's effective demand would be unlimited. If the value of capital is a multiple of the rate of interest, then what determines the rate of interest? If everything is sold at its value, then there is no net profit, as the profits of one person are equivalent to the losses of another. Profits can only exist if one commodity can produce more value than it, itself, costs to produce. If there was no net profit in the capitalist system, as Joseph Schumpeter (2008), a renowned advocate and defender of neoclassical economics, asserted, then capital has no net value. If capital has no net value, there is no net rate of interest. If value is determined by the quantity of money, then what is money a quantity of? If its value is determined by the rate of interest, then it is objective not subjective. If it is objective, then the rate of interest must be known before the physical quantity of money or capital can be valued. If the rate of interest is determined before, and therefore, separately from its physical form, then it is not a physical, but a social construct. If it is an objective social construct, then what is it an objective social construct of? Neoclassical theory had no answer to these basic questions, but this was theory Bergson sought to apply to the USSR.

Consumers must have money or some other commodity like their labour power to sell, with a real objective value, in order to assert their market preference. All market exchanges necessarily, as a precondition for it taking place, increases the sum total of "utility". A useless thing is exchanged for a useful thing. A non-use value for one person has been transformed into a use value for someone else. But this increase in utility does not create "value"; it is the exchange of equivalents, a transfer from one person to another person – even if the total of utility necessarily increases. If one person cheats the other, then what is a gain for one is a loss for the other of the same amount but in the opposite direction. Rather, in a market economy, the value of money is determined by the socially necessary labour time required to produce the commodity that acts as a universal equivalent for all other commodities – gold. As the function of gold in the exchange relationship is purely symbolic, it may be and invariably is, replaced by a worthless symbolic proxy, like a banknote. Value is not created in exchange but is realised there. Simon Kuznets explained, the value of national income is "the *net* value of the goods produced by the given nation during a given time unit" (1941, p.34, emphasis in the original). Production creates value, not consumption, and consequently, the measure of national income excludes temporary windfalls caused by shifts in supply and demand.

The existence of a centrally planned economy, that functioned without markets and consumer preference in any form, and indeed without money as it existed in a market economy, posed a direct challenge to the universal application of neo-classical theory. Bergson observed that "when the government is the master rather than the servant of economic law, the alternative to the labor theory may not be marginal analysis – it may only be no theory" (1964, p.13). This was a polemical jibe at von Mises's assertion that because centrally planned economies were irrational from the point of view of the market, so were any measures of them that treated them as market economies. Bergson continued:

> In sum, if we apply abstract theoretic principles to the U.S.S.R., we should not be surprised if resource use often fails to conform to them. But this is still no argument for an alternative approach often employed in respect to the U.S.S.R.: to apply no principles, or at least none to speak of. After all, one needs some principles even to discover that none prevail. As to the particular principles applied here, I can say no more than has already been said already: Their use seems to facilitate the inquiry. (1964, p.13)

Bergson was determined to measure the USSR by neoclassical categories, because neoclassical theory was the only theory he had, even though the precondition for the application of this theory, a market economy, did not exist in the USSR. Marginalist theory asserted that total output corresponded with the total of "welfare" expressed in "consumers utilities", so Bergson replaced "conventional consumers utilities" with "planners' preferences" (1961, p.39).

In a capitalist economy national income data are compiled in terms of prevailing money values. This was, according to Bergson, entirely in order "where the concern is only to appraise 'monetary' phenomena, i.e. money flows, finance, cost structure etc." (Bergson 1953, p.3). In the USSR where there was no money in the capitalist sense, Bergson nevertheless followed "conventional procedure" and compiled his accounts in the prevailing money values of non-existent money. Bergson modified official "Soviet rouble prices" derived from official subjective "value estimates" but adjusted them by this factor cost, "to clarify the recurring question: 'But what do the rouble figures mean?'" (Bergson 1953, p.3).

An important part of Bergson's argument was that the official data was reliable, albeit in need of interpretation. Bergson said that the "reliability of Soviet financial statistics in current roubles are on altogether a different plane from Soviet national income statistics in 1926–27 roubles" (Bergson 1953, p.6). This was in Bergson's view a distinction of "paramount importance". Bergson repeated Gerschenkron's assertion that

> [a]nyone dealing with Soviet statistics must begin by considering the possibility that the figures may represent sheer invention. If this were the case, no analysis would be possible . . . Soviet statistics are not freely invented: that as a rule they have meaning and significance . . . Mr Jasny's own extensive use of Soviet statistics shows that he shares this view. (Gerschenkron 1950, p.250)

Bergson was supported by the discovery of an official Soviet 1941 planning document. This copy of the annual plan ran to 750 pages and was seized by US intelligence from German occupying forces in the USSR. It was intended for internal use only by planning authorities. Its figures agreed almost exactly with the published record. It confirmed that the Soviet authorities did not engage in "outright falsification" of their financial or other statistical records (Turgeon 1952). Later critics noted that the document was not conclusive; it was at the lowest level of security clearance, and there may have been alternative sets of statistics for the higher ups in the party they claimed (Engerman 2009, p.107). The critics missed the point. The problem with Soviet statistics was not their falsification but that even if they were true from the point of view of the central plan, they were false from the point of view of the market. Bergson's working assumption was that "Soviet statistics are not generally falsified in the sense of being freely invented under a double bookkeeping system" (Kuznets 1963, p.371). He asserted that the "published Soviet data appear to be consistent both internally and with other available information". Where there were differences and inconsistencies these were attributable to methodological differences rather than "free invention" (Bergson 1953, pp.7–8).

Bergson applied marginal value theory to estimate the incomes that should have accrued to the factors of production, land, labour and capital if the USSR had been a capitalist market economy. Marginal utility theory asserted that the three factors of production yield revenue according to their marginal rate of substitution. That is the cost of substituting one factor for the other in the last analysis. In a capitalist economy the failure to redistribute the factors of the production according to this marginal cost results in a loss expressed as an opportunity cost, a loss of revenue incurred by the owner of the factor of production. But the income of these factors of production is a product of a capitalist economy or more precisely private ownership of these factors. Ownership is a human relationship and the revenues derived from the factors of production are products of a human capitalist economy, based on production for exchange. In a centrally planned economy, without capitalists, landlords or bankers the value flows necessary for "property income" to equalise profits, to produce rents and interest did not exist, and neither did "opportunity costs" in the Western sense either.

Kuznets remarked that in the USSR "we could perhaps abandon the (national product) concept entirely, and shift to the notion of increase in national power as the only substance of final product" (Kuznets 1963, p.371), but rejected the idea on the ground that economists did not know enough about national power. Rather, Bergson hypothetically deduced their existence in the USSR. Based on the official Soviet financial statistics Bergson redistributed this non-existent "value" according to the headings of the US Department of Commerce SNA. Bergson stated that his theory did not provide the basis for the precise measurement of "abstract ultimates"; instead, it was a method for "the organisation of broadly meaningful statistical inquiries" (1961, p.41). This formed the basis for his AFC standard, which had the following features:

> i) All commodity prices resolve fully into charges for primary factors, particularly capital, land, and labor. ii) For capital, there is a net charge, corresponding to the average internal return on this factor in the economy generally and an allowance for deprecation of a conventional sort. iii) The charge for land, 'rent', corresponds on the average to the differential return to superior land. iv) 'Wages' are at a uniform rate for any occupation and as between occupations differ on the average in accord with differences in productivity and disutility. v) Similar principles apply in the case of the relation of wages to farm labor income. vi) Commodity prices are uniform in any given market area. (Hoeffding 1954, p.45; Bergson 1953, pp.42–43)

It was besides the point that not a single of these standards actually existed in the centrally planned economy. By redistributing official Soviet aggregate "values", according to the categories of marginalism, Bergson aimed make the figures "real". This was the building block method adopted and applied in a series of studies by the RAND school (Bergson 1953, 1961; Bergson et al., 1954; Chapman 1963; Hoeffding 1954; Powell & Moorsten 1966) and wider by the CIA. It provided a comprehensive analysis of Soviet national income including output, consumption and the capital stock. Bergson estimated "Soviet national income in terms of rouble prices, but attempted to correct the results for outstanding distortions" (1961, p.5). Bergson's measures of "real" national income were derived in two stages: national income was first computed in terms of rouble prices prevailing in different years to account for the Gerschenkron effect, including the adjustment of coverage to include all services. This total was then adjusted for the absence of property income through the AFC.

By far the most significant effect on measurements of industrial growth and national income was the change of index year. Bergson calculated "real" outlays on investments in fixed capital by aggregating measurements of investments in new machinery, capital repairs to machinery, construction and other investments in fixed capital (1961, p.87) and presented series weighted at 1937, 1950 and "given year" that is constant 1928 roubles.

"Real" national income, stated in 1937 roubles (the base year) rather than in 1928 roubles (the given year), markedly reduced the percentage growth in industrial output, simply because 1937 prices were lower than 1928 prices for industrial production. In contrast, a change in base year from 1937 to 1950 had only a very limited effect. "By implication then change in structure was nothing less than radical from 1928 to 1937. Seemingly price changes were also distinctly correlated with production changes" (Bergson 1961, p.95). They were objective not subjective.

Bergson then applied the AFC at 1937 prices. This removed the turnover taxes and profit charges and added subsidies and depreciation charges (Bergson 1961, p.127). As a result of the revaluation, national income "grew more or declined less than it did previously" (Bergson 1961, p.134), but the redistribution of value according to marginal categories made almost no difference to the aggregate totals, as Tables 2.5 and 2.6 show.

Table 2.5 Investments in new machinery, USSR, 1928–55, alternative weights (1937 = 100)

Year	In prices of "given year"	In 1937 prices	In 1950 prices
1928	9.1	18.4	27.1
1937	100	100	100
1944	70	78.2	65.7
1950	214	220	214
1955	353	376	356

Source: Adapted from Bergson (1961, p.95).

Table 2.6 GNP by use, USSR, 1928–55, in 1937 rouble prices and factor cost (1937 = 100)

GNP	1928	1937	1944	1950	1955
1937 prices	64.8	100	108	146	217
1937 rouble factor cost	61.6	100	150	150	216

Source: Adapted from Bergson (1961, p.134).

Bergson conceded that

[t]he effect is far less than that due to the change in base year from 1937 to 1928. The reasons for this difference I believe are twofold. First, when the base year is shifted from 1937 to 1928, the resultant reweighting appears to be more definitely correlated with the trends in different use categories than is the case where one shifts form 1937 prices to 1937 rouble factor cost. (1961, p.135)

The revolution in productivity altered the cost of production and so transformed the structure of the economy:

Secondly, the shift from 1937 prices to 1937 rouble factor cost involves significant change in price structure but by any standard the corresponding change entailed in the shift in base year from 1937 to 1928 is nothing less than revolutionary. (Bergson 1961, p.135)

Bergson's adjustments made almost no difference to the value aggregates. This was inevitable because they were predicated on and used official Soviet data for output, wages and fixed capital assets. The inadequacy of the marginalist critique of Soviet prices was stark indeed. Unable to question the inherent falsity of concrete labour measures, it simply generalised the false prices but changed the headings under which they appeared. Bergson noted that "[a]s computed in this study, outlays in terms of rouble factor cost come to much the same thing as direct and indirect wage costs, including farm and other labor incomes" (1961, p.146). Paradoxically Bergson's theory indirectly confirmed that labour was the source of property income, if not in the capitalist West, then at least in the hypothetical adjusted factor economy of the centrally planned East. Bergson developed hypothetical estimates for what interest, profits, rents and depreciation should have been if the non-capitalist centrally planned economy was the capitalist economy that it was not:

I reclassify Soviet outlays in 1937 as previously computed in rouble factor cost. a) The profit recorded in Soviet accounts in 1937, b) A hypothetical charge of 25 billion roubles for agricultural rent, which amounts to about 40 per cent of total labor income in agriculture in 1937 c) A hypothetical interest charge of10 percent per annum on Soviet fixed capital d) The net of the foregoing, that is, the excess of rent and interest over profits. (Bergson 1961, p.140)

Bergson's estimates for profit rates, assuming a rate of interest between 8% and 20%, formed the basis for later estimates of the value of Soviet fixed-capital stock (Powell & Moorsteen 1966). They included depreciation and the consumption of inputs predicated on the non-existent income streams that they hypothetically represented: "[i]n all cases, the cited figures supposedly represent both direct and indirect incidence, that is, charges not only on final goods but on immediate articles used in production" (Bergson 1961, p.140). Bergson's figures supposedly represented the non-existent reality. This non-existent ideal type was more real than reality or less irrational than the irrational. Strikingly, the aggregate value totals were effectively unchanged.

Bergson conceded the approximation of the AFC to reality "could not be especially close: and it still remains to be seen to what extent the Adjusted Factor Cost Standard itself is realizable with available statistical data" (1953, p.53). His "synthetic" factor incomes were "highly arbitrary". It was perhaps desirable to think of them as not corresponding to relative marginal productivities "as they actually are but as they would be if one abstracts from any special efficiencies or inefficiencies of the social system considered" (Bergson 1963, p.20). Abstracting from the reality of the centrally planned economy as it actually was, Bergson's synthetic and highly arbitrary factors incomes had no objective existence in the real world. Jasny commented that

> [a]ll in all, Bergson's figures in "adjusted roubles" do not represent "real" costs. The arbitrariness of the Soviet price system is too great to hope to eliminate all effects of it. As stated, the percentage distributions of the national income by use and economic sector in different years, even in "real" costs, will remain not comparable because of interrupted changes in relationships between "real" costs in the various sectors of the national economy. Not until the estimates of national income are underpinned with price indexes will the results of such computations become a valuable part of the correct picture of the Soviet economy. (1951a, p.153)

According to Alec Nove (1955) Bergson's adjustment for turnover tax and subsidies, as shown in Table 2.7, was "extremely hazardous" as in the real Soviet accounts interest and rent payments were negligible, investment in state enterprises was not repayable, depreciation allowances were relatively low and the bulk of them were spent on repairs. Worse, Bergson's information on the turnover tax

Table 2.7 GNP in 1937 prices

GNP	1928	1937	1940	1944	1950	1955
1937 prices	64.8	100	118	108	146	217
1937 ruble factor cost	61.6	100	121	150	150	216
1937 ruble factor cost further adjusted						
With profits deducted	60.7	100			150	215
With addition of agricultural rent at 40% of farm labor income	65.4	100			147	211
With addition of interest at 10% of fixed capital	61.1	100			149	216
With profits deducted and rent and interest added	64	100			147	211
1937 ruble factor cost, with allowance for non-labour charges according to 1947 US cost structure	64.3	100			148	213

Source: Adapted from Bergson (1961, pp.134, 140).

was out of date, partial and "highly misleading" (Nove 1955, p.255). Nove gave the example of the Ministry of Armament Production, which made bicycles, civilian radio receivers and washing machines. Even if it were known how much tax was paid by this ministry, it was impossible to know how much of it related to armament production. If turnover tax and subsidies were accurately apportioned there was still the systematically unequal level of profits to be considered, and the transfer through the budget of profits in light industry to investment in heavy industry. Nove concluded that

> [i]t seems very doubtful whether the concept of 'factor cost', at any rate as Bergson uses it, is of any great value in the study of the USSR, and it is certainly liable to be misleading if used in international comparisons. (Nove 1955, p.256)

P.J.D. Wiles provided the substantive critique of Bergson's system from within the neoclassical tradition. Wiles complained that Marx's economics ignored the "correct" Menger–Jevons marginal utility theory, while he considered that Marx's distinction between an exchange value based on private ownership and supply in a centrally planned economy was "an irrelevant distinction, and obscures the fundamental identity of exchange in all societies, so far as it concerns resource allocation" (1962, p.54). This was necessarily so because Wiles viewed marginal theory as a logical, or, more accurately, ideological, device "not at all relevant to the description of facts, but necessary for the development of welfare economics" (1961, p.4). In contradistinction to Bergson, Wiles thought that although planners preferences were irrational, centrally planned retail prices could make "suitable measuring rods in general" whereas, "factor costs on the other hand represent merely the marginal transformation ratios between products (not, to repeat, factors) for enterprises" (1961 p.229). This crystallised the debate for Bergson and his followers. Wiles argument meant that if planned prices departed from true measures of "relative scarcity", then Bergson's adjustments for that divergence did not yield weights appropriate for actual outputs. Irrational relative prices engendered irrational relative outputs. Bergson's "real" and apparently "rational" national income was no more "real" or "rational" than the unreal national income of the irrational planners. Bergson's AFC only corrected weights, "for the relative outputs that would have been established in a free economy employing the current supply of land, labor, and capital to its best advantage" not for the Soviet economy as it actually was (Becker 1969, pp.45–46).

In response, Bergson abandoned the requirement that marginalist theory measured the price at which something was sold. All that was required for marginalist theory to apply to the central plan was that prices needed to correspond to marginal costs. Provided prices corresponded to marginal costs, "then there was no further requirement that the prices that correspond to marginal costs also correspond to marginal utilities or planners' preferences" (Bergson 1961, p.116). But how could they, given that production decisions were made without reference to costs and when planners only knew costs after they had made their decisions? In practice Bergson had dropped both the welfare preferences and their equivalent planners' preferences. This separated price from utility, which was the thing that was supposed to determine price in the first place. Becker in defence of Bergson commented that "the bill of goods produced in a Soviet type of economy, valued at adjusted factor costs, will probably diverge from the optimum, in the sense of failing to maximize an objective function. But such a finding would not invalidate the AFCS" (Becker 1969, pp.45–46). Rather, it would simply highlight Bergson's distinction between production possibility and feasibility and production potential and welfare. Bergson's AFC had failed to meet the the standard set by his own theory, yet none of this mattered, because even when it failed, it succeeded. It was truly immune to verification.

2.13   G. Warren Nutter

In the late 1950s tension mounted between US military establishment, which required high estimates of Soviet growth to support the arms build-up, and the US capitalists who had to pay for it (Engerman 2009, p.117). The Eisenhower administration were concerned about the costs of the arms race and worried that high Soviet growth rates raised questions about the moral superiority of the free enterprise system. The administration provided a research grant for the National Bureau of Economic Research (NBER) to develop an alternative estimate of Soviet output. The NBER hired G. Warren Nutter, Milton Friedman's first graduate student, to develop alternative estimates of Soviet national income. Nutter stood outside the community of Russian-speaking Sovietologists who formed the consensus of Soviet national income estimates. He was sceptical about the application of Western national income measures to a non-market economy.

Nutter reviewed the quality of data, the use of index numbers and the method of various Western measures to develop alternative physical, value and time comparison estimates of Soviet industrial production. Nutter accepted that although Soviet statistics did not accord with Western standards of objectivity in which a "statistic is reliable if it is an accurate magnitude of a definite thing", nonetheless "the internal relations among the statistics demonstrate that they are based on reality, even though they diverge from it" (1962, pp.11–45). Nutter reviewed the Gerschenkron effect and the wider use of index numbers in both Western and Soviet economies. He compared it to "measuring how the caterpillar grows when it turns into a moth". No one figure provided a conclusive measurement of the growth of production in any economy, whether capitalist or otherwise.

Nutter compared the production of swords and plowshares in a two commodity economy. He concluded that it was relative opportunity costs that determined the proportions in which outputs were produced. Nutter took it for granted that in a highly developed market economy, market values, price, unit value added and so on approximated relevant costs, but "this cannot be taken for granted in the Soviet system". Indeed "many Soviet relative prices have no relation whatever to opportunity costs" (Nutter 1962 p.122). Opportunity cost is the measure of lost revenue based on sales. In an economy without sales and in which costs differed across and within industries, this standard could not apply. In the USSR its use was further complicated as "the deficiencies are even graver in the case of data on prices and costs, in particular because Soviet prices bear a more or less haphazard relation to the costs of production" (Nutter 1962, p.112).

Nutter based his estimates of the growth of Soviet output on physical measures of particular industrial sectors and on changes to the size of the manufacturing workforce. Wage breakdowns were not available for individual sectors so labour was assumed to conform to a common standard. Effectively Nutter adopted a kind of labour theory of value but one which was predicated on changes to simple average concrete labour.

For industrial materials the output of each product was weighted by its unit value adjusted for a base year. Each unit value was calculated to exclude the cost of non-industrial intermediate materials, by the removal of a fraction of turnover taxes and profits equal to the ratio of the cost of materials to total "cost", the total of wages and cost of materials. The remaining turnover tax and profits, a fraction equal to the ratio of wages to total "costs", was treated as a return on capital and was left within the adopted unit value.

Nutter noted that "this procedure is obviously arbitrary, but it seems less bad than the alternative available" (1962 p.122). Outputs of industrial groups were combined by value added based on 1928 prices for the weight base year, the last year when market prices existed in the USSR. Accounting for employment, the 1955 weight base year was selected using the official centrally planned prices. Nutter was sceptical about the effectiveness of this procedure. It was

> doubtful whether the use of employment as a weight factor for industrial groups improves the situation, not only because employment is merely an estimate of value added, but also because there is little reason to presume that labor is economically allocated among industries. (1962, p.123)

Prices were based on official Soviet handbooks. A moving weight index was constructed for finished civilian products (Nutter 1962, p.199/200). Nutter concluded that the growth in output in the First Five Year Plan was achieved primarily by expanding employment. Nutter developed a measure of productivity based on common units of physical output produced by a given amount of common labour inputs. The larger the growth in productivity, the greater was the reduction in unit costs (Nutter 1962, p.252). Nutter considered that aside from the defects in basic statistics, it was difficult to construct meaningful measurements of aggregate industrial production because Soviet prices generally did not accurately reflect relative costs of production. The industrial structure had shifted radically over a short period. It had increasingly favoured sectors in which growth is most easily achieved. Growth rates had differed widely from sector to sector and had been interrupted at critical points by major disturbances. Quantitative growth had not been accompanied by the general improvement in the quality of production such as that found during the industrial development of most Western countries (Nutter 1962, p.284).

More fundamentally, Soviet production was not market production. Nutter wanted to "underline" that "the pattern of industrial growth observed in the Soviet Union would never be duplicated by a market economy. Sovereign consumers would not choose the paths of growth chosen by Soviet rulers" (Nutter 1962, p.267). None of Nutter's estimates of Soviet growth, of the increase in physical outputs, of the growth of labour productivity and of the relative size of the Soviet economy to the United States was comparisons of like with like. This raised "the awkward question of whether a highly generalized measure of growth has much meaning even as an indicator of expansion in productive capacity available" (Nutter 1962, p.267). Nutter concluded it did not.

No common measure of economic production could be developed to compare the United States and USSR. "If we bowed to the stern dictates of logic, we would be able to compare Soviet and U.S. industrial growth only if both economies served either consumer welfare or state power. But this is ruled out by the very difference in social order whose influence on growth we wish to assesses", this dilemma could "be mastered only by admitting it – by avoiding the delusion that there is some single-dimensioned, neutral measure of growth, equally meaningful for all types of economies" (Nutter 1962, p.267).

Nutter's estimates developed outside the core group of Sovietologists were sidelined by the majority of neoclassical economists. They preferred Bergson's reconciliation of the central plan with the categories of the market (Engerman 2009, p.127). In any regard, Nutter was not supported by the CIA's vast resources.

2.14   Conclusion

The Soviet-style five-year plans began with the abolition of the NEP in 1928. They transformed the USSR's economy into a non-capitalist bureaucratically centrally planned one in which inputs and outputs were determined by planners in physical terms. Money was not a universal equivalent and the rouble was a nominal unit of account. Market exchange, supply and demand and the capitalist law of value did not exist there. The new economy was not one in which Marx's value categories or the Western SNA could be applied, as the material basis for national income measurements, the objective fact of actual sales, did not exist.

Nevertheless, in the USSR the defeat of the orthodox Marxists by the Stalinists in the 1920s meant that subjective non-market "value" measures were developed to measure the national income of the USSR in the 1930s. Soviet national income figures applied a subjective value to aggregates of concrete labour hours. As less efficient producers were subsidised by more efficient ones, there was no economic pressure to raise productivity.

In the West the debate around the accuracy of official Soviet statistics concluded that Soviet statistics were not freely invented. Soviet data for physical quantities of output was found to be more or less reliable. There was no double counting, and internal estimates corresponded with public published quantities. Soviet financial data corresponded with the physical data. This was necessarily so; otherwise, any form of central planning would have been impossible, and the economy would have collapsed almost immediately. But this debate missed the point. Soviet prices were subordinate to the political priorities of the regime. They regulated the rate of surplus extraction, obscured the privileges of the apparatus and provided propaganda material by exaggerating economic achievements. But even if their nominal totals accurately matched the actual physical output of the economy, they were false from the point of view of the market. They were false as a measure of real national income and false as a basis for the development of alternative Western measures of real Soviet "national income".

Clark's use of international prices bypassed the issue of rouble prices as it transformed physical quantities into UK prices through an early use of PPP. These international prices were predicated on the productivity and price structure of a different capitalist economy not the central plan of the USSR. Jasny used actual official financial data deflated by various price indexes, but only to obliterate the essential distinction between market and non-market production. Bergson reconciled Soviet prices with the categories of neoclassical economics, but only through abstracting from the actual social system considered.

Bergson's idealist method, immune to empirical verification, formed the basis for subsequent Western estimates of the national income of the centrally planned economies. The criticism of Bergson's AFC by economists as varied as Clark, Jasny, Shimkin, Nove and Nutter was ignored and then forgotten. The overtly ideological purpose of Bergson's method, as well as his meticulous, if essentially uncritical, attitude to the data, explains why it was the one ultimately adopted and generalised.

Note

1 Davies was a graduate student of Alexander Baykov. Baykov's early 1947 study of Soviet industrialisation, *The Development of the Soviet Economic System*, supported Stalin's polices and described the purges of 1937–38 as having a "beneficial influence on the development of industry" (1970, p.281). Davies, in his turn, went on to collaborate with Mark Harrison (Davies et al. 1994). By this means, the Stalinist method which permitted the application of value measures to a centrally planned economy was reproduced through the years.

References

Bailey, D., 1990. Accounting in the Shadow of Stalinism. *Accounting, Organizations and Society*, 15(6), pp. 513–25.
Baran, P. A., 1947. National Income and Product of the U.S.S.R. in 1941. *The Review of Economic Statistics* (November), pp. 226–234.
Baykov, A., 1970. The *Development of the Soviet Economic System*. Second edition. Cambridge: Cambridge University Press.
Becker, A.S., 1969. *Soviet National Income, 1958–1964*. Berkeley: University of California Press.
Bergson, A., 1944. *The Structure of Soviet Wages: A Study in Socialist Economics*. Cambridge, MA: Harvard University Press.
Bergson, A., 1953. *Soviet National Income and Product in 1937*. Columbia, NY: Greenwood Press.

Bergson, A., 1961. *The Real National Income of Soviet Russia since 1928*. New York: Harvard University Press.

Bergson, A., 1964. The *Economics of Soviet Planning*. New Haven, CT: Yale University Press.

Bergson A., Heymann, H, Jr., & Hoeffding, O., 1954. *Soviet National Income and Product 1940–48*. New York: Columbia University Press.

Bergson, A. "National Income", in Economic Trends in the Soviet Union, Bergson, A & Kuznets, S, Eds, Cambridge, MA: Harvard pp. 1–37.

Berliner, J.S., 1957. *Factory and Manager in the USSR*. Cambridge, MA: Harvard University Press.

Bukharin, N., 1982. *N.I. Bukharin: Selected Writings on the State and the Transition to Socialism*, R.B. Day, ed. New York: Spokesman.

Campbell, R.W., 1960. Soviet Accounting and Economic Decisions. In G. Grossman, ed. *Value and Plan: Economic Calculation and Organization in Eastern Europe*. Berkeley: University of California Press, pp. 76–104.

Chapman, J., 1963. *Real Wages in Soviet Russia since 1928*. Cambridge, MA: Harvard University Press.

Clark, C., 1939. *A Critique of Russian Statistics*. London: R. & R. Clark, Ltd.

Clark, D., 1984. Planning and the Real Origins of Input-Output Analysis. *Journal of Contemporary Asia*, 14(4), pp. 408–29.

Clarke, S. 1982. *Marx, Marginalism, and Modern Sociology: From Adam Smith to Max Weber*. London: Macmillan.

Cohen, S., 1980. *Bukharin and the Bolshevik Revolution*. Third edition. Oxford: Oxford University Press.

Davies, R. et al., 1985. *Materials for a Balance of the Soviet national economy 1928–30*, S.G. Wheatcroft & R.W. Davies, eds. Cambridge: Cambridge University Press.

Davies, R. & Wheatcroft, S., 1994. The Crooked Mirror of Soviet Statistics. In S.G. Wheatcroft, R.W. Davies, & M. Harrison, *The Economic Transformation of the Soviet Union 1913–45*. Cambridge: Cambridge University Press, pp. 24–37.

Davies, R.W., 1958. *The Soviet Budgetary System*. Cambridge: Cambridge University Press.

Davies, R.W., Cooper, J.M., & Ilic, M., 1991. *SIPS Occasional Paper No.1: Soviet Official Statistics on Industrial Production, Capital Stock and Capital Investment, 1928–41*. Birmingham: University of Birmingham.

Day, R.B., 1988. Trotsky on the Dialectics Democratic Control. In P. Wiles, ed. *The Soviet Economy on the Brink of Reform: Essays in Honor of Alec Nove*. London: Allen & Unwin, pp. 1–36.

Dobb, M., 1948. Further Appraisals of Russian Economic Statistics. A Comment on Soviet Statistics. *The Review of Economics and Statistics*, 30(1), pp. 34–39.

Dobb, M., 1966. *Soviet Economic Development since 1917*. Sixth edition. London: RKP.

Engels, F., 1975. *Anti-Duhring: Herr Eugen Duhrings Revolution in Science*. Sixth edition. Moscow: Progress Publishers.

Engerman, D.C., 2009. *The Rise and Fall of America's Soviet Experts*. Oxford: Oxford University Press.

Gerschenkron, A., 1947. Appraisals of Russian Economic Statistics: The Soviet Indices of Industrial Production. *The Review of Economics and Statistics*, 29(4), pp. 217–22.

Gerschenkron, A., 1950. Jasny and Soviet Statistics. *The Review of Economics and Statistics*, 32(3), pp. 250–51.

Gerschenkron, A., 1951. *A Dollar Index of Soviet Machinery Output, 1927–28 to 1937.* Santa Monica, CA: RAND Corporation.

Gerschenkron, A., 1953. Comments to National Income by Gregory Grossman. In A. Bergson, ed. *Soviet Economic Growth.* White Plains: NY: Row Peterson and Company, pp. 1–36.

Gregory, P.R., 1981. Economic Growth and Structural Change in Czarist Russia and the Soviet Union: A Long Term Comparison. In S. Rosefielde, ed. *Economic Welfare and the Economics of Soviet Socialism: Essays in Honor of Abram Bergson.* Cambridge: Cambridge University Press, pp. 25–52.

Gregory, P.R., 2004. *The Political Economy of Stalinism: Evidence from the Soviet Archives,* Cambridge: Cambridge University Press.

Grossman, G., 1953. National Income. In A. Bergson, ed. *Soviet Economic Growth.* New York: Row, Peterson and Company, pp. 1–36.

Grossman, G., 1960. *Soviet Statistics of Physical Output of Industrial Commodities.* Princeton, NJ: Princeton University Press.

Harrison, M., 1994. National Income. In S.G. Wheatcroft, R.W. Davies, & M. Harrison, eds. *The Economic Transformation of the Soviet Union 1913–45.* Cambridge: Cambridge University Press, pp. 38–56.

Harrison, M., 1996. *Accounting for War.* Cambridge: Cambridge University Press.

Harrison, M., 1998. Prices, Planners, and Producers: An Agency Problem in Soviet Industry, 1928–50. *Journal of Economic History,* 58(4), pp. 1032–62.

Harrison, M., 1999. Soviet Industrial Production, 1928 to 1955: Real Growth and Hidden Inflation. *Journal of Comparative Economics,* 28(1), pp. 134–55.

Hodgman, D.R., 1954. *Soviet Industrial Production 1928–51.* Cambridge, MA: Harvard University Press.

Hoeffding, O., 1954. *Soviet National Income and Product in 1928.* New York: Columbia University Press.

Jasny, N., 1950. Soviet Statistics. *The Review of Economics and Statistics,* 32 (1), pp. 92–99.

Jasny, N., 1951a. *The Soviet Economy during the Plan Era.* Stanford, CA: Stanford University Press.

Jasny, N., 1951b. *The Soviet Price System.* Stanford, CA: Stanford University Press.

Jasny, N., 1952. *Soviet Prices of Producers' Goods.* Stanford, CA: Stanford University Press.

Jasny, N., 1960. *Soviet Industrialization 1928–1952.* Chicago: University of Chicago Press.

Jasny, N., 1972. *Soviet Economists of the Twenties: Names to be Remembered.* Cambridge: Cambridge University Press.

Kaplan, N., 1963. Capital Stock. In A. Kuznets & S. Bergson, ed. *Economic Trends in the Soviet Union.* Cambridge, MA: Harvard University Press, pp. 96–149.

Kaplan, N., 1952. *A Tentative Input-Output Table for the USSR: 1941 Plan.* Santa Monica, CA: RAND Corporation.

Kaufman, A., 1953. The Origin of "The Political Economy of Socialism": An Essay on Soviet Economic Thought. *Soviet Studies,* 4(3), pp.243–72.

Kapuria-Foreman, V., & Pearlman, M., 1995. An Economic Historian's Economist: Remembering Simon Kuznets, *The Economic Journal,* 105(November), pp. 1524–47.

Kennessy, Z., 1994. The Genesis of National Accounts: An Overview. In Z. Kennessy, ed. *The Accounts of Nations.* New York: IOS, pp. 1–15.

Kuznets, S., 1941. *National Income and its Composition 1919–1938* (Vol. I). New York: National Bureau Economic Research.

Kuznets, S., 1963. A Comparative Appraisal. In A. Bergson & S. Kuznets, eds. *Economic Trends in the Soviet Union.* Cambridge, MA: Harvard University Press, pp. 333–82.

Kuznets, S., 1975. *National Income a Summary of Findings*. New York: Arno Press.

Lapidus, I., & Ostrovitianov, K., 1929. *An Outline of Political Economy*. London: Martin Lawrence.

Leontief, W., 1943. *Russian National Income and Defense Expenditures*. Washington, DC: OSS.

Leontief, W., 1951. *Structure of American Economy, 1919–1939*. Second edition. New York: Oxford University Press.

Marx, K., 1976. *Critique of the Gotha Programme*. Moscow: Progress Publishers.

Marx, K., 1982. *Capital Volume I*. Third edition. London: Penguin Classics.

Marer, P., 1985. *Dollar GNPs of the U.S.S.R. and Eastern Europe*. Baltimore and London: John Hopkins University Press.

Meek, R.L., 1956. *Studies in the Labour Theory of Value*. London: Lawrence and Wishart.

Miller, J., 1953. The Political Economy of Socialism in the Making. *Soviet Studies*, 3(4), pp.403–33.

Moorsteen, R., 1962. *Prices and Production of Machinery in the Soviet Union 1928–58*, Cambridge, MA: Harvard University Press.

Murray, P., 1993. The Necessity of Money: How Hegel Helped Marx Surpass Ricardo's Theory of Value. In F. Moseley, ed. *Marx's Method in Capital: A Re-examination*. Atlantic Highlands, NJ: Humanities Press, pp. 37–63.

Nove, A., 1955. Some Notes on Soviet National Income Statistics. *Soviet Studies*, 6(3), pp. 247–80.

Nove, A., 1957. "1926/7" and All That. *Soviet Studies*, 9(2), pp. 117–30.

Nove, A., 1977. The *Soviet Economic System*. London: George Allen and Unwin.

Nutter, G.W., 1962. *Growth of Industrial Production in the Soviet Union*. Princeton, NJ: Princeton University Press.

Powell, R., & Moorsteen, R., 1966. *The Soviet Capital Stock 1928–1962*. Homewood, IL: Richard D. Irwin, Inc.

Preobrazhensky, E., 1965. *The New Economics*. Oxford: Clarendon.

Preobrazhensky, E., 1980. *The Crisis of Soviet Industrialisation*, D. Filtzer, ed. London: Macmillan.

Prokopovich, S.N., 1931 *The National Income of the U.S.S.R.* Memorandum no. 3. University of Birmingham.

Rosefielde, S., 1981. Knowledge and Socialism: Deciphering the Soviet Experience. In S. Rosefielde, ed. *Economic Welfare and the Economics of Soviet Socialism: Essays in Honor of Abram Bergson*. Cambridge: Cambridge University Press, pp. 5–22.

Rosefielde, S., 2004. Post-war Russian Economic Growth: Not a Riddle – a Reply. *Europe Asia Studies*, 56(3), pp. 463–66.

Rubin, I.I., 1990. *Essays on Marx's Theory of Value*. Fifth edition. New York: Black Rose Books.

Samuelson, P., 2004. *Abram Bergson 1914–2003*. National Academy of Sciences Biographical Memoir, 84. Washington, DC: National Academies Press.

Schumpeter, J., 2008. *The Theory of Economic Development*. London: Transaction.

Shimkin, D.B., 1953. *Minerals a Key to Soviet Power*. Cambridge, MA: Harvard University Press.

Spulber, N., 1964. *Soviet Strategy for Economic Growth*. Bloomington: Indiana University Press.

Spulber, N., 1965. *Foundations of Soviet Strategy for Economic Growth: Selected Soviet Essays, 1924–1930*. Bloomington: Indiana University Press.

Stalin, J., 1972. *Economic Problems of the USSR*. Peking: Foreign Language Press. Available at: www.marxists.org/reference/archive/stalin/works/1951/economic-problems/ ch04.htm.

Studenski, P., 1958. *The Income of Nations: Theory, Measurement, and Analysis: Past and Present*. New York: New York University Press.

Turgeon, L., 1952. On the Reliability of Soviet Statistics. *The Review of Economics and Statistics*, 34(1), pp.75–76.

von Mises, L., 1975. Economic Calculation in the Socialist Commonwealth. In F.A. Hayek, ed. *Collectivist Economic Planning*. London: George Routledge & Sons, pp. 87–130.

Wiles, P., 1961. *Price, Cost and Output*. Oxford, Basil Blackwell.

Wiles, P., 1962. *The Political Economy of Communism*. Oxford: Basil Blackwell.

Wiles, P., 1964.*Theory of International Comparisons*. In J. Degras, ed. *Soviet Planning: Essays in Honour of Naum Jasny*. London: Basil Blackwell, pp. 77–115.

Wyler, J., 1946. The National Income of Soviet Russia: A Statistical Puzzle. *Social Research*, 13, pp. 502–18.

Zauberman, A., 1960. The Soviet Debate on the Law of Value and Price Formation. In G. Grossman, ed. *Value and Plan: Economic Calculation and Organization in Eastern Europe*. Berkeley: University of California Press, pp. 17–46.

3   From capitalism and back again

3.1   The CMEA, the MPS and the CIA

Following the Second World War the centrally planned economy of the USSR was able to recover rapidly as resources were directed to replace the wholesale destruction caused by the Nazi invasion. The extension of central planning into the CEE allowed a limited division of labour to develop among the various states and alongside it, a form of non-money trade, or at least the swap of physical outputs, within the Council for Mutual Economic Assistance (CMEA). Consumer living standards began to rise from the early 1950s onwards with growing wages and social consumption provided by enterprises and the state. In 1958 Czechoslovakia submitted two documents to the sixth session of the Conference of European Statisticians (CES). CES/83 described the methodology for the compilation of MPS "national income" while CES/84 presented the scope and structure of the system of balances of the national economy. These documents were the first official presentation of the MPS to the UN from the member countries of the CMEA (Arvay 1994).

The MPS asserted that in the centrally planned economies new value was created in the sphere of material production. Soviet accountants had a similar problem to their Western counterparts, how to measure the "value" of use values that were by their nature incommensurable. They solved it by the aggregation of concrete labour hours. They treated these aggregates as if they were equivalent to aggregates of socially necessary abstract labour measured in exchange. They invented "value" where none existed in reality.

Global Social Product (GSP) was the sum of these imputed values applied to all goods produced in the sphere of material production during the accounting year. Its global reach was limited to the measurement of the output of the centrally planned economies only. These measurements included products used for the production of other products and those used for final uses. National income was GSP less the intermediate consumption of goods and consumption of fixed assets used for the production of other goods or Net Material Product (NMP). National income was divided into two major categories personal consumption, including the depreciation of fixed assets in the service sector and accumulation.

There were no substantial revisions until the MPS was abandoned in the early 1990s when capitalism was restored.

In the late 1950s and early 1960s the United Nations (UN) established a working group to formalise the statistical bridge between the MPS and the SNA. In 1971 the UN published a technical manual originally developed by the CMEA (CIA 1978). This formed the basis for subsequent UN efforts to reconcile the two systems (UN 1986). The enduring nature of the regime received a conservative reflection in the hegemony of Bergson's reconciliation of the MPS with the SNA. This seemed to provide a method of squaring non-capitalist and capitalist value measures. Western researchers remained suspicious of official planned figures but they no longer questioned the viability of developing estimates based on the official figures. Statisticians checked their "corrected" estimates for their internal consistency against physical output indicators, as if this was an adequate control for the essential distinction between market and non-market production.

Abraham Becker (1969) applied Bergson's AFC to an estimate of the USSR's national income for the period from 1958 to 1964. CIA Sovietologists produced regular reports for the Joint Economic Committee (JEC) of the US Congress applying these methods. A CIA team based in Washington, D.C., did the same for China (JEC 1967). In New York, Thad P. Alton et al. (1991) estimated national income for Bulgaria, Czechoslovakia, East Germany, Poland, Romania and Yugoslavia. Alton developed independent estimates of output growth for production and service sectors and then aggregated them into a national income index at factor costs consistent with Bergson's removal of "distorted" centrally planned prices. The AFC synthetic national accounts were contrasted with official value measures.

Western national income estimates were greater than official Soviet national income by the net value of productive depreciation and the net adjustment for the value added of services. Adjustments for non-productive depreciation and losses only rearranged the data (CIA 1978). Western national income increased the nominal value of centrally planned production but produced lower growth rates because they were adjusted for the hidden inflation caused by the introduction of higher priced new goods not on official price lists. There was no real development in Western statistical methods towards the USSR from the early 1960s on. Bergson and Levine ([1983] 2000) anticipated no substantive change in the USSR before the millennium.

3.2   The USSR from stagnation to collapse

From the mid-1960s productivity in the USSR, the amount of physical outputs per quantity of physical inputs, slowed even while rates of investment grew as a proportion of total output (Nove 1977). By the mid-1960s the central plan's tendency towards stagnation began to outweigh possibilities for its quantitative extension (Nove 1989). During the 1970s stagnation was offset by the development of the oil, gas and raw materials production. Between 1970 and 1980 the share of gas and oil in net exports doubled so that by the mid-1980s fuel accounted for more than half of the Soviet Union's exports (Clarke & Fairbrother 1993). Oil and gas prices were based on market rents, so issues of cost and quality did not prevent their sale on capitalist markets. The disruption of Middle Eastern oil supplies by the 1973 Organization of Petroleum Exporting Countries (OPEC) oil crisis, the Iranian revolution of 1979 and the 1980 Iran/Iraq war meant that the USSR's net barter terms of trade improved by 5% per annum between 1976 to 1980 and 3% per annum from 1980 to 1985 (IMF et al. 1991, pp.86, 105).

By the mid-1980s these trends went into reverse. The easiest oil and gas fields, with the most accessible reserves and closest to existing transport infrastructure, were being exhausted. High investment in less productive and more distant fields was required to maintain even existing levels of output. As supplies resumed from Iran and Iraq after 1985, with the end of the war, oil and gas prices fell and this hit the value of the USSR's foreign exchange earnings.

During the period from 1986 to 1990, Soviet gross fixed investment was set to grow at an annual rate of 4.9% up from 3.5% in the previous five-year plan. The proportion of this investment set for modernization and retooling was set to rise to 50.5% from 38.5%. Following the example of the military sector, Gospriemka was established to provide external quality control of Soviet machine production. Improved working class housing and material incentives were combined with a crack down on absenteeism and alcoholism (IMF et al. 1991).

The success of Glasnost undermined the very foundation of the central plan it was supposed to revive. In 1987 Gospriemka rejected some 15% to 18% of output. This particularly hit the machine-building sector, in which 60% of output was subject to inspection compared to 20% elsewhere. The rejection of low-quality production by the new inspectorate caused extensive disruption to production units further down the line who were dependent on the rejected inputs to meet their output targets. The surge in housing construction meant there were inadequate resources available for the retooling, as labour and construction materials were directed away from the machine sector. The proportion of incomplete investment projects rose. This in turn reduced wages as bonus targets were not met. The anti-alcohol campaign stimulated production of illicit alcohol and hit government revenues through falling turnover taxes. These internal problems were compounded by a fall in world oil prices and revenues.

In 1986 at the 17th Party Congress Gorbachev determined to create a system of "market socialism" over the next eighteen months. The solution to the problems created by market reform was to accelerate the pace of market reforms. The Law on State Enterprises in July 1987 abolished mandatory output targets. It allowed enterprises to contract directly with their suppliers and customers. It gave them greater latitude to invest and accumulate capital. But by 1988 state orders still accounted for 80% of output and ministries continued to confiscate surpluses to cross-subsidise loss-making enterprises.

The relative openness of Glasnost and the fracturing of the confederated state encouraged nationalist rivalries, deepening the economic crisis. The rail network was particularly hit. The refusal of national governments to allow the free movement of rail traffic meant bottlenecks in the transport system which prevented the harvest from being gathered. During 1989, half the railways failed to meet transportation targets. Increased imports of food exacerbated the balance of payments shortfall.

The abolition of the monopoly of foreign trade in 1989 was the final nail in the coffin of the central plan. The state monopoly had prevented individual enterprises from trading directly with Western capitalist firms. It was a precondition for the existence of the central plan as it prevented market competition. From 1989 all state enterprises, joint ventures, production cooperatives and other entities which were judged by the Ministry of Foreign Economic Relations to be competent to trade internationally were enabled to do so. By the second half of 1990, 20,000 enterprises had registered, and around a third of that number had begun trading directly with the West.

A brief window of opportunity enabled a small number of enterprises to make significant profits as they bought at subsidised plan prices and sold at market rates. But the substitution of Western for Soviet inputs led to considerable waste and further dislocation. Downstream production units were unable to supply outputs which were now replaced by Western firms. Legal limits on investment and accumulation remained in place, so these profits could not be effectively reinvested in new lines of production. The policy of Glasnost stimulated national and political movements and in 1989 frictions in inter-republic trade grew as shortages of food, consumer goods and fuels spread. The Warsaw Bloc exploded.

Gorbachev's October 1990 report to the Supreme Soviet, *Basic Guidelines for the Stabilisation of the Economy and Passage to a Market Economy*, resolved that the USSR had "no alternative to switching to the market" (Spulber 2003, p.276). There were three other plans for this market transition: Ryzhkov's, Shatalin's, Yeltsin's and Gorbachev's. They differed not over the goal, but the pace of reform (Spulber 2003, p.303). But once again events overtook gradualism.

In June 1991 Yeltsin the liberal outsider opposed by the Communist authorities won the Presidency of the Russian Federation. In July Yeltsin took office and in August conservative generals staged a coup. Gorbachev was arrested and martial law imposed. The failure of the coup after just two days spurred Yeltsin to act. In November the Communist Party was banned. In December the Soviet Union was abolished, and the CIS created. In January 1992 immediate price liberalization and wholesale privatisation or shock therapy was introduced.

Its architect was Yegor Gaidar, the new Prime Minister of Russia. Shock therapy aimed to break the power of the military industrial planners. It destroyed the plan and according to Gaidar created a capitalism that was "repulsive, thievish and socially unjust" (Spulber 2003, p.314). Hyperinflation wiped out savings and destroyed living standards limited by wage restraint policies. Taking 1991 as a base year of 100%, real wages fell to 67% in 1992, 46% in 1995 and 44% in 1998. (Spulber 2003, p.296). The Russian population with incomes below minimum subsistence reached 35 million by 1998 (Spulber 2003, p.313).

By 1998 investment had fallen to less than a quarter of its 1990 level. By 1999 over 96% of machinery was more than five years old, with about two-thirds having been installed before the beginning of Perestroika. Industrial production halved between 1990 and 1999, with the output of light industry falling by 85%,

Table 3.1 Russian Federation: Shares in manufacturing ownership, workforce and output, 1992, 1995 and 1998 (in percentages)

Shares	Ownership		Work force		Output	
	1992	*1998*	*1992*	*1998*	*1992*	*1,998*
State	45.5	3.1	81.3	13.6	84.4	9.9
Private	47.4	88.1	15.4	67.4	14	27
Mixed	0.3	6.3	0.9	46.4	0.7	61.4

Source: Adapted from Spulber (2003, p.344).

faster than it had following the Nazi invasion of 1941 (Clarke 2004, pp.194–96). Table 3.1 shows the share of the state and municipal workforce decreased from 1992 68.9% to 1998 38.3%, while the private-sector workforce increased from 1992 18.3% to 1998 41.8%. The balance was made up of mixed companies often with foreign participation. By 1999 the private and mixed sectors accounted for 82% of ownership and 61% of output (Spulber 2003, p.290). There was nothing stabilising about this stabilisation process.

3.3   The Transition in Central and Eastern Europe

In 1989 Gorbachev renounced the so-called Brezhnev doctrine of military intervention into other "socialist countries" (Lane 1996). It signalled the rapid collapse of the central plan across CEE. The Berlin wall fell on 9 November 1989. On 1 July 1990, the German Democratic Republic (GDR) agreed monetary union with West Germany. Unemployment soared to 10% by 1991 (Lavigne 1999). In July 1989 the G7 summit empowered the European Commission to assist the transition to capitalism, first in Poland and Hungary, to be followed in 1990 by Czechoslovakia, Bulgarian, Yugoslavia and later Romania. The CMEA was abolished under encouragement from the IMF.

In Poland, Solidarity formed the government in 1990. In Hungary the Communist Party's leading role was revoked the same year. East Germany was absorbed into West Germany. Ceauşescu was overthrown in Romania. The break-up of Yugoslavia began. In Czechoslovakia the communists lost the elections.

Price liberalisation caused rapid falls in output, with the largest falls coinciding with the year in which price liberalization began: 1990 in Poland, 1991 in Czechoslovakia, 1992 in Russia and 1994 in the Ukraine. Hungary adopted a gradualist approach but experienced its biggest output fall in the year of CMEA breakdown, that is the year of trade liberalization at the level of the region. The liberalisation of prices was simultaneously the creation of a market economy. As Roland and Verdier pithily noted, "[W]e assume that markets do not exist when prices are liberalized" (1999, p.2). According to the official national income estimates produced by the EBRD, as shown in Table 3.2, every one of the eighteen countries in CEE and the ex-USSR experienced at least three consecutive years of declining GDP: Moldova, Russia and Ukraine each experienced seven or more. In the Eastern European countries,

Table 3.2 "Real" GDP growth in CEE (percentage change)

	1989	1990	1991	1992	1993
Poland	0.2	−11.6	−7.6	20.6	30.8
Hungary	0.7	−3.5	−11.9	−3	−0.9
Czech Republic	1.4	−0.4	−14.2	−6.4	−0.9
Slovakia	1.4	−0.4	−14.5	−7	−4.1
Russia			−13	−19	−12
Ukraine	4	−3	−12	−17	−17
Bulgaria	0.5	−9.1	−11.7	−7.3	−2.4
Romania	−5.8	−5.6	−12.9	−10	1.3

Source: Adapted from EBRD (1995).

GDP stood at 80% of its 1987 level in 1996, while in the republics of the former Soviet Union, it was only 60% (Dayton-Johnson 1999, p.118).

The "stabilisation" measures consisted of price liberalisation through the reduction of subsidies on consumer and producer prices: the deregulation of price fixing and liberalisation of domestic trade: balancing of the government budget through increased taxes and cuts in government spending; a restrictive, high-interest-rate monetary policy; an income policy to limit wage rises; foreign trade liberalisation through the abolition of the monopoly of foreign trade and tariffs; the internal convertibility of internal and external currencies; and the devaluation of the domestic currency. It was supplemented by the privatisation of state industry, reform of the banking system, introduction of welfare payments and limits on subsidies to designated sectors and industries. There were some differences with the pace of change, but these did not affect the result or scope of the measures, simply the timescale over which they took place. By 1995 even Hungary had initiated a big-bang programme (Lavigne 1999, pp.114–15). By the end of 1991 all of the CPEs had adopted a price liberalization and privatisation or "stabilisation" programme to varying degrees. Manufactured exports to the USSR slumped when faced with Western competition. Yugoslavia broke up after the 1988 "stabilisation programme" which saw inflation reach 1200% in 1989. Slovenia and Croatia declared themselves independent in 1991. In 1987 in Eastern Europe and the USSR 2.2 million people lived on less than US$1 a day (in 1985 prices, using PPP exchange rates for each country). By 1993 the number of poor had risen to 14.5 million. Russian male life expectancy fell from 64.4 years in 1989 to 57.3 years in 1994. Not for the first time did capitalism come into the world dripping in blood (Marx 1982, p.926).

In 1994 the EBRD developed a series of liberalisation measures as a benchmark against the capitalist reform process (EBRD 1998), including the extent of privatisation, price liberalisation, legal reform and foreign tariffs. The scale ranged from 1, signalling no reform, to 4+, signalling a standard equivalent with a Western capitalist nation.

Table 3.3 EBRD transition indicators for Russia and Poland selected years

	1989	1990	1995	2000	2005	2010
Russia						
Large-scale privatisation	1	1	2	3	3.7	3.7
Small-scale privatisation	1	1	2.7	3.7	3.7	3.7
Government and enterprise restructuring	1	1	2	2	2.3	2.7
Price liberalisation	1	1	4	4.3	4.3	4.3
Trade and forex system	1	1	4	4.3	4.3	4.3
Poland						
Large-scale privatisation	1	2	3	3.3	3.3	3.7
Small-scale privatisation	2	3	4	4.3	4.3	4.3
Government and enterprise restructuring	1	2	3	3	3.7	3.7
Price liberalisation	2.3	3.7	4	4.3	4.3	4.3
Trade and forex system	1	3	4	4.3	4.3	4.3

Source: Adapted from EBRD (2001).

The indicators demonstrate that by the mid-1990s, all these states had implemented a programme of capitalist restoration. Table 3.3 illustrates the change in Russia and Poland. By the late 1990s the transition economies were capitalist ones, although still shaped by their origin in the central plan and the experience of a phenomenally deep economic crisis. This was now a market economy that produced exchange values not merely things. If national income is a measure of output within the market boundary, then any increase in production within the new market will have increased national income not reduced it.

3.4   World Bank guide to the historically planned economies

In 1992 the World Bank published a statistical guide to the Historically Planned Economies (HPEs; Marer et al. 1992), it was historical in the sense that the centrally planned economies were history, of the past. It summed up the Western statistical consensus for the reconciliation of the MPS and the SNA. It demonstrated how Western experts obliterated the distinctions between market and planned production. It noted that analysts and policymakers from market economies had often struggled to make sense of the administered prices, the value of production and income in the context of a global economy in which markets dominate:

> There are many statistical problems in comparing HPEs and market economies. A major one stems from the changing role of prices in the economy. In both HPEs and market economies, prices generally clear consumer markets and measure value. But in most HPEs, where until recently prices were administered, their purpose was to meet planned financial balance and to transfer income, and they did not usually reflect resource scarcity. The same is true for measures of value. (Marer et al. 1992, p.3)

As a summary of prices in the HPEs this was essentially wrong. A market clears when supply equals demand. A competitive market constricts demand to those willing to pay and those willing to supply at a given price. If supply is too high then prices fall, demand increases and supply falls and vice versa. In the centrally planned economy, quantities of output were allocated without reference to price. Prices were fixed after the event and did not respond to changes in demand or supply. In most sectors physical quantities of inputs were allocated to produce physical quantities of outputs. In the consumer goods sector, the apparatus used a quasi-market mechanism to distribute output, but the quantities of production were determined in advance, as was their price and the level of "wages" allocated to purchase them. Changes in demand made no difference to the price or supply of goods. The mechanism of supply and demand did not exist, there was no real market to clear. The measures of "value" were not an objective record of actual exchanges. The financial measurements were a reflection of them but played no part in determining production decisions. The so-called suppressed inflation expressed in the long queues typical of the USSR and CEE was a deliberate policy too. The queue was a replacement for the direct distribution of rationing and the gulag. The planned prices for consumer goods and the wages to pay for them were deliberately disproportionate.

This disproportion was no more a consequence of economic value than any other prices in the central plan. Without the act of sale, the subjective label of "price" was predicated on the political objectives of the apparatus. Western statisticians had resolved the problem of measuring the central plan by abstracting from the essential difference between planned and market production. The unreal value measurements of the central plan were no more real than the unreal markets that they were supposed to measure.

Indeed whilst the report noted that "HPEs have no economy wide 'markets' for most goods or services", it nonetheless continued "the equivalent of 'market prices' in the SNA is 'established prices' in the MPS, which include net indirect taxes by sector" (Marer et al. 1992, p.14). This was a formal but not an actual equivalence. A correspondence of the accounting systems but not of the real world, prices administered through the state bank "create the conditions for ex-post control of plan realization by the state mono bank system" (Marer et al. 1992, pp.7–8), whereas prices in a capitalist system measure the actual proportions in which use values are exchanged on a market, or, to put it simply, their price.

In the central plan "profits" were a planned or unplanned residual over revenue and costs. They included producer taxes and subsidies, such that profits and net taxes were inseparable. They were not surplus value created in production and realised on sale. The apparatus extracted unpaid surplus labour from the working class: these savings funded their privileged lifestyle and investment. But this exploitation was not market exploitation. In practice enterprise profits were a form of contingency fund allocated by central planners to enable enterprises to work around plan disproportions by the direct purchase of inputs from other production units to meet plan targets. They did not own them and could not accumulate them. Even these semi-official stock transfers were made at planned prices and subordinate to physical plan targets. To complete their physical output targets, enterprises added costs and were automatically reimbursed through price increases, subsidies, lower taxes on profits or write-offs of credit. Enterprises were not permitted to go bust. The absence of market prices affected what was produced, the range of options and the quality of production, such that

> [t]hese qualitative differences complicate comparisons of quantities between planned and market economies. The implication is that if HPE prices do not reflect underlying costs and buyer preferences, and if quantities carry different qualitative meanings, value (their multiple) in an HPE is not strictly comparable with value in a market economy. (Marer et al. 1992, p.11)

Indeed, this was the implication. If value was not strictly or indeed essentially comparable with a market economy, then the entire architecture of Western statistical analysis of the centrally planned economies fell. In effect, Western statistical agencies both recognised and denied the distinction between plan and market prices simultaneously while accepting them both. The incompatibility of the statistical systems was a reflection of the different modes of production. The World Bank noted that "[i]n HPEs the resulting change of added value is not verified by competition because sales are insured by the sellers' market" (Marer et al. 1992, p.13). But verification by competition is verification through the act of sale. This was a seller's market without sales.

The World Bank explained that further "distortions" in the MPS arose due to the underestimation of depreciation in the central plan. In the SNA, assets are valued at their current or replacement cost, the most conservative, highest replacement cost of constant capital. In a capitalist system, depreciation must be high enough to allow the replacement of assets used up through wear and tear or made obsolescent through technological progress so that a continuous circuit of production may take place.

In the central plan assets were not rendered obsolete by technical progress. They were valued, in the sense of a nominal book "value", at their historic or installation cost less wear and tear. Inflation in the capitalist system means that current costs will generally exceed historic costs. In the capitalist system the use of historic costs to measure national income, would mean that depreciation would be underestimated and output over estimated, as depreciation is a deduction from gross output. Because the MPS used historic costs, so it was argued, the NMP (output less deprecation) was overestimated.

But this was only true if Western depreciation measurements were appropriate in the centrally planned economy. They were not appropriate, due to the absence of inflation and the nature of state owned nationalised property. Planned prices did not change for decades, so the distinction between current and historic prices did not apply. More important, means of production were allocated interest free from central government to the given enterprise. The enterprise did not own these means of production. The quantity of the means of production in physical or value terms made no difference to the rate of return as the state already appropriated the entire physical surplus. The nominal book price of the means of production had no economic significance. Means of production were effectively fully depreciated on installation. They used up a certain proportion of available material resources, which if invested in one thing could not be invested in another thing, but nothing was paid for them, and so they cost nothing. The World Bank noted that the same "distorted", or, more precisely, different, measurement arose in the treatment of inventories and concluded that

> [d]isregarding the differences in the treatment of depreciation and inventory replacement, the net increase of the stock of assets (plus the value of losses in the MPS) is equal to the value of capital formation in SNA. (Marer et al. 1992, p.17)

Disregarding the differences between central planning and capitalism, they were the same.

The World Bank repeated the nostrums of Western economics textbooks. It claimed that money in the HPEs as in "other" that is, capitalist economies, was "a unit of account, a means of payment, and a store of value". Money certainly was a unit of account, although a *post factum* subjective one, but money acted neither as a universal means of payment nor as a store of value. Money was no universal equivalent and did not circulate across the economy. In the consumer sector as has been already demonstrated, wages were deliberately out of kilter with the consumption fund.

Outside that sector, money had even less of a role to play. Currency circulated between households and enterprises, between enterprises and the state bank, but not between the households and the state bank. The possession of money did not "automatically command control of resources in the economy's real sector". It was illegal for households or enterprises to accumulate capital. The "deposit money" or credit allocated to enterprises by the state bank was "not fungible under classical planning".

Money had no independent existence. In a capitalist economy, money acts as a store of value in which, in the sphere of circulation, it forms a hoard either to be lent out or thrown back into production. As such it is capable of purchasing any other commodity for the purposes either of productive or unproductive consumption. Not so in the centrally planned economies, in which commodities and money did not share a common value that was transferable between one another. Enterprises did not own the deposit money they had on deposit. Rather, it was allocated by planners for specific uses such as development projects or to specific accounts such as like working capital, investment and social development, with transfers from one to another requiring authorization by the controlling bank that monitored plan fulfilment. Insofar as the money form existed, it maintained the physical non-financial nature of the central plan (Marer et al. 1992, p.23).

Neither was it a store of value. In a capitalist economy the private ownership of the means of production allows capitalists to earn a return based on the value of the capital they own. Capital generates returns in proportion to its amount. A large amount of capital entitles its owner to a large amount of surplus. According to neoclassical theory, the value of capital is the discounted mass of its future revenues, so the rate of interest must be known before the value of capital is. But no rate of interest means no value, hence this capital had no value at all. Between 1990 and 1998 the privatisation of almost the entire Russian economy yielded just US $7.5 billion (Maddison 2006b, p.157).

Trade relations between members of the CMEA repeated the central plan's internal characteristics externally. The USSR charged relatively low prices for energy and raw material exports to the CEE and paid relatively high prices for manufactures imported from them as measured in Transferable Roubles (TRs). This was supposed to be based on a moving average of world market prices, but it was impossible to establish such a relationship empirically. According to the UN Economic Commission for Europe, attempts to estimate a realistic rouble exchange rate against the US dollar were "probably an inherently impossible task" (Marer et al. 1992, p.19). Biases were not systematic across types of output or through time: "[t]hus, official exchange rates have little economic meaning" (Marer et al. 1992, p.20).

3.5   Productive and unproductive labour and the market boundary

According to the World Bank, "[t]here is one fundamental difference between the SNA and the MPS. In the SNA, all sectors of the economy are considered productive; in the MPS only those that yield "material" goods" (Marer et al. 1992, p.66). It noted that the distinction between productive and unproductive labour originated with Adam Smith and was developed by Karl Marx. The World Bank considered this an application of Marx's theory of unproductive labour that meant that only material – that is physical – commodities were productive. The World Bank claimed that Marx services, that is commodities that are consumed as they are produced, are unproductive. This view is common to Western statisticians. John W. Kendrick in the introduction to a series of essays on the 1993 UN SNA explained that

> Smith excluded services from national income, since their labor does not 'fix itself in vendible commodities that can be accumulated as capital for future periods'. Ricardo and J.S. Mill followed Smith's definition. So did Karl Marx, since he could then more readily develop his theory of the materialization of surplus value into capital. Marx's concept was subsequently implemented by the Soviet Union and other Communist nations in the material product system of national accounts. (1995, p.7)

As a summary of the views of Smith and Marx, this is almost completely incorrect. Marx noted that bourgeois economics think capitalist forms of production are absolute, eternal and natural and so consider that "all labour which produces anything at all, which has any kind of result, is by that very fact productive labour"

(1978, p.49). But it is not. Productive labour is productive of surplus value and is predicated on the production and exchange of commodities, that is on the existence of a market economy.

For Smith and Marx, labour in a capitalist economy creates all value and surplus value. Profits, rents and interests are all forms of surplus value. Fixed capital is a stock of the product of past labour. The only labour that is productive is that which was exchanged against capital and not against revenue or labour that produces surplus value or profits for the capitalist. The difference between productive, unproductive and domestic labour is the social context of each. The capitalist social relation whether in production or circulation is defined by two exchanges, the opening purchase and the closing sale. In productive labour, labour power is purchased and set to work and its product is then sold, making up the two exchanges. In unproductive labour, labour power is purchased but its product is never sold, making only one exchange. Finally, with domestic labour there is neither purchase nor sale, no exchange and therefore, only private labour.

If someone makes him- or herself a piece of toast (or pours him- or herself a glass of wine) at home, this person produces a use value, but no exchange value or surplus value. That use value is not measured in national income. If this person pays a servant to make him or her a piece of toast (or to pour him or her a glass of wine) this output has a cost, but not a price. It is measured in national income but is not sold and so not productive of surplus value. If this person buys a piece of toast (or a glass of wine) from a restaurant, this output has an exchange value and is measured by national income and it is productive of surplus value. According to Smith services are unproductive as they "generally perish in the very instant of their performance, and seldom leave any trace or value behind them" (Gough 1972). Marx did not share this view (Shaikh & Tonak 1996); Marx explained that

> [a]n actor for example, or even a clown . . . is a productive labourer if he works in the service of a capitalist (an entrepreneur) to whom he returns more labour than he receives in the form of wages: while a jobbing tailor who comes to the capitalist's house and patches his trousers for him, is an unproductive labourer. The former's labour is exchange with capital, the latter's with revenue. (1978, p.157)

Paul Studenski's classic work on the history of national accounts accurately summarised the distinction between Smith and Marx and concluded that "Marx denied that the form of product – material or immaterial – has anything to do with the distinction between productive and unproductive labour". But Studenski described Marx's view only to deny it in the next breathe. He continued, stating that "Marx chose, nonetheless, in all his subsequent writing to associate productive labor with the creation of material goods alone" (Studentski 1958, p.22). This is not correct. Marx noted in *Capital I* that "[i]f we may take an example from outside the sphere of production of material production, a schoolmaster is a productive labourer when, in addition to belabouring the heads of his pupils, he works himself into the ground to enrich the owner of the school" (1982, p.644). Marx's emphasis on the production of material commodities reflected the relatively undeveloped nature of the service sector in the mid-nineteenth century.

The real distinction between the MPS measurement and GDP measurement was not the material or immaterial nature of the product, the issue of coverage, or the rate of depreciation, but that the MPS did not measure a market economy. The central plan produced use value not value. Nothing produced in it, either material or a service, was ever exchanged against money. There were no independent capitals. There were no nationwide markets and nothing was sold at market prices.

In the centrally planned economy, labour was not productive, in the sense defined by Adam Smith or Marx, because there was no exchange value and so no value at all. The limitation of the MPS to the measurement of the production of only "material" things reflected the prioritisation of the accumulation of means of production over consumption goods such as health, education, administration, business and personal services. Marx opposed the theory paradoxically attributed to him by both the neoclassical and Stalinist statisticians.

Studenski explained that Marx defined the "new produced value" (value added), in a capitalist economy, in income terms, as the sum of wages, profits, and rent. In product terms it is the sum of consumer goods and net investment goods. While gross value added is the sum of wages, profits, rent and capital replacement. The income side of national income is measured by aggregating the incomes derived from production. The production side is the value of the new product plus the value of capital replacement. Gross value added equals the total product less material expenses and capital replacement.

Marx noted that replacement of capital is never a part of income (Studenski 1958, p.23). The "value of the product" is equivalent to the "gross national product" that includes the duplicated values of raw materials and supplies and the replacement of used up capital, whereas net value, what Marx called the "gross income of society", consists of "wages, profit (including interest), and rent" or "net national income". This is reflected in the SNA in which the three forms of national income – production, income and demand – are identical. Production is the sum of value added in different sectors (agriculture, industry and services) net of duplication: income is the sum of wages and surplus value or property income, rents and profits; demand is the sum of final expenditures by consumers, investors and government.

The SNA measures the entire economic activity of the market sector in a capitalist economy. It is predicated on the creation, transformation, exchange, transfer, exhaustion and amortization of value within the market boundary. The 1993 SNA defines the production boundary as "all production actually destined for the market, whether for sale or barter" (UN 1993, 1.20). This production boundary applies even if "the SNA does not present market transactions in a strict sense, but rather in a corrected or completed form" (Lutzel 1986, p.203). The SNA does not differentiate between unproductive and productive labour and considers all labour within the market boundary to be productive. This accords with Marx because the income to pay for production that does not produce surplus value must arise in the productive sector. The 1953 United Nations SNA, itself a development of the original 1947 report from Richard Stone, states:

> Production is a basic concept which can be described as the provision of goods and services. Not all production, however, in this broad sense is included in the concept of economic production which enters into national accounting. It is therefore, necessary to state as clearly as possible the line of distinction between production that is, and production that is not so included. This may be done conveniently by drawing a production boundary . . . In a monetary economy all goods and services are included in the concept of production if they are exchanged for money. (UN 1953, p.4)

Kuznets (who supported the application of market measurements to the non-market central plan) nonetheless considered that the distinction between economic and noneconomic activities is the market:

> The diversity of physical shapes economic goods display and of wants they serve compels us to express them in terms of a common unit that will reveal their economic significance and allow them to be added and subtracted in various combinations. This measurable aspect, common to all economic goods and revealing their economic significance, we designate 'economic value'. The yardstick of economic value is fashioned on the market place. (Kuznets 1941, p.21)

Market prices are a far from perfect measure "but they are the sole practicable basis if the estimator is to follow the consensus of social opinion" (Kuznets 1941, p.55). National income consists of one total, the net value of goods produced. Even if non-economic, non-market activity satisfies the wants of people this production is not included in measures of economic activity, "the yardstick (no matter how it may have to be adjusted) is the market price" (Kuznets 1975, p.124). Transactions with compensation are acts of exchange, transactions without compensation are transfers, valued at the market price of the inputs required to produce them plus or minus profits or losses. Market producers do not care about the functional purpose of the purchase made from them. The general rule in the SNA approach is that "all transactions are recorded in market prices on an accrual basis" (World Bank & Goskomstat 1995, p.9).

The MPS equivalent of "national income", in the sense of a formal accounting identity, was gross output net of depreciation or NMP or Net National Product (NNP) in the SNA. This formal equivalence, achieved in the books but not the real world, reduced the distinction between the economic systems to a statistical issue to be solved through creative accounting. It abandoned the market boundary as an actually existing fact in determining the measurement of economic production. It treated the output of the central plan as market production – without actual markets. The HPE produced a formula to reconcile the two systems:

$$NMP + D(FA) = GMP$$
$$GMP + GV - NMI + Diffs = GDP$$

They took NMP, then added the total value of depreciation of all fixed assets to material production (D(FA)) to arrive at GMP. Then they added the gross value added of non-material services (GV) and deducted the non-material inputs used for material production (NMI) and then adjusted for certain minor differences between the SNA and the MPS (such as travel costs and welfare costs; Diffs) to arrive at GDP (Marer et al. 1992, p.70). Non-material inputs were services not otherwise included in the calculation of net material product. Effectively national income was equal to gross material production plus gross non-material production or national income equals "gross production". Marer claimed that notwithstanding the "arbitrary" nature of depreciation in planned economies their estimates of centrally planned national income were nonetheless, if not true, then at least "truer" (Marer et al. 1992, p.71). By abstracting from the actual social system, statisticians had established a measurement that was, if it were not true, was at least truer than truth.

This formula was an explicit restatement of Bergson's AFC or "building-block" method. It glossed over or ignored the absence of market exchange and actual objective prices. It gave an unwarranted objective significance to the aggregates of concrete labour time that formed the basis for the subjective, *post factum* "value" attributed to planned production by the apparatus. Turnover taxes, subsidies and arbitrary profit mark-ups were "corrected" by "adding subsidies, subtracting turnover taxes, and imposing an economy wide uniform rate of return on fixed and working capital" (Marer et al. 1992, p.71).

Estimates of these quantities were based on sample data in physical units, adjusted when possible for changes in product mix and quality. For value added applied to non-material services in real terms, it was assumed that growth was determined by changes in the number of employees, without accounting for increases in productivity, because the majority of these services were not marketed (Marer et al. 1992, p.75). Indeed, not only were these services not marketed; neither was any of the output of the central plan.

To estimate, or adjust, the value of production on a factor cost basis, the aggregate value of national income was divided into returns to labour and to non-labour factors of production – fixed and working capital and agricultural land. The returns to labour were roughly equal to the sum of wages, salaries, payments in kind, farm income in kind, and social security contributions paid by employees and employers. In calculating factor costs for the USSR (that is the non-existent expenditures on interest and rent to non-existent capitalists and landlords) two basic methods were used. First, the difference between global national income and total return to labour was distributed proportionately according to the stock of fixed and working capital used in each production sector. The valuation of this stock was based on the very same artificial, arbitrary and supposed rate of return imposed to estimate the non-existent profits of the non-existent capitalists. No separate return was attributed to agricultural land. Second, in calculating factor costs for other

European HPES, the non-labour portion of GNP was distributed according to the total stock of capital, including agricultural land. These estimates for national production were then translated into international prices either through comparison with the exchange rates of another country or PPP.

The World Bank, the IMF, the OECD and the newly reformed Goskomstat, now the CIS Statistical Authority, applied this World Bank methodology in a series of reports, which attempted to measure the national income of the Russian economy during the transition to capitalism in the early 1990s. These agencies considered that the key problem with reconciling the MPS or the NMP system with the SNA was one of coverage. The MPS ignored "non-material services". There were further concerns about how to properly measure income, inputs and outputs in market values, how to make historical MPS data comparable with the SNA and how the statistical authorities themselves should operate (Saunders & Wu 2009, p.414). There was no issue of principle in the replacement of planned "prices" with market ones. The collapse of production in CEE and the CIS was synonymous with a collapse of national income.

The OECD in partnership with the CIS Statistical Committee developed production, distribution, use of income and capital accounts for the USSR for the last three years of the centrally planned economy: 1988, 1989 and 1990. They redefined the categories of the MPS as if they were the categories of an SNA market economy (OECD 1993). Youri Ivanov of the Soviet, and then CIS, Statistical Commission considered that

> [i]n both systems major aggregates are valued at market current and constant prices, in both systems capital formation is measured on both a gross and a net basis, i.e. before and after deduction of consumption of fixed assets and there are some similarities in accounting procedures adopted to value non-market output. (1987, p.3).

Although Ivanov understood "the decision (to introduce the SNA) was clearly linked to economic reforms aimed at the transformation of an administrative economy into a market one and the gradual integration of the country into the world economy system" (Ivanov et al. 1993, p.280), he simply assumed that planned production was market production when this was required for ease of measurement.

Ivanov's later comparison of the MPS and the SNA noted that in the MPS, "[e]conomic production is restricted to the production of material goods and material services" whereas in the SNA, "[e]conomic production is defined to include all activities for producing goods and services, except for domestic services that are produced by households for their own use" (UN 2009, p.483). Ivanov abstracted from the market boundary so that the objective nature of real sales on an actual market were indistinguishable from the subjective nature of unreal sales in the non-market central plan. This is reflected in the 1993 joint OECD–CIS Statistical Committee definition of centrally planned productive activity as "one which gives rise the production of goods and services" (OECD 1993, p.9). Sales were assumed whether they occurred or not. The estimates included both material production such as industry, agriculture, forestry, construction, transportation of goods and so on and non-material services such as health care, social security, education and passenger transport.

Value flows, the accounting equivalent of physical production, were imputed at "prices actually used in transactions" when these "transactions" were in fact deliveries, not sales, of physical quantities of pre-allocated inputs and outputs. The prices of direct material inputs into production were the planned prices used in the compilation of MPS estimates. Indirect costs were estimated by specific coefficients for each industry. There was no statistical information available about the purchases of non-materials services, so they were estimated "arbitrarily" after consultation with experts in industrial statistics and accountants.

All items of goods and services including intermediate consumption were valued at "purchasers' prices". Non-marketed goods and services, a misnomer given the absence of markets, were valued by using the "market price of similar goods and services that are marketed where these are available and where not they are valued at the sum of costs of production" (OECD 1993, p.12). Depreciation allowances "were made on the basis of the historical value of fixed assets and the rates of depreciation fixed by government regulation" (OECD 1993, p.37). The annual total of depreciation included allowances for the replacement and major repairs of fixed assets.

The OECD created the categories of a market economy to measure the centrally planned production of the USSR, before a market existed there. The falsity of this method was clear even before these estimates were published. The collapse of the plan after the big bang showed the true effect of transition.

Vincent Koen (1994) for the IMF anticipated the subsequent development of Western statistical analysis of Russia's transition. Koen's intention was to explain away the collapse in production caused by price liberalisation. Koen pointed out that in a period of rapid price change current price indices suffer from base year effects. In Russia the urban consumer price index increased 26-fold from 1991 to 1992, while the producer price index rose 61.9 times. As a result, the nominal value added would be very different in the base or given year. Koen's calculations show that by December 1993 industrial production had fallen to slightly more than half its 1989 level. He pointed out that official statistics that show an 18.5% fall in the 1992 GDP would have been lower if 1992 prices had been used, because of a higher weight for energy production. Similarly, price changes affected estimates of wages, international national income and profits.

Koen and Gavrilenkov developed an alternative real GDP series from the demand side. They claimed official GDP estimates based on the production side exaggerated the fall in GDP. They used revised retail data and alternative estimates of fixed investments, inventory accumulation and government consumption to estimate the scale of the fall from the demand side. They pointed out that private-sector activity was probably not adequately captured in official data, they claimed that investment fell more than consumer production and that "consumer goods that are no longer produced were not desired by consumers" (Koen &

Gavrilenkov 1994, p.iii). Price liberalisation reduced search costs and queuing. Goods were unaffordable, so there was no point queuing for them, and with lower production there was a reduction of waste. Koen and Gavrilenkov showed that the military output of the military industrial complex (MIC) had slumped faster than the consumer output of the MIC. Although notwithstanding this, its consumer output still fell by a cumulative 73%.

They pointed out that either base effects or the use of world market prices altered the scale of the slump substantially and that electricity consumption had not fallen to the same degree as GDP. They searched for any and every method to reduce the scale of the output collapse. This was a nakedly ideological survey but even so it accepted that "It cannot be ruled out *a priori* that the cumulative fall in production was even larger than the one experienced in the United States during the Great Depression of 1929–33, and larger than any downturn registered in Russia during the previous 70 years" including during the German invasion of 1941 (Koen & Gavrilenkov 1994, p.1). Their estimates reduced the rate of decline of real GDP from about a half to about a third, or by 4% to 7% a year, from 1990 to 1994. For all of their attempts to downplay the effects of price liberalisation on output collapse, they failed to differentiate between the creation of real GDP within the real market boundary and the collapse of the central plan. Their alternative series anticipated the report of the World Bank and Goskomstat in 1995 that re-examined official estimates to reduce the estimated fall in GDP almost exactly in line with Koen and Gavrilenkov's estimates (OECD 1997, p.30).

3.6   The World Bank and Goskomstat

The World Bank and Goskomstat (1995) reported on these issues. They reiterated the differences between the MPS and the SNA in terms of the coverage of services and lack of depreciation. They pointed out that under the MPS system the production of material resources was not comparable with the volume and structure of financial resources. The lack of reliable market prices directly shaped how they developed their estimates of Russian national income. The transitional nature of the economy meant that prices were not responsive to supply and demand. Capitalists and workers still did not receive wages, profits or interest proportionate to the output they produced.

As a result they concluded that "[t]he principal method for computing GDP indicators in Russia today is the production approach" (World Bank & Goskmostat 1995, p.11). Although enterprises dramatically increased prices with the abolition of controls in 1992, the new higher prices were still not true market prices. Enterprises used barter to maintain production. They did not take proper account of the value of inputs from stocks. Wages were unpaid. The tax system was only in its infancy. There was a wide gap between the physical and financial measurements of enterprise activity due to delays in payment and high inflation. This was exacerbated by a lack of information because the surveys that formed the basis for information collection in the SNA were not in place, even while the reporting system of the central plan collapsed and was further fragmented by the creation of nation states out of the former USSR. Together all this meant that "a coherent system of price indexes to be used to deflate national accounts is the matter of the future" (World Bank &Goskmostat 1995, p.52).

The quality of national income estimates in current prices depends on the accuracy of the physical indices of output and price indices. Prior to 1994 there were no reliable or actual price indices. The World Bank and Goskomstat used physical output indices to develop their national income estimates, using the output data for comparable prices reported by enterprises. These prices were still modified by the subjective measurements developed in the MPS/NMP. The World Bank applied different measurements to various sectors of the economy in an attempt to circumvent the problem of inaccurate or incomplete price information.

In the construction sector, output was valued on the accrual basis but at mixed prices, partly current market prices and partly costs plus profit margin. In agriculture it was mostly market prices. Non-market services or more accurately, services that would not have been provided by the market in the West, such as general government, non-market health care, education, science and non-market institutions, were valued at cost. Fixed capital consumption was not based on actual data. The output of housing was valued on a cash basis although it was not clear whether prices were market ones or presumably whether this was indeed actual cash, actual payments, actually paid. Intermediate consumption was valued at purchase prices, but the data was unreliable and inconsistent. It was not clear where prices came from (World Bank & Goskmostat 1995, pp.61–62).

Value added in constant prices (that is in the prices of the previous year) were not calculated by the double deflation method (the difference between gross output and intermediate consumption); instead, value added was estimated by applying volume production indices weighted by previous year values of value added, to previous year's value added. Direct estimates were made from physical indicators of production and employment for each economic activity, "due to the unavailability of a comprehensive range of appropriate price indicators for deflating the gross output and intermediate consumption" (World Bank & Goskmostat 1995, p.89).

The unreliability of market prices in this early period of price liberalization was not essentially a problem of statistics. Rather, it was an indicator of the growth of market production and exchange within the planned economy. The reason that the "value" of physical output at planned prices did not coincide with incomes or input–output tables was that there was still no genuine market in the transitional economies. At the beginning of the transition, the share of national income derived from private sector activities ranged from less than 1% in Czechoslovakia and Russia to almost 20% in Poland, compared with about 80% in the United States (Tanzi 1999).

The World Bank and Goskomstat used the physical non-market indicators that measured the central plan. They constructed a 1990 index of GDP at "market prices" for the central plan, before there were any market prices, and from 1991 to 1994, before there were real market prices (World Bank & Goskomstat 1995, p.90). These revised estimates for GDP at constant prices from 1991 to 1994 used either physical volume indicators for production or employment data for each economic activity to extrapolate the base year (World Bank & Goskomstat 1995, p92). According to these estimates of the World Bank and Goskmostat, GDP in constant prices declined by about 35% between 1990 and 1994, less than the former estimate of about 47%. The difference was attributed to under-reporting in the initial estimates.

The World Bank and Goskmostat's estimates measured the decline of the central plan as the decline of market production in a period when market production was rapidly increasing. The use of physical and employment measures, separate from the price mechanism, obscured the growth of the market boundary and with it value production as a proportion of total output. National income increased even as the physical output of the central plan slumped.

Kasper Bartholdy pointed out that the report did not attempt to balance the accounts. He recommended that the discrepancy between production and consumption "should be made transparent" but did not explain how (1997, p.140). Bartholdy's criticism missed the essential point. There were good reasons why the accounts did not balance during the early period of transition. They were an uncomfortable juxtaposition of two different economies. Imputed measures of the rapidly declining output of the centrally planned sector and real value created within the rapidly expanding market boundary.

3.7 IMF national accounts in the transition countries

The problem of how to measure the value of the output of the transitional economies was directly addressed by the IMF (Bloem et al. 1996, 1998). If the OECD had simply assumed market production when there was none, whereas the World Bank had estimated national income on the basis of physical outputs and employment, by 1996 most of the economy was subordinated to production for the market (EBRD 1998). But there remained transitional sectors in which it was still unclear whether much government production was market or non-market. There were issues around the valuation of stocks, the coverage of the service sector and problems with source data. Although social relations inside many enterprises remained largely unchanged from the central planning era, enterprises were now subject to the external operation of the market (Clarke 2007). Value production was no longer a notional construct. This was a real capitalist economy, albeit one shaped by its origin in central planning.

The IMF noted that ministries often continued to organise the production of goods and services which were now sold on the market. There were doubts over the legal status of these institutions and how that legal status would affect the classification of their production in the national accounts. Even if enterprises were legally independent, many of them remained strongly intertwined with the ministries from which they had originated before privatisation. Their fixed capital was financed from ministerial budgets: the prices they charged were often decided by the ministries; ministries compensated them for losses and appropriated surpluses. This had an impact on calculations of value added because non-market production in the SNA was valued as the sum of costs at market prices. The SNA required that, to be considered a separate institutional unit, it should be "capable, in its own right, of owning assets incurring liabilities and engaging in economic activities and in transaction with other entities" (UN 1993, para. 4.3). There should be a complete set of accounts. Where units did not have separate legal status – as in the centrally planned economy of the USSR – "strictly speaking the autonomy implied by the first criterion does not exist" (Bloem et al. 1996, p.7).

The transformation of government owned production units into independent capitalist enterprises was a real transition for the real economy. In the transitional economy of the CIS and of CEE the lack of clarity around whether enterprises met the essential requirements for classification as independent enterprises reflected the actual transition to the market. The IMF noted that applying the criterion for the independence of enterprises "may imply that producing units without an independent legal status" are not independent, as indeed they were not.

The privatisation of these enterprises and their subordination to the market was a key indicator of the growth of market production. The IMF decided to resolve the real ambiguity of the transition, by interpreting this criterion "more liberally" to blur the SNA's definition of a market producer. This obscured the real growth of market production, even though they recognised that it remained important to "avoid inclusion" of government sector units that were not oriented to the market (Bloem et al. 1996, p.7).

The IMF pointed out that in the OECD (1993) report *National Accounts for the Former Soviet Union*, housing services and public utilities were considered to be market services. In contrast in the World Bank and Goskomstat (1995) *Russian Federation: Report on the National Accounts* 80% of the total of housing services and 45% of utilities were considered non-market. This statistical contradiction reflected the nature of the two documents. The OECD/CIS national income estimates measured the final years of the centrally planned economy before a real market existed. The World Bank and Goskmostat estimated national income at the outset of market creation, whereas the IMF could reflect on a process largely complete.

The IMF emphasised that the SNA is quite clear about the distinction between market and non-market output: "[m]arket output is output that is sold at prices that are economically significant or otherwise disposed of in the market" (Bloem et al. 1996, p.8). This repeated the market boundary condition for the SNA that was so conspicuously missing from the OECD and CIS document. They cited the classic example of market production by a government unit, the forestry ministry that sells some timber, which illustrated the point well. Before 1992 essentially nothing was sold in the USSR. The forestry ministry delivered timber according to physical targets not financial ones. When capitalist governments set producer prices below production costs, the SNA requires that these payments be classified as subsidies. This, too, assumes the existence of market producers, market prices and costs: "[a]s regards the recipient, a current transfer made by government cannot be a subsidy unless it is paid to a market producer unit i.e. to a unit producing goods or market services" (Roman 1985, p.42).

Different outputs and inputs are incommensurate as use values. Whether a car is worth more than the labour, rubber, steel and glass that produced it, depends on its price relative to the price of the inputs that created it, and indeed whether underpriced or mispriced, or even sold at all. This requires an objective measure of value measured through exchange. As Leontief noted in his discussion of the US economy between 1919 and 1939:

> [T]he basic properties of an economic system are uniquely determined by the (relative) *value* figures of all different kinds of outputs and inputs. Two systems with identical value patterns will have also the same price and output reactions. Even if the prices and quantities taken separately were quite different . . . For the subsequent empirical analysis, this invariance is of cardinal importance. It makes it possible to determine the most significant properties of the actual economic system on the basis of its value pattern alone. (Leontief 1951, p.65, emphasis in the original)

In a capitalist economy the physical production and exchange of things matters only insofar as it enables the production, circulation and exchange of value. In the centrally planned economy the physical production and distribution of things took place without value at all: "[p]hysical planning refers to the fact that the main attention of planners was concentrated on physical flows (tons of this, cubic metres of that) and not on financial and monetary aspects of economic life" (Estrin et al. 2007, p.21). The price policy of the Soviet Union implied a system of implicit subsidies and taxes (Bloem et al. 1996, p.14) but not explicit ones.

The IMF treated the subjective list prices of the central planners as if they were genuine market prices. Enterprises could "work round" list prices when they did not cover "costs" of production or if they needed "higher values" for their products. The physical completion of output targets was all that mattered in the plan, not their *post factum* reflection in the financial accounts. The transition to capitalism and the introduction of price liberalization meant that list prices were raised in some months "of the order of 300 to 400 percent" (Bloem et al. 1996, p.14). Mark-ups were now at the discretion of the enterprises and were raised on average 70% above costs, up from a pre-transition range of 15% to 20%. This development was not simply a quantitative one. Bergson had pointed out the qualitatively different nature of this planned profit. In the centrally planned economy, enterprises wanted to reduce the proportion of output relative to input – the opposite situation to that of a market economy, in which inputs have a money price. Insofar as this was reflected in the state finance system, this meant that efforts to raise productivity would reduce the planned "profitability" of the enterprise in the next cycle, by reducing the amount of inputs received relative to outputs supplied.

Pre-transition mark-ups were fixed in either physical quantities or measured using a subjective valuation based on concrete labour hours. Post-liberalisation list prices still did not immediately change to reflect market conditions. The state authorities continued to set prices in a number of countries for items such as housing utilities and food staples. Delays in payment and the effect of rapid inflation on the value of stocks of inventories meant list prices were unreliable. This led to further mark-ups of about 20% in Russia and Ukraine. According to the SNA these mark-ups should have been viewed as interest payments, but because they had no relationship to the production process, they did not alter aggregate GDP totals because overpayments in one sector were compensated for by losses in another. The IMF concluded that

> [i]n a sense, in some transition countries the relevant market price is the list price adjusted for inflation over the period over which payment is delayed. But it is by no means clear that this period is known in advance, or even discussed in advance between seller and purchaser. Indeed, the period seems to be dictated more by the circumstances of the purchaser than by an action of the producer. In that sense, it is not clear that there is agreement on price, whereas agreement on price is the foundation of all market behaviour in market economies. (Bloem et al. 1996, p.18)

The economy was not yet a fully capitalist market one. Prices were not yet active indicators that determined the production and distribution of output. They were only becoming so. Before 1990 stocks of raw materials had no value. After 1991 rapid inflation affected the values of stocks and this could have overstated the amount of value added in production by measuring holding gains as value added. This reflected a real change. Stocks had no money price under the central plan, even if they cost the workers that produced them much sweat and labour. By failing to value the stocks at nothing – their actual price in 1990 – the statisticians did indeed understate the growth of capitalist production. The transition to a market economy meant that these stocks now determined in part the value composition of capital. Objective market prices replaced the physical basis of central planning. When there was no information on costs of production, the IMF recommended that stocks be valued at current prices.

The IMF noted that the lack of coverage of the informal economy, the formal unrecorded economy, the hidden economy and the illegal economy meant that the production of the market economy was probably underestimated in the chaotic first phase of transition from 1992 to 1997. This was worsened by the lack of good information. Reporting systems were not in place. Enterprises did not want their activities to be reported and the survey data typical of a market economy did not exist under the central plan. As normal checks based on changes in physical quantities were not reliable, estimates of national income in this period were particularly error prone. But the main error resulted from the confusion of market and non-market production. In the end the issue was not about whether the IMF's estimates were accurate; they were as accurate as could be given the chaos of the economy, the inadequacies of the data and the ideological biases of their own reporters. The problem was that they failed to measure the actual growth of real commodity production inside the market boundary of national income accounting. Although Vincent Koen and Michael Marrese of the IMF noted that the public perception of Russia's economic transition was that the "old system has been successfully destroyed", but it had not been replaced by a "sustainable democracy and an effective market economy" (1995, p.1). Part of the reason the IMF was unable to measure the growth of the market was its failure to differentiate the decline of the central plan from the growth of the market. It applied an aggregated national income measurement that obscured the change. The IMF registered the transformed status of government enterprises into real capitalist firms and the subordination of prices to supply and demand. But all the different estimates measured non-capitalist planned production as if it took place within the market boundary. It failed to track the real growth of capitalist national income within the transitional economies, which increased even as the output of the centrally planned sector slumped. The restoration of capitalism in the CEE and CIS was markedly different to that of China. China experienced no big-bang or IMF-inspired stabilisation programme. Rather, its long road to capitalism began in the late 1970s.

3.8 China: to the plan and back again

The accession of Mao's Chinese Communist Party (CCP) to power in 1949 was rapidly followed from 1953 by the transition to central planning modelled on the USSR. China established the MPS during the First Five Year Plan (1953–57). Skousen summarised the nature of the economic system in a review of Chinese accounting measures:

> Under the centrally planned economy, the government administered the national economy as if it was a single, huge, industrial corporation which did not let operating divisions sell products or develop production plans. Production and cost targets were set through state agencies. Although profit was one of the targets, it was only in name since all prices were set by the state. (1988, p.202)

This was a period of economic recovery after the Japanese invasion and civil war. The transition to a system of bureaucratic central planning was very successful during this early period. Arthur Ashbrook (1967), a CIA analyst writing for the JEC, gave the regime "full marks" for its achievements.

It was followed by the Great Leap Forward (GLF; 1958–65). This was an attempt to raise productivity and output to that of the UK within fifteen years by the forced collectivisation of the peasantry. The apparatus thought that by driving the peasants from the land into small-scale rural industry they could transform the industrial base of the economy. They could not. The GLF failed disastrously and sparked a serious famine. Millions of farmers died as the material basis for collective agriculture did not exist.

This crisis was exacerbated by the Sino-Soviet split in December 1961, which meant that 300 major infrastructural and industrial projects, dependent on both USSR's design expertise and machine tools, were not completed. The GLF was followed by the Cultural Revolution (1966–76) when the state statistics section was abolished. Limited statistical work recommenced in 1974 but its progress was uncertain until after Mao Zedong's death in 1976.

At its third plenum in 1978 the CCP identified the use of market forces as the key to "a historic shift to socialist modernisation" (Hart-Landsberg & Burkett 2005, p.40). At the start of the economic reform, state-owned enterprises (SOEs) delivered 78% of industrial output, employed 76% of all industrial workers and absorbed 84% of investment in industrial fixed assets (Brandt et al. 2008, p.571). From then on, central planning shaped the overall structure of the economy, but a system of dual prices partitioned inputs and outputs into plan and market segments. Plan quotas were fixed and transacted at official prices while surplus output was sold at flexible prices that reflected supply and demand. The share of producer goods transacted at market prices rose from 0% in 1978, to 13% in 1985, to 46% in 1991, to 78% in 1995 (Brandt, Rawski, & Sutton 2008, p.572). In October 1979 the State Council adopted the "Decision on Strengthening Statistical Work and Improving Statistical Organizations" that reinstated national statistics (World Bank 1992, pp.3–4).

In 1979 Deng Xiaoping, the Chinese leader, launched the "Open Door" to foreign multinational corporations to attract foreign direct investment (FDI) from multinational companies. Special Economic Zones (SEZs) that gave these firms special, although initially limited rights, to exploit labour and repatriate profits were launched along the southern coast. Agricultural reform reduced restrictions on private markets and increased the size of privately worked plots on the rural communes. The state raised the prices of compulsory grain purchases by 20% and offered a 50% premium for grain purchases above the quota. By 1983 the decollectivisation of the commune system of agriculture meant that 98% of peasant households produced for the market. Land remained nationalised, but it was placed at the use of the peasant households who farmed it.

The creation of Town and Village Enterprises (TVEs) that fell "outside many of the regulations designed to protect the rights and conditions of urban workers" (Hart-Landsberg & Burkett 2005, p.44) allowed local government bodies to take control of state assets. In 1983 SOEs were ordered to hire new workers on a contractual basis, limiting their job security. By 1984 the private sector employed 3 million workers. A further 6 million workers were put on contracts which reduced their security of employment. By April 1987 these workers accounted for 7.51 million, or 8%, of the industrial workforce. By 1993 there were 25 million TVEs employing 123 million workers. These market reforms produced large increases in output, per capita incomes, based on PPP measures that aggregated centrally planned and market production, doubled between 1978 and 1984.

The transformation of production through the introduction of market forces was reflected in the use of Western accounting methods because "the Chinese could not model these accounting techniques on the Soviet system, since profit centres were more applicable to Western management accounting methods" (Skousen 1988, p.203). As the economic reforms progressed so Western or actually capitalist accounting practices were generalised across the economy. In 1984 at its 12th Congress the CCP adopted the idea of "planned commodity production". SOEs now financed their operations through the retention of earnings and bank loans from the state system. Prices were permitted to move in wider bands (Naughton 1999). Workers' rights to security of contract were limited to regular state employees who now constituted around 40% of the work force. The addition of the Pearl River, Min River and Yangtze River deltas to the SEZs opened the whole southern coast to foreign investment. To encourage foreign companies, taxes were lowered, and companies were given more freedom to hire and fire workers and the ability to acquire foreign exchange.

From 1980 to 1989 China's "real" GDP measured by PPP, aggregated according to Western estimates, grew at 9.7% per annum. But towards the end of the 1980s the rate of agricultural income growth slowed, because the effect of the initial reforms wore off. Significant inflation, alongside the growth of budget deficits started to hit working-class living standards. A sharp rise in unemployment and the erosion of job security led to significant working class unrest. These were contributory factors to the 1989 Tiananmen Square democracy movement. The perceived threat to CCP rule meant the movement was brutally repressed, in so doing removing the last vestiges of resistance to wholesale privatisation of state industry.

In early 1992 Deng Xiaoping during a visit to Shenzhen announced that "as long as it makes money it is good for China" (Hart-Landsberg & Burkett 2005, p.51). At the 14th Party Congress in October 1992 the CCP resolved to establish a "socialist market economy with Chinese characteristics" (Hart-Landsberg & Burkett 2005, p.51). A large-scale policy of privatisation was introduced in all but the 1,000 largest state enterprises. The private sector was awarded preferable tax provisions which taxed the SOEs harder than private firms. The shortfall of tax revenues provided further impetus to the privatisation process and from 1996 it was extended to TVEs. By the end of the 1990s SOEs employed just 12% of total employment accounting for 38% of national income. The influx of multinational corporations into the SEZs meant that by 2003 these firms accounted for 57% of total exports. By the mid-1990s these reforms had created a truly capitalist economy. The overwhelming majority of exchanges took place at market prices. Hart-Landsberg and Burkett concluded that:

> Once the path of pro-market reforms was embarked upon, each subsequent step in the reform process was largely driven by tensions and contradictions generated by the reforms themselves. . . . that has created an economy that has little to do with socialism. (2005, p.61)

The dominance of market prices, the transition to commodity production and exchange, is demonstrated by the proportion of total output undertaken at market prices. In 1978, 100% of producer goods, 100% of retail sales, and 93% of farm commodities were valued at state "prices". By 2003, 87% of producer goods, 96% of retail sales and 97% of farm commodities were valued at market prices.

The transition to capitalism produced some similar features to those of the CEE and CIS. Unemployment among state owned manufacturing workers grew rapidly alongside income inequality. From 1996 to 2001 36 million SOE and 17 million TVE workers were laid off (UN Conference on Trade and Development [UNC-TAD] 2005). The Gini co-efficient, a standard inequality measure, rose from 0.33 in 1980 to 0.46 in 2000. But the low level of development of the Chinese economy with a predominantly agricultural population and the rapid growth of the export-oriented sector based in the SEZs meant that the growth of these two sectors more than compensated for the decline of the privatised industries.

As the rate of productivity growth outstripped the rate of decline of consumption, workers' wages rose even while the proportion of wages in national income fell. The number of consumer goods per 100 households rose: for 1984 and 2003, TVs from 4/100 to 94/100 in 2003, washing machines from 1/100 to 59/100 and refrigerators from 0/100 to 46/100, respectively (Dayton-Johnson 2005; OECD 2005). By the end of the 1990s, China's average level of daily per capita calorie intake fell only 10% short of the level of developed countries.

Vietnam's path from central planning to capitalism was similar to that of China. Vietnam's first movements away from a planned economy came in 1979 in agriculture and 1981 in industry. Beginning in 1981, SOEs were allowed to sell outside the plan, and to keep a share of profits. Reforms in SOEs were deepened through the 1980s. The 1988 land law allowed for the household use of land for agricultural production. It led to the rapid dismantling of collectives between 1989 and 1993. In 1990 the law on private enterprises and the law on companies were passed, establishing legalized ownership forms, proprietorships, limited liability companies and joint-stock companies. Employment in the private sector grew from 3.8 million in 1988 to 10.2 million in 1992 and to 12.6 million in 1995. The number of private firms grew by 40% a year between 1992 and 1996. By 2003 the domestic private sector accounted for 23% of industrial output in Vietnam (Woodruff 2004).

3.9   Western estimates

In 1958 W.W. Hollister developed the first published Western estimates of China's national income. Hollister used a final expenditures method, but it was based on a narrow range of data. Hollister (1958) assumed stable input–output relationships, based on official Chinese wage and price indices, and his estimates were close to official rates of growth. In 1961 Alexander Eckstein, with the support of Simon Kuznets and Abram Bergson, published national income estimates for 1952, the final pre-plan year. Ta-Chung Liu and Kung-Chia Yeh were part of the US Air Force's Project RAND. They worked with Simon Kuznets on the first proper Western attempt to reconstruct the output of China's centrally planned economy, to correct for "obvious biases" by conforming to Bergson's standard definitions according to the categories of the SNA (Liu & Yeh 1965, p.125).

They addressed typical issues of coverage, depreciation and the treatment of taxes and subsidies. They noted that communist policy in 1955 was "designed to wipe out whatever free market activity was left in rural areas" (Liu & Yeh 1965, p.14) and that by the end of the First Five Year Plan in 1958, private enterprises' share of industry and retail trade had declined to zero. Although market prices no longer existed, the authors nonetheless explained that centrally planned national income was measured at market prices, rather than factor income. They concluded that the

> Communist concept of national income appears to be essentially the same as that of net domestic product at market prices as defined in the U.S. Department of Commerce, except for the narrower scope of economic activities covered in the Communist definition. (Liu & Yeh 1965, p.215)

This definition of market activity was no longer one based on actual market activity, but of imputed non-activity. Although Liu and Yeh questioned the reliability of the data for the period from 1952 to 1956, they nonetheless considered it reliable enough to form the basis of their work (Liu 1968; Liu & Yeh 1973). They estimated the gross value of output in four sectors and then extrapolated input–output coefficients from 1961 to 1970, based on the 1952–57 figures to arrive at their measurement of Chinese national income (Liu & Yeh 1973, p.217).

Kuznets next supervised Dwight H. Perkins's (1975) estimate of China's GDP for the period up to 1971. Perkins discussed China's growth under the central plan in terms of the modern era. He took Western estimates of industrial production as the lower end and China's estimates as the upper end. Perkins noted that beginning in the 1950s, China's growth was sustained but uneven. He estimated that national income had tripled between 1952 and 1971 and that per capita national income had doubled.

Kravis (1981) undertook a PPP estimate of China's national income based on a limited comparison of Chinese and US goods and services. Kravis's estimates used official Chinese prices to establish Chinese per capita GDP. They formed the basis for the Penn World Table estimates developed by Robert Summers and Alan W. Heston in 1988 and 1991 (Lardy 1994, p.15). Kravis did not directly address the issue of planned prices and market prices but compared his acknowledged rough estimate in terms of measuring other poor, capitalist developing nations such as South Korea.

Jeffrey R. Taylor (1991) used PPPs to estimate Chinese GDP. He ignored the question of the market boundary but following convention converted the official figures from the 1981 input–output table into US dollars and subtracted these from gross value added. These were used to derive double deflated estimates of value added in residual dollars. These dollar estimates were then aggregated into primary, secondary, and tertiary sectors to obtain a total dollar GDP estimate for the 1981 benchmark year. GDP for earlier and later years was then calculated using constant price output indices for the components of GDP.

3.10 China measures of transition

The relatively smooth nature of China's transition to capitalism contrasted with the post-liberalization collapse in the USSR and CEE. But for all their differences the transition of China's statistical system from the MPS to the capitalist SNA both anticipated and mirrored the experience of the USSR. As in the USSR, China's MPS reported physical output and those services that made a direct contribution to the production of that physical output. Depreciation was treated as an intermediate input category. Physical outputs were valued according to a list of constant prices based on a standard set of 2,000 products published by the State Statistical Bureau (SSB). There were five sets of prices between 1949 and 1990.

Thomas Rawski, a Harvard sinologist, summarised the consensus opinion in 1976 that "most foreign specialists now agree that statistical information published in Chinese sources provides a generally accurate and reliable foundation on which to base further investigations" (Holz 2004, p.381). By the mid-1980s, as the proportion of output produced by the market sector increased, China introduced a hybrid system with the aim of introducing the "SNA with Chinese characteristics". The hybrid system was based on the reporting mechanisms of the MPS but increased coverage to include the output of the "non-material" service sectors such as health care, education, passenger transport, government administration and residential housing and depreciation estimates to form its official GDP measures (World Bank 1992, p.v.).

In 1994 Albert Keidel attempted to remove central plan price "distortions" based on the work of the World Bank's statistical mission to China in 1990. Keidel estimated an unofficial 32% increase in Yuan national accounts, 14% for statistical shortcomings and 18% for China's non-market price system (1994, p.v). Keidel adjusted existing Chinese "prices" to establish a more equal rate of return across different sectors. Keidel's method was paradoxically similar to the transfer of value between capitals of different organic compositions demonstrated by Marx in *Capital III*, except this was not the work of the market, but of a reimagining of Chinese output as if were that of the market. Keidel accepted that "in general there is no 'correct' or 'accurate' choice for what China's profitability patterns might look like" (1994, p.23). After all, there was no real rate of profit in the Chinese economy. Keidel's reworked prices diverged from the original list prices and made the application of PPPs based on original prices more difficult. Keidel pointed out the problem of establishing direct comparisons between physical outputs was affected by China's plan output which was measured through quantitative targets with less emphasis on quality. Higher quality is more expensive in a market economy, so this affected direct comparisons of physical commodities.

The World Bank (1992) reported on the transition of China's statistical system from the MPS and the SNA. It showed how Western statisticians sought to reconcile the decline in planned production with the growth of the market. In its view, the most serious distortions in China's price reporting system resulted from the disproportionate quantity of both subsidized low-price transactions and of high-price transactions on periodic markets outside the subsidized plan system. They noted that while the SNA was predicated on the existence of market prices, the central plan "distorted" the measurement of economic activity as it undervalued many goods. The nature of transactions was that they were not market transactions:

> The fundamental difficulty with relying so heavily on MPS valuation principles is that although they refer to actual *transactions*, many transactions in China are not *market* transactions. That is to say, goods and money change hands in many transactions, but the amounts involved are determined by bureaucratic regulations, and prices implied by the transactions frequently have little bearing on the social usefulness of the goods and services involves. (Marer et al. 1992, p.12, emphasis in the original)

"The social usefulness of goods" was World Bank code for market price. In the classical central plan, money did not change hands even when output did. The financial measures of production were nominal units of account that were registered with the state bank. State prices even dominated the shadow planned area, in which production units used informal but tolerated channels to barter inputs to complete their planned targets, as the World Bank report itself recognised, "not all prices in China are used for transactions" (1992, p.52). Different sets of prices existed for the same product in different "markets" decreed by "political/administrative fiat, rather than being determined by economic forces" (Marer et al. 1992, p.15). Official constant prices were accounting prices used to calculate and report the "value" of output according to various price manuals (Ruoen & Kai 1995, p.14). If there was a zero price or a situation where deliveries were based on the allocation of inputs and outputs under the central plan this, "value" was strictly notional and derived after the event.

This non-market production by definition lay outside of the market boundary measured by the SNA. Strictly speaking, it should not be included in the measurement of national income. But rather than measure the actual growth of real capitalism in China, the World Bank created a version of capitalism in the accounts. They increased the valuation of the rented housing sector, reinterpreted government subsidies as government purchases and converted output valued at government list prices into "values based on more meaningful market oriented transactions" to represent the "true extent of economic activity" (Marer et al. 1992, p.13).

The distinction between non-market and market production was obliterated. The World Bank stated that "[i]t is important to stress that reworking China's GDP by subsector as described below is not recalculating China's GDP according to some ideal price system" (but this was exactly what they did); the World Bank continued, stating,"[h]owever, some elements of the present valuation system reflect conceptual biases and distortions which must be adjusted in estimating GDP" (1992, p.86).

The abolition of mandatory purchasing quotas for most goods in the mid-1980s and the strict limit on the physical quantity of centrally planned production meant that as the economy grew the proportion of output subject to supply and demand rapidly increased (Naughton 2007, p.93). By the early 1990s negotiated prices were no longer just a "non-plan" category. Planned production was subject to the operation of the market, according to whether they were "state-set" or "state-guided" prices. State-set prices were fixed at one value. They were not really prices at all, but the traditional units of account. State-guided prices were set by local state enterprises and government departments within certain range and were subject to supply and demand. In their turn, non-plan prices had three sub-categories: consultative, negotiated and periodic market prices. In general, these were decided by the parties to the transaction but were subject to government guidelines and monitoring. The official segmentation of many markets allowed the use of a product's planned or list price in some transactions and the negotiated price in others (Marer et al. 1992, p.50).

The Chinese SSB and Institute of Economic Research at Hitotsubashi University (1997) issued national income estimates for the period from 1952 to 1995. These estimates considered that:

> The totality of spheres of material production and non-material services essentially conforms to the coverage of economic activities in SNA. The major difference between the two systems is that the separation of non-material services from material production constitutes the basis of economic analyses in MPS methodology. (National Accounts State Statistical Bureau of the People's Republic of China [SSBC] & Hitotsubashi 1997, sec.1.2)

Following the methodology of the World Bank's guide to the data of the centrally planned economies (Marer et al. 1992) the study considered all planned production as market production, whether it was or not.

Ren Rouen applied two methods to estimate China's national income developed by the UN International Comparison Project (ICP). First, Rouen built calculations from the expenditure side and, second, from the output side he applied the International Comparison of Output and Productivity (ICOP) project of Groningen University, developed under the supervision of Angus Maddison (Ruoen 1997). The advantage of both these methods over the exchange rates used by the World Bank was that they measured the "actual" growth of the economy, or, more accurately, changes in the quantity of physical output measured as if it were capitalist production. During the 1980s the fall in the Yuan's exchange rate offset the growth in the economy. The disadvantage was that it made it impossible to distinguish between non-planned and planned production. It prevented the measurement of actual market production or real national income. Rouen compared the various alternative estimates of China's output made by Western theorists, adjusted where necessary into current prices for the purposes of comparison. No great discrepancies appeared between them. This was unsurprising as all of them adopted the same theoretical method that regarded centrally planned as if it were market production.

Harry X. Wu and Angus Maddison separately and together published a series of papers which attempted to provide a definitive alternative estimate of China's national income to the official statistical series. Both Maddison and Wu (1993) recognised that during the plan period:

One cannot talk meaningfully about prices that reflect consumer preferences or factor costs for either consumer or producer goods in China because there was (and still is to a certain extent) no market through which such consumer preferences or factor costs could influence the prices of these commodities. (Wu 1993, p.70)

Angus Maddison according to his own account applied Abram Bergson's methods to the period of China's centrally planned economy to estimate the real level of China's growth (Maddison & Wu 2008, p.14). Actually, Maddison's estimates owed less to Bergson than to Colin Clark's PPP. The use of PPPs facilitated Maddison in abstracting from China's centrally planned economy, by measuring China's planned output in the prices of comparative capitalist nations. This was Bergson's original objection to using the prices of a capitalist state to measure the output of the USSR. Wu reconstructed China's GDP from 1952 to 1977 based on the official output estimates from 1978 to 1990 by establishing a relationship between GDP and MPS at a sectoral level (Wu 2000, p.477).

Maddison's final paper with Wu (2008) superseded earlier estimates. It used physical estimates of agricultural output and a volume index for industrial production based on physical quantities and official price series. It included estimates of non-material services: banking, insurance, housing services, administration of real estate, social services, health, education entertainment, personal services, research and development activities, the armed forces, police, government and party organisations that used employment growth as a proxy for real value added. Maddison assumed that there was no productivity growth in services, in contrast to the official figures which "show improbably high rates of growth of labour productivity (5.1 per cent a year for 1978–2003)" (Maddison & Wu 2008, p.23). This was predicated on the generalisation that there is typically little growth in service sector productivity. Whether such an assumption holds in the period of the transition from central planning to capitalism is a moot point. The service sector was completely transformed in this period from the old iron rice bowl, in which enterprises provided services directly to their staff, to an *ad hoc* informal sector or nothing at all.

The Maddison–Wu estimates were very similar to China's official figures for the period of the central plan but diverged slightly during the 1990s. Maddison confirmed official estimates of agricultural production and a reworked set of official statistics to estimate industrial production. The OECD had previously commented on Maddison's earlier estimates that "[a] reasonable assessment might be that the official growth estimates represent an upper bound and the Maddison estimates represent a lower bound, with the true growth rates lying somewhere between the two" (OECD 2000, p.17). This was itself a controversial assessment and one that was disputed by Maddison (2006a) and, from the opposite side, Carsten Holz (2006). Holz broadly speaking defended the official estimates whereas Maddison criticised them. Given the subjective comparative nature of this dispute, there could be no definitive answer.

Wu sought to close, if not settle, the debate by a "data fundamentalist" approach (2011, p.4). Wu did not question the correctness of neoclassical orthodoxy but rather explained the contradictory results of various studies by the problems of Chinese statistics, inconsistent definitions and classifications, methodological problems and data fabrication. Wu complained that consumer services like passenger transport were excluded from the MPS because "they are considered 'unproductive' in the Marxian orthodoxy" (Wu 2011, p.8). Wu noted that neo-classical studies had concluded that official Chinese national income estimates typically underestimated the size of the economy, due to coverage, but overestimated growth, due to base year effects, as in the USSR.

Wu estimated Chinese capital stock. He noted that Maddison (1998) had previously used a hypothetical capital/output ratio based on the lower bound of the international standard and some pre-war estimates by Yeh. Wu replaced it with information from the 1951 National Asset Census. Neither estimate can really resolve the problem. Mao's CCP expropriated the capitalists without compensation. If the value of the capital stock is measured by its purchase price on transfer or by a multiple of the revenue it generates, then the value of the capital stock was nil. It cost the state nothing and means of production accumulated under the plan earned no revenue. Wu pointed out that the value of gross fixed capital formation in the SNA is the amount "when the ownership of the fixed assets is transferred to the institution unit that intends to use them in production" (UN 1993, p.223). As nothing was paid, so the fixed capital stock was worthless. The return on capital, capital share and wage share of the centrally planned economy are all subjective inventions of the plan apparatus.

Wu analysed the Total Factor Productivity (TFP) of China's economy during the centrally planned and capitalist market period. TFP seeks to explain the contribution of technical progress or productivity to the growth of value separate from other inputs. It measures the transfer of values between capitals of different compositions. Wu cited Felipe (1997), who explained that the TFP is predicated on free competition and profit maximisation. Felipe's paper does not address the operation of the centrally planned economies at all. In a centrally planned economy with neither competition nor profits, TFP cannot by definition apply. Rather, Felipe's paper was concerned with the growth of East Asian "tiger" economies.

Paul Krugman (1994) similarly explained the stagnation of the USSR by a rising capital output ratio. According to Krugman the USSR demonstrated the law of diminishing returns. For every additional unit of capital invested, the marginal increase in value added slowed. This law was proved by the fall off in the rate of increase in sales for every unit of additional investment. In the USSR there were no sales capable of influencing supply and demand and so no real markets. The capital labour ratio did not exist either. Its existence was according to Krugman "imputed" by economists.

But an imputed law is no law at all. William Easterly and Stanley Fischer (1994) attributed the stagnation of the USSR to a decline in TFP, but what applies to the capital/labour ratio applies just as well to total factor productivity (Easterly & Fischer 1994). If there are no sales, how can TFP, a measure of sales, stagnate? Wu conceded: "Nevertheless it is perfectly reasonable to argue that the neoclassical framework used in this study is questionable or unacceptable in terms of the discovery of the truth" (2011, p.47). But he offered no alternative framework to explain the truth which neoclassical economics could not explain.

Thomas Rawski resolved this problem by removing any distinction between planned and market prices altogether. He said that

> [t]o obtain a long term measure of Chinese growth that avoids the biases inherent in domestic prices during the plan era, we combine official time series for real value added in the primary, secondary and tertiary sectors with nominal sectoral output for 2000 to form a new series of aggregate output valued in 2000 prices for the entire period 1952–2005. (Rawski 2009, p.835)

Rawski abstracted from the Maoist overthrow of capitalism and expropriation of the capitalists and landlords in 1953 to develop his estimates of the fixed capitalist stock in 1952. Rawski dismissed a 1952 incomplete estimate of the value of the fixed capital stock. Instead, he assumed that the capital output ratio was either 1:1 or 2:1 relative to GDP. This had little effect on the growth rate of the capital stock in the 1978 post-reform period, but it did influence growth rates for the 1950s (Rawski 2009, pp.835–36). Mao paid nothing for the fixed capital stock. It was expropriated without compensation on the accession of the CCP to power. Debates about its price miss the point.

Western statisticians treated the reconciliation of the MPS and the SNA as a statistical anomaly to be corrected ideally. These statisticians considered that Chinese state list prices were a convenient measure for changes of the "value" of gross output measures over time. Whereas net values were considered to be more problematic because input prices could not be identified, it was not clear on what basis new products were valued. As with estimates of the USSR and CEE, they worked around these problems through a comparison of changes in physical quantities of output with similar price series in capitalist economies. Western statisticians extended the coverage of their national income estimates to the service sector and reduced the "price" of industrial production and increased the "price" of agricultural output and collective working class consumption such as housing (Wu 2000, pp.422–27). Standard SNA procedure eliminated changes in the price level to show changes in volume, but these adjustments were based on the objective fact of market sale. When applied to the MPS these procedures created a commodity economy in the books where none existed in the world.

3.11 Conclusion

Maddison and Wu, like Holz, Kravis, Keidel and Liu, abstracted China's output from the plan. They abstracted exchange value from exchange. They abstracted the SNA (a measure of the commodity economy) from the commodity economy it measured. As a comparative exercise the various other attempts to measure "real" – meaning unreal – Chinese national income during the plan period add something to the picture of the development of the Chinese economy, provided that it is clear that all of the alternative totals are counter factual in the sense of fictional, subjective not objective, indeed not real but "real". For the Western statisticians the switch from the MPS to the SNA was exactly that, the superseding of one basically inadequate system of measurement for another much better one. This was not the creation of a value where previously there had been none, but in the case of the material production sectors at least "primarily a task of asking production units to manipulate accounting items in new ways" (Holz 2004, p.387).

During the 1990s the rapid growth of non-plan production outside of the traditional reporting system, the redefinition of economic categories and data falsification among low ranking officials meant that the quality of statistics declined (Holz 2004, p.392). The reporting system of the central planning apparatus was not replaced in time by a comprehensive survey system typical of the SNA. Paradoxically at the very moment when market prices replaced list prices, the concern of statisticians about the falsification of data with China's centrally planned economy came true. As the data began to measure real GDP, its accuracy declined; it was no longer false, even if it was now falsified.

According to Angus Maddison, Bergson's AFC aimed to "create a counter factual estimate of what Soviet prices would have been if the economy were run on capitalist lines, removing the "distortions" created by the command economy, and getting a better picture of the real cost of production" (1998, p.312). As we have seen, it claimed quite a lot more than that. Bergson's followers thought that by revaluing planned prices according to the rules of the SNA they could actually measure the "real" value of the centrally planned economy, when there was actually no value to measure. They created a fictional version of reality as if the thought was the deed, rather than the mother of it.

In the Soviet Union, CEE and China, the official agencies blurred over the distinction between central planning and capitalism. Their attempts to measure non-capitalist production as capitalist production meant that they failed to measure the growth of economic production within the market boundary during the transition to capitalism. They did not do the very thing for which the SNA is designed. In the CIS and CEE they measured the collapse of the plan as a collapse of capitalism, when it was the creation of capitalism out of the plan. They measured the slump in use values measured by the MPS, as a slump of values measured by the SNA. Their figures measured the growth of market production as a decline of it. They turned the world on its head.

All the disputes between the various theorists around the correct weighting scheme, the comparison of physical outputs, the measurement of quality, the evaluation of the service sector and the appropriate level of depreciation try to value the central plan as if it were capitalist are essentially irresolvable. Unlike real market economies there was no objective standard, a market price, against which to assess these claims. They all missed the essential point – the only way real national income could be measured was by measuring the actual growth of real commodity production.

In China the development of capitalist production began in 1978 and was completed by the mid-1990s. In the USSR and in CEE it began after 1989 and was completed by the late 1990s. In the next chapter developing some estimates of the actual growth of commodity production in the CIS/CEE and China is attempted, to show how the transition to capitalism increased the size of market production and therefore of national income.

References

Alton, T., et al., 1991. *Occasional Papers Nos. 115–119 of the Research Project on National Income in East Central Europe*. New York: L.W. International Financial Research.

Arvay, J., 1994. The Material Product System (MPS): A Retrospective. In Z. Kenessey, ed. *The Accounts of Nations*. New York: IOS, pp. 218–36.

Ashbrook, A. Jr., 1967. Main Lines of Chinese Communist Economic Policy. In *An Economic Profile of Mainland China*. Washington, DC: Joint Economic Committee Congress of the United States, pp. 15–45.

Bartholdy, K., 1997. Old and New Problems in the Estimation of National Accounts in Transition Economies. *Economics of Transition*, 5(1), pp. 131–46.

Becker, A.S., 1969. *Soviet National Income, 1958–1964*. Berkeley: University of California Press.

Bergson, A., & Levine, H.S., eds., [1993] 2000.*The Soviet Economy towards the Year 2000*. London, George Allen and Unwin.

Bloem, A.M., Cotterell, P. & Gigantes, T., 1996. *National Accounts in Transition Countries: Distortions and Biases*. IMF Working Paper, 96 (130). New York: IMF.

Bloem, A.M., Cotterell, P. & Gigantes, T., 1998. National Accounts in Transition Countries: Balancing the Biases? *Review of Income and Wealth*, 44(1), pp. 1–24.

Brandt, L., Rawski T. & Sutton J., 2008. China's Industrial Development. In L. Brandt & T. Rawski, eds. *China's Great Economic Transformation*. Cambridge: Cambridge University Press, pp. 569–632.

CIA, 1978. *USSR: Toward a Reconciliation of Marxist and Western Measures of National Income*. Washington, DC: CIA.

Clarke, S., 2004. Globalisation and the Subsumption of the Soviet Mode of Production under Capital. In A. Saad-Filho, ed. *Anti-Capitalism: A Marxist Introduction*. London: Pluto, pp. 187–98.

Clarke, S., 2007. *The Development of Capitalism in Russia*. London: Routledge.

Clarke, S., & Fairbrother, P. 1993. *The Crisis of the Soviet System*. In S. Clarke, P. Fairbrother, M. Burawoy, & P. Krotov, eds. *What about the Workers? Workers and the Transition to Capitalism in Russia*. London and New York: Verso, pp. 33–58.

Dayton-Johnson, J., 1999. The Transition from Soveitism: Today's Depression Tomorrow's Growth? *Review of Income and Wealth*, Series 45(1), pp. 117–30.

Dayton-Johnson, J., 2005. *China 2005*, J. Dayton-Johnston, ed. Paris: OECD.

Easterly, W., & Fischer, S., 1995. The Soviet Economic Decline. *World Bank Economic Review*, 9(3), pp. 341–71.

EBRD, 1995. *Transition Report 1995: Investment and Enterprise Report*. London: EBRD.

EBRD, 1998. *Transition Report 1998: Financial sector in transition*. London: EBRD.

Estrin, S., Kolodko, G., & Uvalic, M., 2007. The Rise and Fall of Socialist Planning. In S. Estrin, G. Kolodko & M. Uvalic, eds. *Transition and Beyond*. London: Palgrave Macmillan, pp. 17–34.

Felipe, J., 1997. *Total Factor Productivity Growth in East Asia: A Critical Survey*. EDRC Report Series No. 65. Manila: Asian Development Bank.

Gough, I., 1972. Productive and Unproductive Labour in Marx. *New Left Review*, 1(76), pp. 47–72.

Hart-Landsberg, M., & Burkett, P., 2005. *China and Socialism*. New York: Monthly Review.

Hollister, W.W., 1958. *China's Gross National Product and Social Accounts, 1950–57*. Glencoe, IL: The Free Press.

Holz, C., 2004. Chinas Statistical System in Transition: Challenges, Data Problems and Institutional Innovations. *Review of Income and Wealth*, 50(3), pp. 381–409.

Holz, C, 2006. China's Reform Period Economic Growth: How Reliable Are Angus Maddison's Estimates? *Review of Income and Wealth*, 52(1), pp. 85–119.

IMF et al., 1991. *A Study of the Soviet Economy* (Vol. 1–3). Paris: OECD.

Ivanov, Y., 1987. Possibilities and Problems of Reconciliation of the SNA and the MPS. *Review of Income and Wealth*, 33(1), pp. 2–14.

Ivanov, Y., Rjabushkin, B. & Homenko, T., 1993. Introduction of the SNA into the Official Statistics of the Commonwealth of Independent States. *Review of Income and Wealth*, 39(3), pp. 280–92.

Joint Economic Committee Congress of the United States (JEC) 1967. *An Economic Profile of Mainland China*. Washington DC: US Government Printing Office.

Kendrick, J.W., 1995. Introduction and Overview. In *The New System of National Accounts*. Boston: Kluwer Academic Publishers, pp. 1–23.

Koen, V., 1994. *A User's View on National Accounts in Russia*. IMF Working Paper No. 94/6. New York: IMF.

Koen, V., & Gavrilenkov, E., 1994. *How Large Was the Output Collapse in Russia?* Working Paper No. 94/154. New York: IMF.

Koen, V., & Marrese M., 1995. *Stabilization and Structural Change in Russia. 1992–94*. IMF Working Paper No. 95/13. New York: IMF.

George Kopits, G., 1993. *Lessons in Fiscal Consolidation for the Successor States of the Soviet Union*. IMF Working Paper 93/54 (June). New York: IMF.

Kravis, I.B., 1981. An Approximation of the Relative Real per Capita GDP of the People's Republic of China. *Journal of Comparative Economics*, 5, pp. 60–78.

Krugman, P., 1994. The Myth of Asia's Miracle: A Cautionary Fable. *Foreign Affairs*, 73(6), pp. 62–79.

Kuznets, S. 1941. *National Income and Its Composition 1919–1938* (Vol. I). New York: National Bureau Economic Research.

Kuznets, S., 1975. *National Income a Summary of Findings*. New York: Arno Press.

Lane, D., 1996. *The Rise and Fall of State Socialism*. Cambridge: Polity.

Lardy, N.R., 1994. *China in the World Economy*. Washington, DC: Institute for International Economics.

Lavigne, M., 1999. *The Economics of Transition: From Socialist Economy to Market Economy*. Second edition. Basingstoke: Palgrave.

Leontief, W., 1951. *Structure of American Economy, 1919–1939*. Second edition. New York: Oxford University Press.

Liu, T., 1968. Quantitative Trends in the Economy. In A. Eckstein, W. Galenson, & T. Liu, eds. *Economic Trends in Communist China*. Chicago: Aldine, pp. 87–182.

Liu, T., & Yeh, K., 1965. *The Economy of the Chinese Mainland: National Income and Economic Development, 1933–1959*. Princeton, NJ: Princeton University Press.

Liu, T., & Yeh, K., 1973. Chinese and Other Asian Economies a Quantitative Evaluation. *The American Economic Review*, 63(May), pp. 215–23.

Lutzel, H., 1986. Market Transactions in the National Accounts. *Review of Income and Wealth*, 32(2), pp.202–09.

Maddison, A., 1998. Measuring the Performance of a Communist Command Economy. An Assessment of the CIA Estimates for the USSR. *Review of Income and Wealth*, 44(March), pp.1–27.

Maddison, A., 2006a. Do Official Statistics Exaggerate China's GDP growth? A Reply to Carsten Holz. *Review of Income and Wealth*, 52(1), pp.121–26.

Maddison, A., 2006b. *The World Economy, A Millennial Perspective*. Second edition. Paris: OECD.

Maddison, A., & Wu, H.X., 2008. Measuring China's Economic Performance. *World Economics*, 9(2), pp.13–44.

Marer, P., et al., 1992. *Historically Planned Economies: A Guide to the Data*, Washington, DC: World Bank.

Marx, K., 1978. *Theories of Surplus Value I*. Fourth edition. Moscow: Progress Publishers.

Marx, K., 1982. *Capital Volume I*. Third edition. London: Penguin Classics.

Naughton, B., 1999. *Growing Out of the Plan: Chinese Economic Reform 1978–93*. Fourth edition. Cambridge: Cambridge University Press.

Naughton, B., 2007. *The Chinese Economy Transitions and Growth*. Cambridge, MA: MIT Press.

Nove, A., 1977. *The Soviet Economic System*. London: George Allen and Unwin.

Nove, A. 1989. *An Economic History of the USSR*. Fifth edition. London: Penguin Classic.

OECD, 1993. *National Accounts for the Former Soviet Union*. Paris: OECD.

OECD 1997. *OECD Economic Surveys: Russian Federation, 1997*. Paris: OECD.

OECD, 2000. *China in the Global Economy: national Accounts or China, Sources and Methods*. Paris: OECD.

OECD, 2005. *OECD Economic Surveys China*. Paris: OECD.

Perkins, D. H., 1975. Growth and Changing Structure of China's Twentieth-Century Economy. In Perkins, D.H, ed. *China's Modern Economy in Historical Perspective*. Stanford, Calif: Stanford University Press.

Rawski, T., 2009. Forecasting China's Economic Growth to 2025. In T. Rawski & L. Brandt, eds. *China's Great Economic Transformation*. Cambridge: Cambridge University Press, pp. 829–86.

Roland, G., & Verdier, T., 1999. Transition and the Output Fall. *Economics of Transition*, 7(1), pp. 1–28.

Roman, J.C., 1985. Treatment of subsidies in National Accounts. *Review of Income and Wealth*, 31(1), pp. 38–43.

Ruoen, R., 1997. *China's Economic Performance in an International Perspective/* Paris: OECD Development Centre.

Ruoen, R., & Kai, C., 1995. *China's GDP in U.S. Dollars Based on Purchasing Power Parity*. World Bank Policy Research Paper No. 1415. Washington, DC: World Bank.

Saunders, P., & Wu, H., 2009. Measuring Growth, Productivity, Income Distribution and Poverty in Transition Economies: Progress, Challenges and Prospects. *Review of Income and Wealth*, 55(1), pp. 413–22.

Shaikh, A., & Tonak, E., 1996. *Measuring the Wealth of Nations*. Cambridge: Cambridge University Press.

Skousen, C.R., 1988. Western Management Accounting and the Economic Reforms of China. *Accounting, Organizations and Society*, 13(2), pp. 201–06.

Spulber, N., 2003. *Russia's Economic Transformations: From Late Tsarism to the New Millennium*. Cambridge: Cambridge University Press.

SSBC & Hitotsubashi University, 1997. *The Historical National Accounts of the People's Republic of China 1952–1995*. Ministry of Education and Sciences of Japan. Available at: www.ier.hit-u.ac.jp/COE/Japanese/online_data/china/china.htm [Accessed June 29, 2012].

Studenski, P., 1958. *The Income of Nations: Theory, Measurement, and Analysis: Past and Present*. New York: New York University Press.

Tanzi, V., 1999. Transition and the changing Role of Government. *Finance and Development* 36(2). Available at: http://www.imf.org/external/pubs/ft/fandd/1999/06/tanzi.htm.

Taylor, J.R., 1991. *Dollar GNP Estimates for China*. Washington, DC: World Bank.

UN, 1953. *A System of National Accounts*. New York: United Nations.

UN, 1986. *National Accounts and Balances: Links between the System of National Accounts (SNA) and the System of Balances of the National Economy (MPS): Conceptual Framework*. New York: UN.

UN, 1993. *The System of National Accounts 1993*. Brussels and Luxembourg: United Nations.

UN, 2009. *National Accounts 2008*, New York: United Nations.

UNCTAD, 2005. *China in a Globalizing World*, C. Fortin, ed. Geneva and New York: United Nations Publications.

Woodruff, S., 2004. Symposium on Transition in Vietnam. *Economics of Transition*, 12(2), pp. 193–99.

World Bank, 1992. *China's Statistical System in Transition*. Washington, DC: World Bank.

World Bank ECA Country Department III & Goskomstat of the R.F.S.S.C., 1995. *Russian Federation: Report on the National Accounts*. Washington, DC: World Bank.

Wu, H. X., 1993. The "Real" Chinese Gross Domestic Product (GDP) for the Pre-Reform Period 1952–77. *Review of Income and Wealth*, 39(1), pp. 63–70.

Wu, H.X., 2000. China's GDP Level and Growth Performance: Alternative Estimates and the Implications. *Review of Income and Wealth*, 46(4), pp. 475–99.

Wu, H.X., 2011. *Accounting for China's Growth in 1952–2008: China's Growth Performance Debate Revisited with a Newly Constructed Data Set*. The Research Institute of Economy, Trade and Industry. Available at: www.rieti.go.jp/en [Accessed June 21, 2012].

4 Empirical evidence

4.1 National income

National income measures the value of the final production of goods and services within the market boundary. The output, income and expenditure approaches to national income are alternative versions of the same value measurement. The output approach establishes the total value of final production. GDP at market price equals the value of output in an economy in a particular year less intermediate consumption. The income approach equates the total output of a nation to the total income. It consists of wages and property income or the compensation of employees plus net interest plus rental and royalty income plus profits. The expenditure approach measures the total value of all goods as equal to the total amount of money spent on goods: GDP equals $C + I + G + (X - M)$, where C equals household consumption expenditures/personal consumption expenditures, I equals Gross domestic investment, G equals government consumption less taxes and gross investment expenditures, X equals gross exports of goods and services and M equals gross imports of goods and services. Although both transfer pricing and the unofficial nature of black market transactions can lead to an underestimation of national income.

Andre Vanoli discussed the measurement of value in the various systems of national accounts established since the Second World War. He considered that "market exchange is the touchstone of evaluation in monetary terms: goods or services against money" (Vanoli 2005, p.147). Statisticians have imputed values to owner occupied dwellings and agricultural own account consumption where no exchange takes place, but "exchanges are fundamental, because they allow delineation of social monetary values", because "it is only by referring to market values, or more generally to the value of actual monetary transactions, that it is possible to strive to assign a monetary value to non-market non-monetary flows" (Vanoli 2005, p.151). The existence of these imputed values does not mean that "an exchange or a payment is imputed" only that a "value" is. To impute an exchange to an imputed value "will only blur the scheme of analysis". Actually to impute a value to an imputed exchange has the same effect.

It blurs the market boundary and implies that value can be created from thin air. Vanoli could not resolve what this "value" was that was being measured. He considered that the 1993 UN SNA clarified the issue by defining economic flows as having the effect of "creating, transforming, exchanging, transferring or extinguishing economic value (1993, SNA 2.24)" (Vanoli 2005, p.151). This defined value as a form of value – a tautology, not a definition. This problem struck at the heart of marginal value theory predicted on a subjective value definition based on utility not exchange.

Alfred Marshall and Arthur Pigou both recognised that, even given the assumptions of their own marginalist theory, although prices may – or may not – reflect marginal utility, there was no monetary measurement of the average utility of products. The total of utility had no price or value. It is an aggregate of different subjective, conflicting, contradictory and counterposed assessments of usefulness. It can no more be quantified against a single objective standard than beauty can be. But if total utility cannot be measured in money, then utility cannot be the basis of monetary measures. Need does not create value; production for exchange does. The nature of value, as the specific form of social labour in a capitalist economy was forgotten. Marx explained that in a capitalist economy, predicated on generalised commodity production and exchange:

> The gross income is the portion of value and the part of the gross product measured by this, which remains over after deducting the portion of value, and the part of the total production measured by it, which the constant capital advanced and consumed in production replaces. Gross income, therefore, is equal to wages (or the part of the product destined to become the workers' income again) + profit + rent. Net income, on the other hand, is the surplus-value, and hence the surplus-product that remains after wages are deducted, and so it expresses in fact the surplus-value that capital realises and has to share with the landowners, and the surplus-product measured by this. (Marx, 1981, p.979)

According to Studenski, "[n]ational income is an expression, in monetary terms of the current achievements of the national economy" (1958, p.163). It is strictly separated from non-economic production that "does not possess economic value" such production has a use value but not a market price; it is consumed but is neither bought nor sold. The distinction between economic and non-economic production is not defined by the usefulness of the output but by its social relationship to capital. This means that the output of subsistence farmers, who produce and consume foods stuffs and domestically produced handicrafts, is not within the market boundary and the notional "value" of this output should not be measured in national income. Marginal theory that attributes exchange value to use value cannot explain the logical significance of the market boundary, which rests on the distinction between use and exchange value, a distinction that it claims does not exist. Studenski noted that if the output of subsistence farmers were included in measures of national income, then according to this standard, household production should be too and that

[l]ogical consistency would demand reaching out even further to include similar free services rendered outside the family, e.g. neighbourly advice and co-operation versus paid professional services . . . But such a supercomprehensive concept of national income, taking all these human actions into account, would embrace the entire content of human life and would, for all practical purposes, rob the national income concept of any meaning and render it useless as an expression of economic production. (1958, p.178)

When applied to the capitalist economies the logical application of neoclassical economics was illogical. How much more so for the non-market central plan? Paradoxically, such a super-comprehensive concept of national income was developed by Studenski himself. He estimated the output of the Soviet Union and claimed that the distinction between measures of planned and capitalist economies was "not very great" (Studenski 1958, p.353). In practice national income statisticians ignore the logic of their illogical system and proceed perfectly logically so that the output of goods and services is evaluated first "at the market prices or costs of the goods and services sold" (Studenski 1958, p.169).

Logically and in reality, the output of CPEs was outside the market boundary and logically and in reality it produced no national income. The central plan produced physical output, or use value – there were no market prices and so exchange value or *value*. The entire attempt to measure the output of a non-market economy by imputing market values to it was illogical and unreal, a contradiction in terms.

To measure the growth of national income during the transition period it is necessary to separate market from non-market production. This is the actual amount of real commodity production, the proportion of total output inside the market boundary that is produced and sold. The transition to the market in CEE and the CIS led to the collapse of the plan. The output of use values slumped. This slump was real. However, this was not a fall in capitalist output. It was not a fall in market production, but a fall in centrally planned production. It was a collapse in use values not in exchange values. It precipitated the creation of national income, which is production within the market boundary, where previously there had been none. The growth of the market was synonymous with the collapse of the plan. Although the total quantity of output of physical production slumped during the transition to capitalism, the value of production within the market boundary simultaneously increased. National income rose even as output fell.

4.2 Official statistics

The Soviet critique of Western official statistics considered them unreliable as the need for business secrecy and the ideological priorities of government agencies effectively prevented the accurate measurement of the capitalist economy. The Western critique of Soviet official statistics considered them unreliable as subordinate agencies concealed the true levels of production from their superiors and the ideological priorities of government agencies effectively prevented the accurate measurement of the centrally planned economy. Retrospective analyses of Soviet output with unlimited access to former Soviet archives such as those of Masaaki Kuboniwa (1997) of the Hitotsubashi University re-estimated Soviet output from official labour force statistics. The trends and levels moved in a systematic pattern that differed from the original only because of a change in the underlying assumptions. The overall accuracy of the (suitably modified) figures was vindicated.

This study deliberately uses the official estimates of physical output and national income developed by Western agencies to demonstrate that the data themselves were not at fault but that it was the way in which they were misused by Western, Soviet and CIS agencies. It insists that the key methodological mistake was a failure to distinguish between the output of the centrally planned economy and the output of the capitalist market economy. This failure underpinned the systematic underestimation of the growth of world capitalism and of national income with capitalist transition in the 1990s.

4.3   The transition in CEE and the CIS

In CEE and the CIS the big-bang privatisation of the early 1990s meant that market prices were not reliable indicators of market output until the late 1990s. Western agencies used national income estimates from the production side. Changes in employment were used as a proxy for output change. Prices, although liberalised, only became real market prices after a number of years. By applying the market boundary deflators, as illustrated in the following, it is possible to make a rough estimate of the growth of real market production in the transition economies. The EBRD developed estimates of the growth of private production during the transition period in its annual "Transition Reports" (EBRD 1999). The EBRD's "private sector shares" of national income were approximations based on available statistics from both official (government) sources and unofficial sources. Its term *private companies* referred to all enterprises in which a majority of the shares was owned by private individuals or entities. The underlying concept of private-sector value added included income generated byte activity of private registered companies as well as by private entities engaged in informal activity, in those cases in which reliable information on informal activity was available. The EBRD estimates occasionally differed quite markedly from available data from official sources on the contribution to GDP made by the "private sector" or by the "non-state sector". This was usually because the definition of the EBRD concept differed from that of the official estimates. Specifically for the CIS countries, official data in most cases refer to value added in the "non-state sector", a broad concept which incorporated collective farms as well as companies in which only a minority stake has been privatised. Accepting the limitations of these estimates – that they are general figures indicative of a trend rather than definitive totals – they nonetheless provide a good proxy for the growth of market production inside CEE and the CIS. The totals for any given year are not in any respect decisive. For the purposes argued here, it is enough that they prove that at the outset of the

Table 4.1 Private-sector proportion of GDP% in CEE and the CIS

Country	1989	1990	1991	1992	1993	1994	1995	1996	1997	1998	1999	2000
Albania	8.1	11.7	24.2	36.7			60	75	75	75	75	75
Armenia							45	50	55	60	60	60
Azerbaijan	5.1	5.5	6.8	8.1			25	25	40	45	45	45
Belarus							15	15	20	20	20	20
Bosnia and Herzegovina										35	35	35
Bulgaria	0	0	16.6	25.3	35.9	40.2	45	45	50	50	60	70
Croatia							45	50	55	55	60	60
Czech republic	11.2	12.3	17.3	27.7	45.1	56.3	70	75	75	75	80	80
Estonia	0	0	17.7	45	50.6	58	65	70	70	70	75	75
FYR Macedonia							40	50	50	55	55	55
Georgia	17.6	28.1	27.3	49	56.9	60	30	50	55	60	60	60
Hungary	14.9		33	44	52		60	70	75	80	80	80
Kazakhstan	15	7.2	12.2			20.2	25	40	55	55	55	60
Kyrgyzstan					56.4	58	40	50	60	60	60	60
Latvia	10.4	11.6					60	60	60	60	65	65
Lithuania			16	37	57	62.3	55	65	70	70	70	70
Moldova							30	40	45	45	45	50
Poland	28.6	31.4	45.3	48.2	53.5	56	60	60	65	65	65	70
Romania	12.8	16.4	23.6	26.4	32	35	40	60	60	60	60	60
Russia	5.3	6	10.1	14	21	25	40	60	70	70	70	70
Slovakia				22	24.6	43.8	60	70	75	75	75	75
Slovenia	8.1	11.4	15.7	19.5			45	45	50	55	55	55
Tajikistan							15	20	20	30	30	40
Turkmenistan							15	20	25	25	25	25
Ukraine		7.6	7.8	5.6	7.5		35	40	50	55	55	60
Uzbekistan				38.8	46.7	54.2	30	40	45	45	45	45

Sources: Adapted from EBRD (1995, 1996, 1997, 1998, 1999, 2000, 2001).

Note: FYR = Former Yugoslav Republic. The CIS was formed from the USSR in 1991.

transition, there was little or no market production and that by the end of it, the market had subordinated the vast bulk of economic output to it.

When there are missing data between two known points, the mean average annual trend point is used. When there is one country known, but another unknown, the closest equivalent is used. Lithuania substitutes for Latvia, and Latvia for Lithuania, the Czech Republic for Slovakia. These are in any event small nations with little impact on the aggregate. The change to the wider institutional framework through the liberalisation of prices, the introduction of private property law, the wider growth of market relations and so on are reflected in the assumption that after 2001 centrally planned production no longer existed. State output was by then subordinated to market prices as in the West. A more finished analysis could synthesise the growth of private production with changes to the wider institutional framework and in particular the extent to which liberalised prices became market prices.

Table 4.1 demonstrates that in CEE the process of capitalist restoration was already underway by 1989. Poland and Czechoslovakia had high proportions of private-sector production that grew to dominate the economy by the very early 1990s. In the CIS the process was slower and more uneven. By the 2000, the majority of production was located in the private sector with Russia, Ukraine and the Baltic states. The process was generally slower in Central Asia, Uzbekistan, Tajikistan and Turkmenistan and in parts of Europe, notably Belarus. These estimates of the growth of market production can be combined with the EBRD Transition Indicators to measure the degree of transition on a scale of 1 to 4 (EBRD 2011). They demonstrate that even in countries such as Turkmenistan, Bosnia and Herzegovina and Tajikistan, where as late as 2001, the private sector produced only a minority of output, market prices dominated the economy. In 2001, the EBRD score for the liberalisation of market prices was 2.7 for Turkmenistan, 4 for Bosnia and Herzegovina and 3.7 for Tajikistan. This justifies what might appear to be the somewhat arbitrary assumption made here that after 2001, all production in these economies is subordinated to market prices. East Germany is missing from this table because its entire economy was incorporated into West Germany in 1989.

4.4   The transition in China

In China pro-market price reforms began in 1978. Over the next three decades this process created a market economy, but with the control of the CCP intact. The largest 1000 state enterprises remained nationalised. The proportion of centrally planned output was fixed and surplus above this minimum target was sold at market prices. The deflators used are based on an empirical survey undertaken by the OECD, the empirical data and methodology underpinning it is described in detail by (Dougherty & Herd 2005, p.6). The OECD survey utilizes the industrial firm database of the Chinese National Bureau of Statistics (NBS) based on a survey of 140,000 valid firms in 1998 and 180,000 by 2003. For each firm, detailed balance sheet data were available in addition to basic information on its ownership

Table 4.2 The proportion of Chinese output at market prices by sector

Year	% producer goods at market prices	% producer goods in total output	% market price producer goods in total output	% retail sales at market prices	% retail sales in total output	% market price retail sales in total output	% farm commodities at market prices	% farm commodities in total output	% market price farm commodities in total output	% total output at market prices
1978	**0%**	**29%**	**0%**	**3%**	**29%**	**1%**	**6%**	**42%**	**3%**	**3%**
1985	**13%**	**30%**	**4%**	**34%**	**36%**	**12%**	**40%**	**34%**	**14%**	**30%**
1989	35%	32%	11%	58%	38%	22%	52%	32%	17%	50%
1990	40%	33%	13%	64%	39%	25%	55%	31%	17%	55%
1991	**46%**	**34%**	**16%**	**69%**	**39%**	**27%**	**58%**	**28%**	**16%**	**59%**
1992	54%	36%	19%	74%	39%	29%	63%	26%	16%	65%
1993	62%	38%	24%	79%	38%	30%	68%	24%	16%	70%
1994	70%	40%	28%	84%	38%	32%	73%	22%	16%	76%
1995	**78%**	**42%**	**33%**	**89%**	**37%**	**33%**	**79%**	**20%**	**16%**	**81%**
1996	80%	43%	34%	92%	38%	35%	79%	17%	13%	83%
1997	82%	43%	35%	94%	38%	36%	79%	17%	13%	84%
1998	84%	44%	37%	97%	39%	38%	79%	16%	13%	87%
1999	**86%**	**44%**	**38%**	**99%**	**39%**	**39%**	**79%**	**15%**	**12%**	**88%**
2000	88%	44%	39%	99%	39%	39%	79%	15%	12%	89%

Sources: Adapted from Naughton (2007, p.155) and OECD (2005).

Note: Official figures in boldface; author estimates are in lightface.

structure, industry, location and employment. This high level of detail allowed for several types of adjustment for value added, intermediate inputs, profit and capital concepts to ensure correspondence with international practice. Total production as measured by Western statisticians combines non-market planned production – imputed market production – and actual market production. The proportion of each sector at market prices is disaggregated by multiplying the proportion of total output in that sector by the proportion of market prices in that sector. The total for the entire economy is a simple addition of these three totals. This provides the total output real national income deflator that shows the proportion of total output produced at market prices. This shows the actual increase of national income within total production. When official state figures were unavailable then the mean average between two known dates was used to develop an estimate of annual change.

Table 4.2 demonstrates that the proportion of output at market prices increased very rapidly during the early 1980s; from effectively no market production in 1978, it rose to 30% of total output by 1985. Retail sales and agricultural production were liberalised faster than the industrial sector. By 1991 the economy was already a predominantly capitalist one. The dismantling of the iron rice bowl, the provision of social services by industrial plants, meant that the proportion of market prices in the producer sector had increased to 78% by 1995, while total market output rose to 81%. Total output grew rapidly but the capitalist sector grew even more rapidly. By 1989, 89% of total output was at market prices, a proportion higher than in the US. By tracing the growth of the market sector separately from the aggregate of total economic activity, the real expansion of market production and national income is revealed. China is taken as a proxy for Vietnam, a much smaller albeit fast growing economy, that followed a similar path to capitalist restoration (Hayton 2010).

The growth of capitalist production can be estimated by both physical and value quantities. In a market economy, physical quantities of use values represent actual amounts of value. Although there is not a direct correlation between physical and value aggregates, the direction of change of the economy can be established by the amount of physical output produced by it. In 1936 Trotsky used them to describe the growth of industrial production in the USSR:

> If in view of the instability of the rouble as a unit of measurement, we lay aside money estimates, we arrive at another unit which is absolutely unquestionable. In December 1913, the Don basin produced 2,275,000 tons of coal: in December 1935, 7,125,000 tons. During the last three years the production of iron has doubled. The production of steel and of the rolling mills has increased almost 2½ times. The output of oil, coal and iron has increased from 3 to 3½ times the pre-war figure. In 1920, when the first plan of electrification was drawn up, there were 10 district power stations in the country with a total power production of 253,000 kilowatts. In 1935, there were already 95 of these stations with a total power of 4,345,000 kilowatts. In 1925, the Soviet Union stood 11th in the production of electro-energy: in 1935, it was

second only to Germany and the United States. In the production of coal, the Soviet Union has moved forward from 10th to 4th place. In steel, from 6th to 3rd place. In the production of tractors, to the 1st place in the world. This also is true of the production of sugar. (1936, pp.6–7)

Physical outputs further provide the basis of PPP GDP measures. This study uses estimates of aluminium, electricity, steel, concrete, automobiles and PPP GDP deflated by the growth of market production to estimate the growth of "real" GDP separate from the total output of the transition economies. For a point of comparison, the G7 core Western industrialised economies of the United States, German, the United Kingdom, France, Italy, Canada and Japan are contrasted.

4.5 Electricity

Stern and Davies (1998) in a study of the privatisation of the electricity industry noted the crucial role of electricity in Soviet economic thinking. It was an index of modernisation, equated with the creation of a modern industrial economy. Just as it had been a measure of the transition of the market to the plan, so now it was a measure of the reverse. Stern and Davies assessed the extent of market reform in electricity production against several key criteria, whether the main consumer groups pay the full economic cost of the production, distribution and supply of the electricity they consume, whether electricity companies were commercially viable and whether firms were able to finance investment without subsidy or other state assistance.

By the mid-1990s, budget subsidy in the Czech Republic, Hungary, Poland and Slovakia and Slovenia had declined from 10% to 3% of national income, similar to West Europe. This confirmed that the privatisation of the electricity sector had followed a similar path to that of private sector production as a whole. Prior to 1989, prices bore no obvious relationship to the cost of production. Consumers were charged low prices for essential goods. After the big bang, electricity companies were required to cover their current costs in accounting terms and to earn a positive operating profit. Depreciation rates remained very low as the required rate of return and depreciation were calculated based on historic book values, not current replacement cost as in the West. This reflected the fact that before 1989 the capital stock had no value. If firms charged depreciation at current rates they "would earn sizeable revenues but without the dividend or debt payment obligations of an OECD utility . . . this would leave the companies with potentially very large amounts of retained earnings" (Stern & Davies 1998, p.444). The low organic composition of capital in the newly created fixed-capital stock would result in high rates of profit.

Dobozi and Pohl (1995) argued that changes in electricity consumption provided a more accurate proxy for changes in real national income than official national income estimates. The collection of electricity consumption data did not rely on output surveys or census and the ratio of electricity consumption to national income is constant or in decline. They concluded (based on changes to electricity consumption) that real national income fell by 21% between 1989 and 1994.

Table 4.3 The CIS, CEE, Chinese and Vietnamese total, capitalist and centrally planned electricity production 1990–2010

Year	CIS & CEE total	CIS & CEE capitalist	CIS & CEE CPE	China & Vietnam total	China & Vietnam capitalist	China & Vietnam CPE	Transition total	Transition capitalist	Transition CPE
1990	1,987	172	1,866	630	290	340	2,617	461	1816
1991	1,937	271	1,666	687	316	371	2,624	587	2,037
1992	1,820	310	1,509	764	412	351	2,583	723	1,860
1993	1,735	416	1,319	822	510	312	2,557	926	1,632
1994	1,608	473	1,135	940	658	282	2,548	1,131	1,418
1995	1,597	773	823	1,021	797	225	2,618	1,570	1,048
1996	1,572	855	718	1,098	879	220	2,671	1,733	937
1997	1,542	962	580	1,124	921	202	2,666	1,883	783
1998	1,527	962	565	1,185	996	190	2,712	1,958	754
1999	1,538	987	551	1,221	1,050	171	2,759	2,037	722
2000	1,589	1,036	553	1,382	1,216	166	2,971	2,252	719
2001	1,621	1,621	0	1,511	1,511	0	3,133	3,133	0
2005	1,746	1,746	0	2,554	2,554	0	4,300	4,300	0
2010	1,850	1,850	0	4,307	4,307	0	6,157	6,157	0

Source: BP (2012).

Note: twh = terawatt-hours.

Whether this was indeed a more accurate assessment of the change in the notional value of centrally planned output, depends on the extent to which electricity does indeed provide a reliable indicator of changes in production. Most electricity is used for domestic consumption or transport, and only a minority goes to industrial output. During an industrial crisis, electricity used in consumption and transport will not collapse to the same degree as that of industrial production. More to the point, their method aggregated the electricity production of the central plan and the market sectors. That is production inside and outside the market boundary. As such, it could not by definition be a more accurate measure of the growth of output within the market boundary when it did not measure it.

In Table 4.3 and the other tables that follow, "Total" production is the combined centrally planned and capitalist output. "Capitalist" production is the total of market production deflated as described above. "CPE" production is the non-market centrally planned production. Table 4.3 contrasts the growth of capitalist electricity production in the CIS, CEE, China and Vietnam. All the physical estimates of Chinese and Vietnamese physical production deflate the total by the proportion of market production in producer prices.

Total electricity production in the CIS and CEE fell from 1,987 terawatt-hours (twh) to 1,621 twh between 1987 and 2001, or by 18%. By 2010 it had recovered to 1,850 twh, still 6% below its 1990 level. This fall obscures the growth of distinctively market production. The output of the market sector grew rapidly as prices were liberalised. Between 1990 and 2001 it increased from 172 twh to 1,621 twh, or by 1,029%. Centrally planned electricity production fell from 1,820 twh in 1990 to 0 twh in 2001. The stagnation in total output confused the growth of the market with the collapse of the plan.

In 1990, 46% of Chinese producer goods were already sold at market prices. The total output of these economies was just 31% of the combined total of the CIS and CEE, but market production was actually larger, at 290 twh in 1990 compared with 197 twh in the CIS and CEE. By 2010 China's total – now capitalist electricity production – had far surpassed the CIS and CEE at 4,307 twh, an increase of 583% in total output from 1990. The growth in total production still obscured the growth of capitalist production, which grew by 1,386% in the period.

The entry of the CEE, CIS, China and Vietnam into the world market had a significant impact on world capitalist electricity production. In 1990 the capitalist electricity production of the transition economies amounted to just 5% of world capitalist production. What remained of centrally planned production still amounted to 22% of the capitalist total. By 2000 the proportions were almost entirely reversed. Centrally planned production amounted to just 5% of world capitalist production, whereas transition capitalist production had risen to 20% of world capitalist electricity production. Over the next decade, transition capitalist electricity production rapidly increased to 29% of world capitalist output by 2010. The growth of the transition economies was mirrored in the proportionate decline in electricity production within the G7 from 62% of world capitalist electricity production in 1990 to 50% in 2000 and 37% in 2010.

Table 4.4 World electricity production 1990–2010

Year	Total World	Transition capitalist	CPE	World capitalist	CPE % world capitalist	Transition cap % world capitalist	G7	G7 % world capitalist
1990	11,861	461	1,816	9,701	22%	4%	6,011	62%
1991	12,108	587	2,037	10,049	21%	5%	6,136	61%
1992	12,223	723	1,860	10,376	18%	6%	6,174	60%
1993	12,484	926	1,632	10,869	15%	7%	6,310	58%
1994	12,813	1,131	1,418	11,413	12%	9%	6,462	57%
1995	13,256	1,570	1,048	12,228	8%	12%	6,644	54%
1996	13,685	1,733	937	12,771	7%	13%	6,825	53%
1997	13,977	1,883	783	13,191	6%	13%	6,901	52%
1998	14,350	1,958	754	13,625	5%	14%	7,062	52%
1999	14,731	2,037	722	14,038	5%	14%	7,198	51%
2000	15,394	2,252	719	14,703	5%	15%	7,407	50%
2001	15,640	3,133	0	15,640	5%	20%	7,345	47%
2005	18,339	4,300	0	18,339	0%	23%	7,924	43%
2010	21,325	6,157	0	21,325	0%	29%	7,975	37%

Source: BP (2012).

Note: twh = terawatt-hours.

Table 4.5 Total, capitalist and centrally planned electricity production, decade growth

	Total production	World capitalist production	CPE
1990–99	24%	45%	–68%
1999–2010	45%	52%	–100%

Source: BP (2012).

Table 4.5 shows the effect of aggregating capitalist and non-capitalist production. From 1990 to 1999 total world electricity output grew by 24%, but world capitalist production increased by 44%. At the same time centrally planned output fell by 68% and ceased entirely after 2001. Total world electricity production increased by 45% between 1999 and 2010 but in the same period, world capitalist production increased by 52%.

4.6 Aluminium

Aluminium use is widespread in modern industry as a lighter and more flexible alternative to steel. Its production requires modern infrastructure and uses massive quantities of electricity in the Hall–Heroult process. The transition to capitalism in the aluminium sector was less traumatic than within the economy as a whole. Table 4.6 contrasts the effect of disaggregating capitalist and centrally planned aluminium production from the total, in China, Vietnam, the CEE and the CIS.

CIS and CEE aluminium production fell from 4,146 thousand metric tons (tmt) in 1989 to 3,417 tmt in 1995, or by 18%. It recovered to 4,378 tmt by 2001 and then grew to 5,069 tmt in 2010. Capitalist output increased much faster, from 270 tmt in 1989 to 4,378 tmt in 2001 and then to 5,069 tmt in 2010, or by 1,777%.

In 1990 total Chinese aluminium production of 750 tmt was 20% of the CIS and CEE total of 3,692 tmt. Chinese total production rose rapidly during the 1990s. It was 1,680 tmt in 1995, or 49% of the CIS and CEE total of 3,417 tmt. By 2000 China's production total had reached 2,800 tmt, 64% of the CIS and CEE total of 4,331 tmt, but by 2010, it had reached 16,200 tmt compared to 5,069 tmt, or 320% larger. China's capitalist aluminium production rose 4,596% between 1990 to 2010.

Total world production is a category that aggregates the aluminium output of the central plan and capitalism. Table 4.7 illustrates the growth of world capitalist aluminium production by separating distinctively capitalist production from the aggregated total. Total world production rose from 19,010 tmt in 1989 to 40,800 tmt in 2010, an increase of 114%. The agglomeration of the output of these two distinct modes of production hides the relative increase in capitalist production that rose from 14,729 tmt in 1989 to 40,800 tmt in 2001, or by 177%. In 1989, centrally planned output was 26% of world capitalist production. By 2001 the now capitalist production of the transition economies was 31% of world capitalist

Table 4.6 The CIS, CEE, Chinese and Vietnamese total, capitalist and centrally planned aluminium production, 1990–2010

Year	CIS & CEE total	CIS & CEE capitalist	CIS and CEE CPE	China total	China capitalist	China CPE	Transition total	Transition capitalist	Transition CPE
1989	4,146	270	3,876	750	345	405	4896	615	4,281
1990	4,234	319	3,915	850	391	459	5,084	710	4,374
1991	3,873	461	3,412	963	442.98	520	4,836	904	3,932
1992	3,635	558	3,077	1,100	594	506	4,735	1,152	3,583
1993	3,551	732	2,819	1,220	756	464	4,771	1,488	3,287
1994	3,367	821	2,546	1,450	1,015	435	4,817	1,836	2,981
1995	3,417	1,740	1,678	1,680	1,310	370	5,097	3,050	2,048
1996	3,565	2,029	1,536	1,770	1,416	354	5,335	3,445	1,890
1997	3,659	2,396	1,263	1,960	1,607	359	5,619	4,003	1,616
1998	3,857	2,592	1,265	2,340	1,966	374	6,197	4,558	1,639
1999	4,092	2,746	1,346	2,530	2,176	354	6,622	4,929	1,700
2000	4,331	2,919	1,412	2,800	2,464	336	7,131	5,383	1,748
2001	4,378	4,378	0	3,250	3,250	0	7,628	7,628	0
2005	5,041	5,041	0	7,800	7,800	0	12,841	12,841	0
2010	4,746	4,746	0	12,900	12,900	0	17,646	17,646	0
2011	5,069	5,069	0	16,200	16,200	0	21,269	21,269	0

Source: USGS (1989–2011).

Note: tmt = thousand metric tons.

Table 4.7 World aluminium production, 1990–2010

1989	19,010	615	3,854	14,729	4%	26%	7,231	49%
1990	19,299	710	3,990	14,925	5%	27%	7,244	48%
1991	19,535	904	3,585	15,603	6%	23%	7,449	48%
1992	19,467	1,152	3,583	15,884	7%	23%	7,459	47%
1993	19,800	1,488	3,283	16,517	9%	20%	7,394	45%
1994	19,200	1,836	2,981	16,219	11%	18%	6,883	42%
1995	19,700	3,050	2,047	17,653	17%	12%	6,921	39%
1996	20,700	3,445	1,890	18,810	18%	10%	7,242	39%
1997	21,600	4,003	1,616	19,984	20%	8%	7,354	37%
1998	22,600	4,557	1,640	20,960	22%	8%	7,584	36%
1999	23,600	4,921	1,701	21,899	22%	8%	7,728	35%
2000	24,400	5,383	2,257	22,143	24%	10%	7,627	34%
2001	24,300	7,628	0	24,300	31%	0	6,869	28%
2005	31,900	12,841	0	31,900	40%	0	7,035	22%
2010	40,800	21,269	0	40,800	52%	0	5,799	14%

Source: USGS (1989–2011).

Note: tmt = thousand metric tons.

Table 4.8 World total, capitalist and centrally planned aluminium production, decade growth

	Total	CPE	Capitalist
1980–89	24%	48%	18%
1989–99	24%	–61%	49%
1999–2010	73%	–100%	86%

Source: USGS (1989–2011).

production before reaching 52% by 2010. The G7 traced the opposite path, falling 19% as a proportion of total world production between 1989 and 2010. As a proportion of world capitalist production it declined even faster from 49% in 1989 to 14% in 2010.

Table 4.8 shows that world aluminium production grew by 24% between 1980 and 1989 and by 24% between 1989 and 1999. The relative stability of the total change conceals the growth of capitalist production. The 1980s increase was in large part due to the growth of centrally planned production which rose 48% between 1980 and 1989, a period in which capitalist market production only rose 18%. During the 1990s the centrally planned output fell by 61% while capitalist production increased by 49%. Between 1999 and 2010 total output rose by 73%, but capitalist production increased by 86%.

4.7 Hydraulic cement

Hydraulic cement is a key material for both residential and infrastructural construction. Relatively cheap to produce but expensive to transport, its output is closely related to the physical quantity of construction in a given national economy. It provides a very clear idea indicator of the distinction between total output and capitalist output. Construction in the CIS and CEE collapsed during the transition to capitalism. Table 4.9 shows that total CEE and CIS cement production was 90,185 tmt in 2001, a fall of 54% compared to 197,884 tmt in 1989. By 2010 it had recovered to 129,651 tmt, still 34% below its 1989 level.

If total production, the aggregation of centrally planned and market output, is elided with production within the market boundary, then the introduction of the market led to a fall of market production. As national income measures economic activity within the market boundary, the growth of output within the market boundary led to a fall in it. This absurd assumption forms the empirical basis for the official fall in national income measures during the transition to capitalism. Production within the market boundary increased from 17,223 tmt in 1989 to 55,353 tmt in 2001, or by 221%; by 2011 it had reached 129,651 tmt, a rise of 653%. In China and Vietnam total production increased by 223% between 1989 and 2001 before rising by 821% in 2010. Even this very sharp increase conceals the rise in capitalist production, which rose twenty-fold between 1989 and 2010, or by 1,903%.

Table 4.10 shows that over the same period, the transition capitalist economies came to dominate world capitalist hydraulic cement production. By 1989, almost exclusively because of China's early transition to the market, capitalist transition hydraulic cement production already amounted to 13% of world capitalist output. By 2010 this had risen to 62%. Meanwhile, the G7 fell from 30% of world capitalist production in 1989 to 12% in 2005 and then to just 7% in 2010.

The amalgamation of centrally planned and capitalist production during the transition period provides a very misleading picture of the growth of the world market production of hydraulic cement. Table 4.11 shows that total hydraulic cement output grew 26% in the period from 1980 to 1989 and 30% in the period from 1989 to 1999. It would appear that the creation of a global market made almost no difference to capitalist production during the 1990s. Total output increased 106.9% from 1999 to 2010, but this aggregation conceals the growth of specifically capitalist market production. Capitalist market production expanded by 52% between 1980 to 1989, by 60% from 1989 and 1999 and by 122% from 1999 and 2010.

4.8   Steel

Steel is a fundamental material in modern industrial production and a proxy for industrial production itself. The total output of steel in CEE and the CIS fell by 39.9% between 1989 and 2001. By 2011 it was still 36% below its 1989 level. Nonetheless, CIS and CEE capitalist steel production increased by 970% between 1989 and 2001 and by 1,033% in the next ten years. The amalgamation of centrally planned and capitalist production transforms this eleven-fold rise into a 40% fall. While China and Vietnam both saw total steel production expand very

Table 4.9 The CIS, CEE, Chinese and Vietnamese total, capitalist and centrally planned hydraulic cement production, 1990–2010

Year	CIS & CEE total	CIS & CEE capitalist	CIS & CEE CPE	China & Vietnam total	China & Vietnam capitalist	China & Vietnam CPE	Transition total	Transition capitalist	Transition CPE
1989	197,884	17,223	173,451	209,500	96,370	120,340	422,384	127,243	295,141
1990	183,260	16,033	160,627	205,500	94,530	117,570	398,490	118,943	279,547
1991	163,389	22,348	134,921	255,610	117,821	143,909	421,999	141,396	280,603
1992	141151	28,323	114,728	359,000	194,260	162,840	498,251	221,676	276,575
1993	116,721	29,823	88,158	372,080	231,026	139,794	488,501	263,148	225,353
1994	97,898	31,235	68,073	425,880	298,116	126,354	523,678	332,324	191,354
1995	92,599	43,355	50,388	481,110	375,266	104,700	573,609	422,036	151,573
1996	82,352	43,079	40,413	496,890	397,512	98,238	579,157	444,382	134,775
1997	82,839	47,956	35,963	498,600	408,852	88,668	581,348	460,608	120,740
1998	83,915	50,053	35,420	545,738	458,420	85,760	629,453	511,971	117,482
1999	86,991	53,435	35,024	583,489	501,801	80,220	670,138	558,603	111,535
2000	88,549	55,353	35,058	610,298	536,796	71,640	698,499	595,395	103,104
2001	90,185	90,185	0	676,414	676,414	0	766,299	766,299	0
2005	121,584	121,584	0	1,099,658	1,099,658	0	1,220,792	1,220,792	0
2010	129,651	129,651	0	1,930,000	1,930,000	0	2,058,794	2,058,794	0

Source: USGS (1989–2011).

Note: tmt = thousand metric tons.

Table 4.10 World hydraulic cement production, 1989–2010

Year	World Total	Transition capitalist	CPE	World capitalist	Transition capitalist % world cap	CPE % world capitalist	G7	G7 % world capitalist
1989	1,235,693	127,243	295,141	929,402	14%	32%	282,859	30%
1990	1,160,000	118,943	279,547	881,803	13%	32%	286,300	32%
1991	1,180,000	141,396	280,603	901,170	16%	31%	279,696	31%
1992	1,240,000	221,676	276,575	962,432	23%	29%	276,429	29%
1993	1,290,905	263,148	225,353	1,062,953	25%	21%	278,936	26%
1994	1,373,013	332,324	191,354	1,178,586	28%	16%	293,333	25%
1995	1,443,328	422,036	151,573	1,291,583	33%	12%	281,926	22%
1996	1,488,262	444,382	134,775	1,353,445	33%	10%	288,056	21%
1997	1,515,442	460,608	120,740	1,394,661	33%	9%	291,347	21%
1998	1,540,000	511,971	117,482	1,422,438	36%	8%	283,005	20%
1999	1,600,000	558,603	111,535	1,488,329	38%	7%	286,658	19%
2000	1,650,000	595,395	103,104	1,546,756	38%	7%	289,460	19%
2001	1,730,000	766,299	0	1,730,000	44%	0%	282,472	16%
2005	2,350,000	1,220,792	0	2,350,000	52%	0%	288,497	12%
2010	3,310,000	2,058,794	0	3,310,000	62%	32%	223,227	7%

Source: USGS (1989–2011).

Note: tmt = thousand metric tons.

Table 4.11 World total, capitalist and centrally planned hydraulic cement production, decade growth

	Total	CPE	Capitalist
1980–89	26%	−16%	52%
1989–99	30%	−64%	60%
1999–2010	107%	−100%	122%

Source: USGS (1989–2011).

rapidly, total Chinese and Vietnamese output increased by 1,008% between 1989 and 2001. This eleven-fold rise still underestimated the increase in distinctly capitalist production of 2,628%, a twenty-seven-fold rise.

Total world steel output rose by 82% between 1989 and 2011 while world capitalist steel production rose by 171%. As transition capitalist steel production increased, the output of the G7 declined. In 1989 the G7 produced 61% of world capitalist steel, falling to 38% by 2001, before falling further to 22% by 2010. Over the entire period, G7 steel output fell by 4%, from 332,457 tmt to 308,146 tmt. At the same time the transition capitalist economies grew from 7% of world capitalist steel in 1989 to 31% in 2001 and 53% in 2010. Total transition capitalist output grew twenty-fold by 1934%. Table 4.13 shows that in six years, China added steel capacity equivalent to the entire G7.

Steel particularly demonstrates why it is so misleading to amalgamate the output of the central plan and the capitalist market. The conflation of total and market steel production implies that the growth of market production in the 1990s actually led to a slowdown in market steel production. Table 4.14 shows that total steel output grew by 10% between 1980 and 1989 before stagnating between 1989 and 1999, during which output grew just 0.3%. It increased by 81% between 1999 and 2010. But the decline on the 1990s was not because of the stagnation of capitalist production but because of the collapse of the central plan. Capitalist production grew by 13% between 1980 and 1989, and then 39% between 1989 and 1999, before accelerating again by 96% between 1999 and 2010.

4.9   Automobiles

The poor quality of Eastern European and Soviet automobiles was a standing joke from the 1930s onwards when Soviet tractor factories began the production of large numbers of badly made and already obsolete American models. In 1991 centrally planned production of passenger cars and commercial vehicles were only 6% of the capitalist total.

Unlike the output of basic infrastructure that requires high quantities of steel, concrete and electricity, the introduction of capitalism in CEE and the CIS enabled capitalists to use existing infrastructure to transplant new plant and equipment for more sophisticated manufacturing. Table 4.15 shows that after an initial collapse in total production by 31% between 1990 and 1994, CIS and CEE auto

Table 4.12 The CIS, CEE, Chinese and Vietnamese total, capitalist and centrally planned steel production, 1990–2010

Year	Total	Capitalist	Centrally planned	Total	Capitalist	Centrally planned	Total	Capitalist	Centrally planned
1989	215,732	12,124	203,608	61,672	25,286	36386	277,404	37,409	239,995
1990	201,458	18,285	183,173	66,451	30,567	35884	267,909	48,852	219,057
1991	169,306	23,074	146,232	71,183	32,744	38439	240,489	55,819	184,670
1992	383,341	23,579	359,763	81,154	43,823	37331	464,495	67,402	397,093
1993	128,358	29,418	98,940	89,809	55,682	34127	218,167	85,100	133,067
1994	110,026	34,797	75,229	92,914	65,040	27874	202,940	99,837	103,103
1995	113,090	57,206	55,884	95,631	74,592	21039	208,721	131,798	76,923
1996	110,631	60,974	49,657	101,548	81,238	20310	212,179	142,212	69,967
1997	114,521	72,914	41,607	109,225	89,565	19661	223,746	162,479	61,267
1998	107,968	68,244	39,724	114,894	96,511	18383	222,862	164,755	58,107
1999	114,119	73,688	40,431	123,568	106,268	17300	237,687	179,957	57,730
2000	127,879	79,321	48,558	127,542	109,686	17856	255,421	189,007	66,414
2001	129,731	129,731	0	151,225	151,225	0	280,956	280,956	0
2005	145,838	145,838	0	356,680	356,680	0	502,518	502,518	0
2010	132,754	132,754	0	641,714	641,714	0	774,468	774,468	0
2011	137,450	137,450	0	687,579	687,579	0	825,029	825,029	0

Source: WSA (1989–2011).

Note: tmt = thousand metric tons.

Table 4.13 World steel production, 1989–2010

Year	Total	Capitalist world	Transition capitalist	CPE	CPE % capitalist world	Transition capitalist % world capitalist	G7	G7 % capitalist
1989	785,968	526,021	37,409	239,995	46%	7%	322457	61%
1990	770,458	542,949	48,852	219,057	40%	9%	319,555	59%
1991	733,592	539,806	55,819	184,670	34%	10%	311,241	58%
1992	719,680	593,445	67,402	397,093	67%	11%	301,980	54%
1993	727,547	593,445	85,100	133,067	22%	14%	308,395	52%
1994	725,107	619,840	99,837	103,103	17%	16%	313,861	51%
1995	752,271	673,758	131,798	76,923	11%	20%	326,433	48%
1996	750,090	680,627	142,212	69,967	10%	21%	314,676	46%
1997	798,954	735,226	162,479	61,267	8%	22%	333,775	45%
1998	777,328	719,427	164,755	58,107	8%	23%	320,925	45%
1999	785,968	730,157	179,957	57,730	8%	25%	315,970	43%
2000	847,670	788,602	189,007	66,414	8%	24%	339,891	43%
2001	850,345	850,345	280,956	0	0%	33%	319,682	38%
2005	1,146,686	1,146,686	502,518	0	0%	44%	339,158	30%
2010	1,428,711	1,428,711	774,468	0	0%	54%	308,146	22%

Source: WSA (1989–2011).

Note: tmt = thousand metric tons.

Table 4.14 World steel production, decade growth

	Total	CPE	Capitalist	G7	Transition capitalist
1980–89	10%	4%	13%	−4%	4,931%
1989–99	0%	−78%	39%	−2%	381%
1999–2010	81%	−100%	96%	−3%	323%

Source: WSA (1989–2011).

Table 4.15 The CIS, CEE, Chinese total, capitalist and centrally planned automobile production, 1991–2010

Year	CIS & CEE total	CIS & CEE capitalist	CIS & CEE CPE	China total	China capitalist	China CPE	Transition total	Transition capitalist	Transition CPE
1991	2,880	422	2,458	709	326	383	3,589	748	2,841
1994	1,999	725	1,274	1353	947	406	3,352	1,672	1,680
1995	2,047	1,162	885	1435	1119	316	3,482	2,281	1,201
1996	2,065	1,298	767	1466	1173	293	3,531	2,471	1,060
1997	2,153	1,477	676	1578	1294	284	3,731	2,771	960
1998	2,514	1,712	802	1628	1368	260	4,142	3,080	1,062
1999	2,769	1,941	828	1805	1552	253	4,574	3,493	1,081
2000	2,596	1,823	773	2009	1768	241	4,605	3,591	1,014
2001	2,468	2,468	0	2332	2332	0	4,800	4,800	0
2005	3,172	3,172	0	5668	5668	0	8,840	8,840	0
2010	4,518	4,518	0	18265	18265	0	22,783	22,783	0

Source: OICA (1990–2010).

Note: thv = thousands of vehicles.

Table 4.16 World automobile production, 1991–2010

Year	Total world	World capitalist	CPE	CPE % world capitalist	Transition capitalist	Transition capitalist % world capitalist	G7	G7 % world capitalist
1991	47,262	44,493	2,769	6%	748	2%	35,902	81%
1994	49,658	48,036	1,622	3%	1,672	4%	36,257	76%
1995	50,046	48,901	1,145	2%	2,282	5%	36,173	74%
1996	51,496	50,475	1,021	2%	2,470	5%	36,476	72%
1997	53,474	52,566	908	2%	2,771	5%	37,034	71%
1998	52,093	51,082	1,011	2%	3,080	6%	36,581	72%
1999	54,948	53,910	1,038	2%	3,493	7%	38,382	71%
2000	58,946	57,961	985	2%	3,591	6%	37,986	66%
2001	56,325	56,325	0	0%	4,800	9%	36,319	65%
2005	66,085	66,085	0	0%	8,840	13%	37,583	57%
2010	76,148	76,148	0	0%	22,783	30%	29,791	39%

Source: OICA (1990–2010).

Note: thv = thousands of vehicles.

Table 4.17 World automobile production, decade growth

	Total	Capitalist	CPE	G7	Transition capitalist
1991–2000	24.7%	30%	–64%	6%	380%
2000–10	29.2%	31%	–100%	–22%	534%

Source: OICA (1990–2010).

output rose to 4,518 thousands of vehicles (thv) in 2010, which was an increase of 56% over the plan period. This increase was far smaller than the rise in China's production. China's total auto output jumped by 2,476.2% between 1991 and 2010, but China's capitalist production increased fifty-six-fold, or 5,500.4%, between 1991 and 2010.

The shift in world automobile production is pronounced. Table 4.16 demonstrates that the transition economies are displacing the West in advanced manufacturing sectors, even while much of this production is still dominated by global multinational corporations. Transition capitalist auto production rose from 2% of world capitalist production in 1991 to 9% in 2001 and 30% in 2010.

Table 4.17 shows that the growth of total capitalist production at 24.7% is still larger than the growth of total production of 30% between 1991 and 2001. The relatively small quantity of automobiles in centrally planned production in 1991 means that the disaggregation of centrally planned and capitalist production is not as marked as in other sectors.

4.10   Gross domestic product – purchasing power parity

The use of physical indicators provides strong evidence for the importance of the distinction between total, centrally planned and capitalist (GDP) production. Physical indicators enable the comparison of national economies and allow the practical demonstration of the growth of capitalist production during the transition period. The aggregation of centrally planned and capitalist production systematically underestimates the growth of output within the market boundary.

These measures underpin the widely used PPP estimate of national income. PPP provides an alternative measurement standard to exchange rate based conversion factors such as the World Bank "Atlas" method. Atlas uses a conversion factor which is the average of the exchange rate for that year and the exchange rates for the two preceding years, after adjusting them for differences in relative inflation between the country in question and the United States. In 1992 the World Bank pointed out that there was "no fully satisfactory way to compare per capita income of the Former Soviet Union (FSU) with that of most other economies". The "root cause" was that "the FSU had a non-market and exceptionally isolated economy". This was exacerbated by the collapse of information reporting systems. It concluded that the "seemingly simple case for using official exchange rates proves untenable because, like other planned prices, such rates prove to be artificial and misleading" (World Bank 1992, p.i). The World Bank proposed a PPP bridge from the planned to the market economies. This enabled the measurement of the FSU but obliterated the distinction between the collapsing central plan and the growing market. Koen and Meyermans for the IMF noted that

> [t]he adoption of a unified exchange regime in July 1992 was a major step in opening Russia to the world economy and moving toward a market system. Notwithstanding political turmoil, collapsing output, very high inflation, large scale dollarization and occasional rumors about an imminent return to a system of multiple exchange rates, this decision has not been reversed. (Koen & Meyermans 1994, p.10)

This led to very large fluctuations in the exchange rate as a market in foreign exchange was created from almost nothing. Based on real exchange rates in 1992 the Russian economy was smaller than Denmark's, while fluctuations in the interbank rate meant that the size of Russia's economy in US dollars more than doubled from the first to the second quarter of 1992. This effectively prevented the use of exchange rates to produce comparative national income estimates during the transition period.

PPP is defined as the number of currency units required to purchase an amount of goods and services in the subject country, equivalent to what can be bought with one unit of the object base-country currency. This is usually the US dollar. PPP addresses the problem of comparing different national economies, with different price structures, wages and productivity. This study uses the GDP estimates developed by the Conference Board of the Groningen Growth and Development Centre (GGDC; University of Groningen, The Netherlands; GGDC 2012). The Conference Board's Geary Khamis (GK) GDP estimates adjust values to reflect the productive capacity of different economies (GGDC 2012). Geary Khamis PPP gives a greater weight to more developed economies.

They use detailed categories of outputs matched for quality and specified price information for representative items intended for consumption, investment and government services. The goods should be equivalent, of physically identical, quality, use, taste and standard – irrespective of variations in the mode of production. Coverage of national and international measures should be made to a common standard.

PPP estimates are sensitive to the sample of products, prices, regions and periods. The country-reversal test means that in a given bilateral comparison, it should not matter which country is used as the base country. The product of the price and the quantity ratios should equal the expenditure ratio. For the test to be met, both the price and quantity indices must be computed independently.

By applying the market boundary deflators developed earlier, it is possible to determine the actual value of market production in them and by so doing to separate non-market centrally planned production from capitalist market production during the transition period. This will then allow an estimate of the real value of the transition to capitalism to be estimated.

4.11 China and Vietnam

In 1978 China introduced market measures that had transformed the economy into a capitalist one by the early 1990s. The GK PPPs used by the GGDC (2012) conflate the output of the central plan with that inside the market boundary. At the

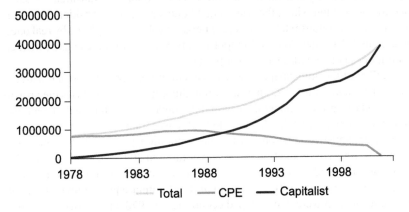

Figure 4.1 China's and Vietnam's capitalist transition from 1978–2001

Table 4.18 China and Vietnam during the transition: total, centrally planned and capitalist output, 1978–2010

Year	Total	CPE	Capitalist
1978	765,376	739,353	26,023
1984	117,2536	855,951	316,585
1989	1,653,718	843,396	810,322
1990	1,712,820	787,897	924,923
1991	1,825,141	751,958	1,073,183
1992	2,001,868	720,672	1,281,195
1993	2,194,362	658,309	1,536,053
1994	2,413,016	579,124	1,833,892
1995	2,772,557	512,923	2,259,634
1996	2,837,100	482,307	2,354,793
1997	2,989,790	448,469	2,541,322
1998	3,005,042	390,656	2,614,387
1999	3,200,069	374,408	2,825,661
2000	3,486,171	348,617	3,137,554
2001	3,853,199	0	3,853,199
2005	6,027,030	0	6,027,030
2010	10,183,399	0	10,183,399

Source: GGDC (2012).

Note: GDP in millions of 1990 US$ (converted at GK PPP).

outset of the transition the overwhelming bulk of production took place within the centrally planned sector. By 2001 all production was subordinate to market prices. In the figures for national income presented in Table 4.18 and all subsequent tables, the "Transition total" is the aggregate of the imputed national income applied to the output of the centrally planned economy and the actual national income within the real market boundary of the capitalist economy. The value allocated to the "CPE" is imputed national income only, while the value of "Capitalist transition" is actual economic production within the real market boundary. As the transition from central planning to capitalism takes place, the imputed values are replaced by real ones. It is assumed that after 2001, all output is subordinated to the capitalist market, even if it does not take place at market prices.

The effect of the adjustment between total and market production is illustrated in Table 4.19. and Figure 4.2. They show that this adjustment increases the growth rate of capitalist production by the original imputed value of the total of centrally planned production in 1978. This imputed value was transformed into or replaced with real capitalist production during the restoration process. CPE output fell from nearly 100% of production in 1978 to nothing in 2001. Meanwhile capitalist production increased as a proportion of total output until all output was subordinate to the market in 2001. At this point, total output equalled market output. China and Vietnam were undeveloped economies in 1978, but the disaggregation still adds 20% to the growth of real national income between 1978 and 2001.

Table 4.19 The CEE and CIS during the transition, total, centrally planned and capitalist production, 1989–2010

Year	Total	CPE	Capitalist
1989	231,3850	2,169,710	144,140
1990	2,250,508	2,082,435	168,073
1991	2,091,179	1,845,810	245,368
1992	2,146,467	1,690,713	455,753
1993	1,982,668	1,469,736	512,933
1994	1,806,026	1,219,235	586,791
1995	1,773,634	992,449	781,184
1996	1,766,336	800,017	966,319
1997	1,811,148	690,959	1,120,189
1998	1,803,852	667,274	1,136,579
1999	1,871,436	679,035	1,192,401
2000	2,002,065	708,555	1,293,510
2001	2,111,998	0	2,111,998
2005	2,524,359	0	2,524,359
2010	3,252,669	0	3,252,669

Source: GGDC (2012). GDP in millions of 1990 US$ (converted at GK PPP).

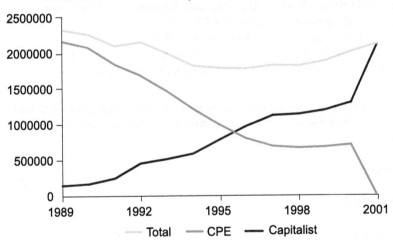

Figure 4.2 CEE and the CIS capitalist transition from 1989–2001

4.12 CEE and the CIS

The effect of this differentiation is even more significant in CEE and the CIS. Their economies were more developed in 1989, and the effect of the big-bang transition was more traumatic. Janos Kornai (2006) claims that the superiority of capitalism is demonstrated by comparing growth rates for the transition economies with those of Western Europe for 1995 and 2003. This was after the "transformational recession" that destroyed a third of the economy. There is no doubt that by excluding capitalist crises, growth rates will increase. Whether such a method proves anything about the superiority of capitalism or otherwise is moot. Kornai's real mistake is more fundamental. He confuses a collapse of the plan with the creation of the market, a decline of use values with the creation of exchange values.

According to the official Western estimates the total national income of the transition economies fell by approximately 23% of GDP between 1989 and 1996. In fact, output within the market boundary and therefore national income increased by 570%.

In 1989 at the outset of the restoration process, the nominal total national income attributed to the transition economies imputed "value" to the output of the central plan. But nothing can exist before it exists, and neither did capitalist production. The creation of market production requires the creation of a market. The collapse of the central plan in CEE and the CIS was real. But it was a collapse of the physical output of the centrally planned economy, not the collapse of value production but of its genesis. By 2001 the entire economies of these nations was subordinated to market prices, hence the one-off jump in capitalist production in that year. More sophisticated estimates than this one could develop some formula to demonstrate the transformation of state production to the market, but there would be no change to the aggregate. Western statisticians underestimate the growth of capitalist production in CEE and the CIS, by $2,111,998 million in 1990 US dollars (converted at Geary Khamis PPP).

Figure 4.3 shows the combined effect of the transition in the CEE, CIS, China and Vietnam. Capitalist production in China and Vietnam grew through the course

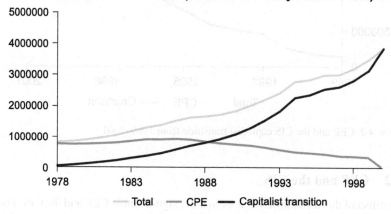

Figure 4.3 CEE, the CIS, China and Vietnam capitalist transition from 1978–2001

Table 4.20 World capitalist transition, 1978–2010

	Capitalist world economy	Transition capitalist	Transition capitalist % world capitalist	G7	G7 % world capitalist	Transition capitalist % of G7
1978	15,180,771	26,023	0%	8,988,470	59%	0%
1984	17,978,359	316,585	2%	10,361,297	58%	3%
1989	22,129,022	954,462	4%	12,539,019	57%	8%
1990	22,942,130	1,092,996	5%	12,844,077	56%	9%
1991	23,592,861	1,318,551	6%	12,973,151	55%	10%
1992	24,651,285	1,736,949	7%	13,244,411	54%	13%
1993	25,494,791	2,048,986	8%	13,423,941	53%	15%
1994	26,740,572	2,420,683	9%	13,842,205	52%	18%
1995	28,153,140	3,040,819	11%	14,171,665	50%	22%
1996	29,384,653	3,321,112	11%	14,555,118	50%	23%
1997	30,703,763	3,661,510	12%	15,027,098	49%	24%
1998	30,018,400	3,750,966	13%	15,429,080	51%	24%
1999	31,167,487	4,018,062	13%	15,938,345	51%	25%
2000	32,741,742	4,431,063	14%	16,528,165	51%	27%
2001	34,784,288	5,965,196	17%	16,733,768	48%	36%
2002	36,007,527	6,531,796	18%	16,953,922	47%	39%
2003	37,695,795	7,316,895	19%	17,264,936	46%	42%
2004	39,700,129	7,986,986	20%	17,754,826	45%	45%
2005	41,676,065	8,708,522	21%	18,157,424	44%	48%
2006	44,040,756	9,681,605	22%	18,623,797	42%	52%
2007	46,639,453	10,867,770	23%	19,024,093	41%	57%
2008	48,161,221	11,761,504	24%	18,969,008	39%	62%
2009	48,300,661	12,368,806	26%	18,197,707	38%	68%
2010	50,976,329	13,436,068	26%	18,735,787	37%	72%
2011	53,172,579	14,494,526	27%	19,000,590	36%	76%

Source: GGDC (2012).

Note: total GDP in millions of 1990 US$ (converted at GK PPP).

Table 4.21 World employment, 1978–2010

Year	Capitalist world	Transition capitalist	Transition capitalist % world capitalist	G7	G7 % world capitalist
1978	1,038,113	16,549	2%	197,439	19%
1984	1,313,752	155,250	12%	211,198	16%
1989	1,786,859	340,728	19%	228,744	13%
1990	1,831,526	381,536	21%	231,751	13%
1991	1,889,757	424,523	23%	232,817	12%
1992	1,989,659	481,358	24%	234,301	12%
1993	2,052,821	533,171	26%	235,066	12%
1994	2,124,419	589,496	28%	239,694	11%
1995	2,187,146	652,277	30%	242,569	11%
1996	2,232,691	688,041	31%	245,551	11%
1997	2,279,111	723,360	32%	249,264	11%
1998	2,326,036	747,297	32%	251,646	11%
1999	2,369,476	764,010	32%	253,854	11%
2000	2,422,450	786,511	33%	255,659	11%
2001	2,538,908	935,036	37%	255,673	10%
2005	2,707,142	961,538	36%	258,644	10%
2010	2,905,803	987,338	34%	257,621	9%
2011	2,945,357	991,265	34%	258,753	9%

Source: GGDC (2012).

Note: employment in thousands of persons.

of the 1980s as the proportion of output at market prices expanded. Following the big bang in the CIS and in CEE after 1991, the growth of transition economy national income accelerated until the central plan was entirely negated by 2001. From that time, all economic production was within a real market boundary. It is real rather than imputed national income and real value production, too. In 1992 the total imputed value of the still basically centrally planned economies was 17% of the world capitalist total. By 2001 when the transition process was completed the total still amounted to 17% albeit of what was now a larger world economy. This was real national income created in a real market economy. Between 1989 and 2001 this expansion of real capitalist value production raises nominal growth by half to 64%, compared to 44% for the aggregated output of both centrally planned production and capitalist production.

What enabled this one-off addition to have such a qualitative impact was not simply the one off transformation of centrally planned production into capitalist production: it was the availability of huge quantities of labour as shown in Table 4.21, often well educated but always low paid and masses of very cheap or free means of production and infrastructure that had no value. It had been constructed without payment during the central plan period. These economies had a very low organic composition of capital and consequently, once the circuit of capital accumulation process had begun to operate by the late 1990s, very high rates of profit.

During the first decade of the twenty-first century, these economies took off. The national income of the transition economies as a proportion of the G7 rose from 10% in 1991 to 36% in 2001 and 76% in 2010.

In 1991 the transition economies already included 22.5% of the world employed population compared to 12.3% in the G7. By 2010 this was 33.7% and 8.8%, respectively.

4.13   Conclusion

Globalisation aptly describes the creation of a global world market in the 1990s. The transition of the central plan to capitalism extended the rule of capital across the whole world for the first time since the Bolshevik Revolution of 1917. This was perhaps the greatest single and exceptional one off increase in the size of world capitalism in history. By 2001, when the process of capitalist restoration was complete, the transition economies accounted for 37% of world capitalist employment, 31% of aluminium, 44% of hydraulic cement, 24% of steel, 16% of electricity, 8.5% of cars and passenger vehicles and 17% of GDP (GK PPP). Far from the 1990s being a decade of capitalist stagnation world capitalist aluminium production increased 60.3%; hydraulic cement, 96%; steel, 56%; electricity, 61%; automobiles, 27%; and GDP (GK PPP), 52%. These trends accelerated markedly up to 2010.

This expansion of world capitalism with the transition of the centrally planned economies to capitalism was concealed by the national income measurements of the Western statistical agencies. They had transformed national income from a measure of real market exchanges within a real market boundary into a statistical construct outside of the real world. Through an imaginary imputed market they created exchange value in a centrally planned economy without exchange. They measured national income in an economy without national income. When the capitalist transition created a real market economy, they could not measure the growth of the market, because for them, it already existed in the books.

By separating the output of the central plan from that of the capitalist market, it is possible to demonstrate the qualitative impact of this capitalist transition on the world capitalist economy. It solves the riddle of how to measure the increase in national income during the transition period. It is the measurement of the growth of production in the expanding capitalist market. It is a real phenomenon rather than an imputed one.

References

BP, 2012. *BP Statistical Review of World Energy 2012*. London: BP. Available at: www. bp.com/assets/bp_internet/globalbp/globalbp_uk_english/reports_and_publications/statistical_energy_review_2011/STAGING/local_assets/pdf/statistical_review_of_world_energy_full_report_2012.pdf [Accessed April 1, 2012].

Dobozi, I., & Pohl G., 1995. Real Output Decline in Transition Economies – Forget GDP, Try Power Consumption Data. *Transition: The Newsletter about Reforming Economies*, 6(1–2), pp.17–18.

Dougherty, S., & Herd, R., 2005. *The Fast-Falling Barriers and Growing Concentration: The Emergence of the Private Economy in China.* OECD Economics Department Working Papers, No. 471. Paris, OECD

EBRD, 1995. *Transition Report 1995: Investment and Enterprise Report.* London: EBRD.

EBRD, 1996. *Transition Report 1996: Infrastructure and Savings.* London: EBRD.

EBRD, 1997. *Transition Report 1997: Enterprise Performance and Growth.* London: EBRD.

EBRD, 1998. *Transition Report 1998: Financial Sector in Transition.* London: EBRD.

EBRD, 1999. *Transition Report 1999: Ten Years of Transition.* London: EBRD.

EBRD, 2000. *Transition Report 2000: Employment, Skills and Transition.* London: EBRD.

EBRD, 2001. *Transition Report 2001: Energy in Transition.* London: EBRD.

EBRD, 2011. *Transition Indicators by Country.* EBRD Transition Indicators. Available at: www.ebrd.com/downloads/research/economics/macrodata/tic.xls [Accessed June 8, 2012].

GGDC, 2012. *The Total Economy Database.* GGDC. Available at: www.conference-board.org/retrievefile.cfm?filename=TEDI_Jan20121.xls&type=subsite [Accessed May 1, 2012].

Hayton, B., 2010. *Vietnam Rising Dragon.* New York: Yale University Press.

Koen, V., & Meyermans E., 1994. *Exchange Rate Determinants in Russia 1992–93.* IMF Working Paper No. 94/66. New York: IMF.

Kornai, J., 2006. The Great Transformation of Central and Eastern Europe: Success and Disappointment. *Economics of Transition,* 14(2), pp.207–44.

Kuboniwa, M., 1997. Economic Growth in Post War Russia: Estimating GDP. *Hitotsubashi Journal of Economics,* 38(1), pp.21–32.

Marx, K., 1981. *Capital Volume III.* London: Penguin Classics.

Naughton, B., 2007. *The Chinese Economy Transitions and Growth.* Cambridge, MA: MIT Press.

OECD, 2005. *OECD Economic Surveys China.* Paris: OECD.

OICA, 1990–2010. *World automobile production statistics.* Paris: OECD. Available at: http://oica.net/category/production-statistics/ [Access April 1, 2012].

Stern, J., & Davies R. Jnr., 1998. Economic Reform of the Electricity Industries of Central and Eastern Europe. *Economics of Transition,* 6(2), pp.427–60.

Studenski, P., 1958. *The Income of Nations: Theory, Measurement, and Analysis: Past and Present.* New York: New York University Press.

Trotsky, L, 1936. *The Revolution Betrayed.* New York: Dover.

UN, 1993. *The System of National Accounts 1993.* Brussels and Luxembourg: UN.

USGS, 1989–2011. *Minerals Yearbook Area Reports International.* Washington, DC: USGS. Available at: http://minerals.usgs.gov/minerals/pubs/commodity/myb/ [Accessed May 1, 2012].

Vanoli, A., 2005. *A History of National Accounting.* Amsterdam: IOS Press.

World Bank, 1992. *Measuring the Incomes of Economies of the Former Soviet Union.* Washington, DC: World Bank.

WSA, 1989–2012. *Annual Crude Steel Production Archive.* Brussels: WSA. Available at: www.worldsteel.org/statistics/statistics-archive/annual-steel-archive.html [Accessed February 1, 2012].

5   After the fall

5.1   Bergson and the CIA reassessed

The failure of Western experts to predict the post-1991 collapse of the CIS re-opened the question of the meaningfulness of their estimates of Soviet national income. How could their imputed prices be "real" when output collapsed with the introduction of real market prices? There were essentially two sides to the debate, those who attempted to explain away the collapse in output and those who defended the conventional wisdom despite its failure to anticipate the crash.

Those who were most critical of the Bergson synthesis sought to deny the reality of Soviet output. They elaborated the argument of Lev Navrozov (1988), a Soviet exile who developed a critique of the CIA's national income estimates during the 1970s and 1980s. Navrozov argued that the CIA was gullible. It set too much store by official statistics. It did not use its network of spies efficiently. It underestimated the USSR's military expenditure and failed to adequately account for differences in quality between the market and centrally planned production.

After the fall, Navrozov's complaints were echoed by Nicholas Eberstadt (1995). Eberstadt recognised that it may not be possible to measure a command socialist economy in a market framework, but offered no alternative framework with which to measure it. Eberstadt argued that the CIA's assessment was insufficiently critical and that it accepted official Soviet data too readily. Anders Aslund (1995), a neo-liberal adviser to Yeltsin's administration, argued that the collapse of the central plan demonstrated that Soviet national income was much smaller than originally understood. It was not really a collapse at all but was a "myth" (Aslund 2001). Aslund had several interrelated points. He asserted that the output of the central plan was over reported by as much as 5%. He pointed out that if the first year of collapse were moved from the peak output year, then the collapse would be smaller. He followed Ronald McKinnon and argued that much of the Soviet economy was value destroying, not value creating (McKinnon 1991). He considered the example of fresh fish. He pointed out that fresh fish were nicer than Soviet canned fish. He did not consider whether rotten fish are nicer than canned fish. He believed that unofficial output was underestimated, while trade subsidies to partners in the CMEA were eliminated during the transition: "[t]he wrong things were traded for the wrong reasons between the wrong people in the wrong places at the wrong prices" (Aslund 2001, p.8).

Certainly the end of Russia's trade subsidies to the CMEA may have increased the output of the CIS compared with the former USSR, but it reduced the output of those partners by the same amount. "Subsidies" were not subsidies in any Western sense. The net flow of outputs was from the USSR to its CEE partners. But there was no monetary exchange and the value of those outputs fluctuated according to the political, not economic priorities, of the Soviet Union. Either way, it was a zero-sum game. As the "subsidies" from the CIS to CEE declined, so did the benefits from them, in the opposite direction but to the same amount. This transfer of resources was not actually foreign trade at all, as understood in a market economy; no payments took place between and within the CMEA. Transferable Roubles were not transferable or Roubles (Lavigne 1999).

Aslund repeated the point of Johnson, Kaufman, and Shliefer (1997), that as the decline in electricity consumption was not as great as the measured fall in output so the collapse in output was not as large. Aslund concluded with a definite indefinite that "because of all the methodological problems it is not possible to have precise knowledge of the actual development of output during the transition" (2001, p.1).

Massaki Kuboniwa (1997) of Hitotubashi University used previously unavailable official output and employment data to re-estimate Russian output from 1961 to 1990. Her estimates reduced Soviet output growth by a quarter; it grew three not fourfold. Kuboniwa followed a similar method to the World Bank and Goskomstat (1995). Kuboniwa's intention, and the result of her re-estimates, was to reduce both the original size of Soviet centrally planned output and its decline following price liberalisation. Kuboniwa based her assertion on the observation that electricity output "only" fell by 25% between 1990 and 1994 while official industrial output estimates fell 50%. If there was a constant relationship between electricity consumption and value output, then the fall in industrial output was overestimated. But there was no such constant relationship, not least as the majority of electricity production is consumed in the household and transport sectors. The physical decline in industrial output was far greater than the physical decline in electricity production. The physical production of metal cutting machines fell between 1989 and 1996 by 83%, lorries by 80%, refrigerators by 70% (OECD 1997, p.32). In 1990, 29.4% of machines were less than four years old; the proportion had fallen to 10.9% by 1995. The average age of machinery increased from 10.8 years to 14.1 years (Gavrilenkov 1997). The installation of means of production effectively halted. In a capitalist economy, sectors of production with a higher technical and organic composition of capital sell their output above its value, as capital seeks out the highest rate of profit. In the national accounts the production appears to add more value than sectors with a lower organic composition of capital, because the equalisation of profit rates means it claims a higher proportion of social labour time, it incorporates a higher quantity of past labour in the form of depreciation and it uses larger quantities of raw materials. The collapse of exactly these high volume and highly priced sectors implies the fall in nominal imputed national income may have been larger, not smaller, than official estimates. Generally, in a capitalist economy as the supply of a commodity declines, its price rises. This is exactly the opposite of what happened in the USSR during the early transition period.

There was no genuine market production in 1990 as there were no genuine markets. As national income is a measure of production within the market boundary, there was by definition, no national income in 1990. There was a fall in output which was probably far larger than that estimated by Kuboniwa, but this was the destruction of the central plan and the creation of capitalism. It was not the destruction of national income: but its creation where previously there had been none.

Kuboniwa and Gavrilenkov produced an analysis of the attempt to create a "real capitalist system" in Russia (Kuboniwa & Gavrilenkov 1997, p.v). This presented a more refined version of their earlier analysis. They emphasised that the informal sector was probably under-reported during the transition period. The fall in household consumption was not as large as the fall in production. They disaggregated the use of electricity by physical sector, on the assumption that input coefficients and the consumption coefficient of electricity were stable. This reduced the decline in industrial activity from the official 50% to 28.5% between 1991 and 1994 (Kuboniwa & Gavrilenkov 1997, p.140). This, of course, assumed a stable price structure alongside a stable industrial coefficient, the condition which was precisely absent in the early 1990s.

Ultimately, this argument cannot be settled definitively. There is no objective standard against which it can be measured. No quantities of real things sold for real market prices. What was missing was precisely the fact of sale, of real market prices valuing real quantities of output. Kuboniwa's and Gavrilenkov's guesstimates showed originality and were thought provoking. But they missed the essential point. Value production did not exist in a centrally planned economy. The price of something is only established by the amount of one thing being exchanged for another thing. In a capitalist economy this is the socially necessary labour time required for its production modified by the movement of capital to equalise profit rates. It is predicated on the act of sale. Without buying or selling there can be no price based on value. The collapse of the central plan was the collapse of use values not of exchange values and it led to the creation of exchange value where previously there had been none.

Steven Rosefielde was to revisit many of the assumptions that underlay Bergson's AFC. Rosefielde and Pfouts provided mathematical proof that output in the USSR could not coincide with the neo-classical production function because in the absence of the free movement of capital, prices could not redistribute value according to opportunity costs: "[i]f production is not responsive to prices, then no mechanism exists to reliably connect prices, official, adjusted, or otherwise, with the marginal rate of transformation (1995, p.381). As enterprise managers did not know the adjusted factor prices to which they were supposed to respond, they could not determine the allocation of resources in response to price signals that did not exist.

Rosefielde and Pfouts effectively demonstrated that a centrally planned economy was not subordinate to the laws of the market. They confirmed that both Bergson and the CIA's alternative estimates of Soviet output were "virtually the same" as the official statistics (Rosefielde & Pfouts 1995, p.387). After 1991, the exposure of centrally planned production to the world market demonstrated that its output was both too expensive and of too low a quality to be sold – it could not be "given away". The CIA's 1989 estimate that Soviet GNP was 67% of what the United States was, Rosefielde claimed, "calculated at imputed quality-adjusted dollar production cost on the erroneous assumption that everything manufactured or manufacturable could be sold in the West at these cost prices" (1996, p.979).

If in the real world this output could not be sold, then the "dollar cost price estimates of aggregate growth in controlled economies greatly overstate value growth". This reassessment of Soviet output could be applied right back to 1928, so that although the physical quantity of output grew in the first two five year plans, the "value of these gains was slight". The putative worthlessness of Russia's manufactured export production had "profound" implications for the valuation of "Stalin's capital stock". As neo-classical theory insists that the value of assets is equal to the present discounted value of their future earnings, "the value of the capital stock is correspondingly small" as they had little international value (Rosefielde 1996, p.979). Rosefielde was inconsistent even here. The Soviet capital stock was not capital at all because the means of production was supplied to enterprises interest free. If their value was the discounted total of their future earnings, they had to be worthless on delivery as there were no earnings in the USSR. This capital was not capital at all.

Abraham Becker (1994) a leading CIA Sovietologist, argued that there was little evidence that CIA estimates had been seriously mistaken. Abram Bergson (1997) himself reiterated the fundamentals of the CIA's analysis. But Mark Harrison provided the most consistent defence of Bergson and the CIA. Harrison asserted that as Soviet output was not useless and so it was not valueless, he concluded that "it is perfectly plain that Soviet consumer production was not valueless, just as the collapse of consumer supply since 1991 has been a real collapse, not just the elimination of valueless or value-subtracting activity" (Harrison 1996, p.3). Harrison effectively inverted Rosefielde's method, but to no greater effect. The collapse of Soviet consumer production was a real collapse, but of use values, not exchange values.

Rosefielde considered that the root of the problem with Bergson's estimates stemmed from their use of planned prices: "suspicion has fallen properly on the system's Achilles heel – price formation" (2003, p.474). The issue was not one of exchange value versus use value, but of the inability of planners to adequately account for the introduction of new goods at higher prices. This was a repetition of the point that Gerschenkron and Jasny had demonstrated decades earlier. Rosefielde explained that this was in its turn a consequence of Soviet statisticians' adherence to Marx's labour theory of value:

Like many of his contemporaries, Marx believed that value was intrinsic, and inhered in the quantity of labour. The prices of goods and services accordingly could be computed by aggregating direct and indirect (capital services) labour time, allowing for skill differentials if desired. Philosophical qualms aside, this labour theory of value made no allowance for some types of product and service improvements. If better designs vastly enhanced quality (utility) without altering labour input, original and improved product prices must be the same, even though superior items were clearly preferable. (2003, p.474)

As a summary of Marx's views this was almost completely wrong. Marx was writing about a system of generalised commodity production and exchange – a capitalist system not a centrally planned one, hence the title of his work – *Capital*. In a capitalist system the quantity of labour time did not determine value, but the quantity of socially necessary labour time established by exchange or sale. The labour theory of value was predicated on rising productivity and improvements in products and services. Competitive pressure forced capitalists to continually raise productivity in order to lower their cost of production below that of their rivals in order to garner a profit above the average rate.

In a bureaucratically centrally planned economy, none of this applied. For Rosefielde, CIA estimates that adjusted official industrial volume figures by physical output indices were no real improvement as "the agency's physical series indicate that spurious innovation is concentrated in machine building, while civilian consumer goods are implausibly distortion free" (2003, p.475). Harrison pointed out that here at least Rosefielde was mistaken (2003). But this does not alter Rosefielde's essential point that Sovietologists were victims of "the delusion that fiat ruble factor cost prices, or mechanical adjustments thereof, permitted them to reliably gauge Soviet economic growth and development". Soviet economic statistics could not "be made meaningful by adjusted factor costing" (Rosefielde 2003, p.478).

Harrison viewed Rosefielde's critique as a reflection of his ideological commitment to the "Washington Consensus", the term coined by John Williamson for the market reform package promoted by the IMF, the World Bank and US State Department. Harrison (2003) argued that there was Soviet growth under the central plan and that the Bergson and CIA national income estimates measured something real. Part of the problem was a loose and inappropriate use of categories. In Harrison's chapter in *The Soviet Market for Weapons* he explains that "in writing about the internal market for weapons we do not mean that there was a market relationship between the Army and Industry Units" (Harrison & Markevich 2008, p.157). When asserting the relevance of the category "market", there was not actually a market for this "category".

The Western estimates of Soviet national income did measure something real, the growth of the output of use values in the central plan, but this measure did not give those use values real "value" in the real world. Rosefielde may have been motivated by an ideological commitment to the free market, but his point about the absence of market exchange and value production in the USSR was well made. Without production within a market boundary, there could be no corresponding measure of production within a market boundary and therefore no national income measurement either by adjusted factor cost or otherwise:

> The bottom line after half a century of analysis therefore is that both Bergson's 1953 and 1963 axioms were wrong. Soviet economic performance cannot be . . . transformed to a Western accounting basis, revalued at adjusted ruble factor cost and discounted by replacing value sub-series with indices of physical growth at each analyst's discretion . . . Bergson's axiology could always generate 'reasonable' results by bending rules while disregarding reality, but it could not scientifically determine Soviet performance or potential. (Rosefielde 2004, pp.463–466)

During the transition period Western statisticians were faced with two distinctly different problems. First, the measurement of Soviet imputed national income, which by 1992 was an entirely historical problem and secondly, the measurement of the national income of the transitional CIS economy. To resolve this problem, they needed to separate out the rapidly declining centrally planned economy from the new market production. How to distinguish between the two (in a dynamic and fast-moving situation) was a practical problem, which they did not concern themselves with, as they set out to measure central planned production as if it were already capitalist market production. They confused the two different systems and as a result, were unable to measure either accurately.

Bergson and Rosefielde agreed that use value determined exchange value and was synonymous with it. Bergson (and Becker and Harrison) noted the obvious: that the central plan from the mid-1930s massively expanded the quantity of use values of physical product, of output. Bergson concluded that if the amount of use values had grown then by manipulating official Soviet statistics to cure them of their "distortions", this physical product could be valued as if it were commodity production. Rosefielde simply inverted this logic. Rosefielde (and Eberstadt and Aslund) agreed that use value determined exchange value. Rosefielde also noted the obvious: that this output could not be sold on the open market because there were no markets for it to be sold in. He then concluded that because the product could not be sold, it could not be useful either.

Both sides demonstrated how marginalist theory, that conflates use and exchange value, is unable to adequately account for a centrally planned economy, in which things are produced but not values. They differed only to the degree that they emphasised that confusion. Either they denied that the USSR produced anything useful and its output was therefore valueless or they pointed out that the USSR did produce useful things and therefore its output was valuable. In fact the central plan produced use values, but never exchange values.

The transition of the centrally planned economies into capitalist market ones during the 1990s vindicated Marx's argument that different methods or modes of production produce distinct forms of society. The growth of world value production measured in national income demonstrates the expansion of the market across the entire globe. The application of value measures to the centrally planned economies obscured this expansion as it imputed market production and exchange to planned economies in which this did not take place.

5.2 Globalisation and the expansion of the world market

The creation of a global world market was a direct result of the transition of the central planned economies to capitalism. The collapse of the USSR and CEE was a result of the inherent stagnation of the bureaucratic central plan. Once the quantitative gains available because of the extension of the scope of the plan were exhausted, the plan stagnated, due to the inability of the bureaucracy to raise the quality of production. In China the extremely backward nature of the economy meant that market measures introduced after 1978 rapidly took on a dynamic of their own. They provided the personal incentives to subsistence farmers not available in the collective farms. As the marketable surplus increased, so a migrant workforce was released from the land to be employed in the growing export oriented sector in the SEZ.

By disaggregating market from non-market production, it has been demonstrated that the growth of actual capitalist production during the 1990s was much faster than the official series. The restoration of capitalism in the centrally planned economies increased the size of the world market by around a quarter up to 2010. By 2010 the transition economies produced most of the world's aluminium, hydraulic cement and steel. This very rapid expansion of world capitalist production and the relative diminution of the economic power of the older G7 nations enabled capitalism to escape the stagnation of the 1970s and 1980s. Globalisation is a new super cycle or long wave of capitalist development.

The destruction of the Soviet Union and CEE not only opened the formerly centrally planned economies to capitalist accumulation, but it removed the only rival military and economic power to the United States, thus limiting the negotiating strength of emerging nations such as Brazil and India. Without the USSR, these dependent capitalist nations no longer had a material counterbalance to US hegemony. Trade barriers that had protected domestic manufacturing virtually disappeared.

This reduced the cost of transport and enabled the vertical and horizontal integration of manufacturing irrespective of national borders. This was the pre-requisite for the opening of the entire globe to the capitalist market. In the transition economies, the fall in tariffs occurred before 1991 with the abolition of the monopoly of foreign trade in the late 1980s. Elsewhere, the most dramatic falls in tariff levels were in the emerging markets of Brazil and India, but the decline occurred everywhere, including in the developed capitalist powers of Japan, the EU and the United States.

When data for the year were unavailable, the closest available year was selected.

Table 5.1 Manufactured goods tariffs, effectively applied rate, simple average of simple averages

	1991	2001	2011
Argentina	14.8	13.49	9.98
Australia	13.87	5.78	3.05
Brazil	28.75	15.15	14.08
Canada	10.65	5.1	3.16
China	40.8	15.28	7.86
India	79.92	30.7	8.62
Japan	2.77	2.4	2.06
Poland	11.44	2.4	..
Russia	9.51	10.89	7.48
USA	5.59	3.68	2.87
Viet Nam	13.69	18.98	6.91
EU	4.31	3.21	1.37

Source: UNCTAD (2012).

The removal of trade barriers in its turn raised productivity and lowered the circulation time of capital which in turn raised profit rates. It was reflected in the adoption of free-trade treaties the provided a register of the extent of the integration of these states into the capitalist world economy. It was a precondition for the ICT revolution which saw the general application of a series of mainly electronic technological discoveries – the Internet, graphical user interface and the personal computer – made during the long downswing of the 1970s and 1980s, which required a global market for their production and sale.

World trade increased absolutely by about fivefold between 1991 and 2011 and as a proportion of GDP from around 18% in 1991 to 32% in 2011, or by around two thirds (UNCTAD 2012). The nominal dollar totals of trade are affected by the phenomenon of transfer pricing, in which multinational corporations ship components, actually or virtually, around the world for tax purposes and by changes in raw materials prices in general and in particular oil. But the freedom of major corporations to shift value between their subsidies is itself a feature of the abolition or significant reduction of tariffs during the period of globalisation. It remains indicative of general trends which demonstrate very strong trade growth from the early 1990s as the transition economies began capitalist trade and as a global market enabled firms to exploit comparative advantages to the full. Trade recovered very strongly even after the recent recession. The increase in trade to and from the now capitalist transition economies outstripped the general growth in total trade as central planning was replaced by commodity production.

Before 1991 these statistics combine the internal "trade" of the CMEA and external trade with the capitalist nations. The CMEA "trade" was not sold at market prices; indeed, it was not sold at all but was bartered on an *ad hoc* basis. It was not part of world capitalist trade. This "trade" collapsed with the fall of the CMEA and collapse of the central plan in the CIS and CEE. From the early 1990s genuinely capitalist trade emerged and grew from around 6.5% of the world total

Table 5.2 G7 percentage of employment in industry and services

Year		1971	1981	1991	2001	2011
France	Industry	39.3	35.5	29.2	24.6	20.9
	Services	44.7	54.2	64.2	70.9	76.1
Canada	Industry	29.4	26.9	22	21.7	19.1
	Services	63.1	68.3	73.7	75.5	78.8
Germany	Industry	48.7	42.2	39.8	32.3	27
	Services	44.3	52.8	56.1	65.1	71.4
Italy	Industry	38.8	36.5	31.4	30.4	27.3
	Services	40.9	50.2	60.1	65	69
Japan	Industry	35.7	35.1	34.2	30.1	24.9
	Services	48.6	55.2	59.4	65.2	71.3
UK	Industry	42	34.3	31.3	22.3	17.7
	Services	54.8	63	66.4	76.6	81.1
USA	Industry	31.7	28.9	23.4	21.3	17.3
	Services	64	65.2	73.8	77	81.1

Source: Bureau of Labor Statistics (2012).

in 1991 to 37% in 2011. This increase in capitalist trade mirrors the rise in the proportion of key physical commodities and world GDP produced by the transition economies.

The total amount of FDI rose by 635% between 1990 and 2011. The proportion of total FDI directed into the transition economies increased even faster than the total, from almost nothing in 1991 to around 15% of the world total by the mid-1990s. There was a marked fall in FDI after the East Asia financial crisis of 1997 which was reversed thereafter and not even interrupted by the high-tech recession of 2001, growing back to the 15% level. Outward FDI, investments from the transition countries and in particular China and Russia, began to rise sharply from the mid-2000s, as Russia sought to export its oil and raw material surplus and China sought to invest its huge balance of payments surplus by securing raw materials and technology abroad.

The rise of financial profits as a proportion of total profits in the United States, was a consequence of the decline and restructuring of old core industries like shoes, textiles, food and beverages, as well as automobiles and steel. The shift to high-tech global manufacturing, with rising productivity offsetting the reduction in manufacturing as a proportion of total output and finally the growth of professional and business services, related to the growth of finance. The significance of this shift towards the transition economies both as centres of manufacture and as centres of markets is reflected in the rapid decline of manufacturing industry in the West, as factory jobs were replaced by services.

This has an important consequence for the statistics of Western economies. Services tend to have a lower technical and value composition of capital than manufacturing. The technical composition of capital is the physical configuration of buildings, machines and labour required to produce a given output, while its value composition is the price of that technical composition in value terms. Once a barber's shop has fitted out the décor and paid for the chairs, there are almost no raw materials costs. A restaurant will pay something for food, but this is still a relatively small part of overall costs compared to staffing. Once a call centre is operational its overwhelming cost is the labour of the operatives who staff the phones and maintain the technical capacity of the computer systems and so on. Services such as railways with a high organic composition of capital are the exception. Even a small manufacturer has machines that are constantly depreciating, and raw materials are a key cost of production relative to labour. Labour productivity is the physical amount of use values produced by a given period, but this too has a reflection in value terms. In a capitalist economy sectors with a lower organic composition of capital transfer value to sectors with a high organic composition as capital moves in search of a higher rate of profit. As a result every unit of labour in a high organic composition sector will "add" more value than sectors with a low composition, as that labour includes part of the value transferred to it from a lower organic composition sector. As services make up a larger proportion of the economy, so the rate of productivity growth, whether measured by the quantity of output, labour productivity or total factor productivity, will fall.

The destruction of domestic Western manufacturing and its replacement by imports not only lowered the domestic Western organic composition of capital and raised profits but also lowered the growth of total factor productivity and productivity in general. It appears that this shift causes a further stagnation of the economy, when it is actually a sign of a more thorough domestic restructuring of capital only made possible by globalisation.

This had a further positive knock-on effect for the capitalists by consolidating the defeats of the workers inflicted by the Thatcher and Reagan neo-liberal offensive. After the defeat of these workers, their manufacturing plants were closed and they were physically dispersed, making it far more difficult for workers to organise without the industrial core of the domestic working class, thereby weakening trade union organisation, working-class parties and general militancy. This in turn helped drive down wages and undermined the ability of labour organisations to oppose speed-ups and productivity drives. Trade union density, the proportion of workers covered by collective bargaining declined precipitously, as did the number of strike days lost. This added to the ideological disarray caused by the defeat of "really existing socialism" in the USSR and CEE. It now seemed that there was no alternative to capitalism for the mass of the population. All these effects combined to raise the rate of profit in the major Western economies.

The integration of East Germany into a united Germany in 1991 meant a one off increase in West German GDP of around 16% which was not included in figures for German GDP growth due to the same statistical glitch that caused the underestimation of the transition in general. After large subsidies to cushion the collapse of the plan, the new United Germany is now reaping the fruits of what it sowed then. The influx of skilled East German workers drove down wage costs and allowed Germany manufacturing to take advantage of cheap centrally planned infrastructure all of which drove down costs. The United German government established the Treuhand to oversee the privatisation of East German

Table 5.3 German per capita GDP, unemployment and manufacturing unit labour costs, 1991–98

Year	Per capita GDP (East/West in %)	Unemployment rates		Manufacturing unit labour costs (East/West %)
		East	West	
1991	31.3	10.3	6.3	159.7
1992	38.9	14.8	6.6	139.6
1994	52.3	16	9.2	120.6
1996	56.8	16.7	10.1	115.9
1998	56.1	19.5	10.5	108.8

Source: Adapted from Council of Economic Advisers (1999).

state assets. It assumed ownership of 95% of East German enterprises which then were given away (Dornbusch & Wolf 1994). There were significant subventions from the German government totalling around €2,000 billion by 2007 or around €100 billion a year (Boyes 2007), but this relatively small amount – US post-credit-crunch bank loans amounted to $21 trillion – bought an entire nation and transformed the German economy.

The close links of East Germany to Poland and other transition economies allowed further movement of cheap skilled labour. Throughout the first decade of the twenty-first-century Germany unit labour costs fell, in contrast to the rise in labour costs throughout Southern Europe despite the inflow of cheap money from the EU there. The current crisis is largely a product of Germany's political determination to drive down wage costs and government spending throughout the southern periphery of the EU. Outside East Germany, the transition cost even less. Entire countries and all their assets, including fifty years' worth of infrastructure, were privatised for next to nothing. By 2006 China was the second largest capitalist economy in the world, employed 112 million industrial workers (Bannister 2009), as well as millions more in the former USSR and CEE.

The decline in the rate of capacity utilisation was another product of growth of services in the United States. As services are produced as they are consumed there are material limits to the extension of work time and therefore, of capacity utilisation. A barber's shop cannot open all night. A car factory can. The growth of the market enabled Western capitalists to complete the destruction of much of their domestic heavy industrial manufacturing.

Capitalism is measured in value terms, but it requires a mix of physical inputs in order to function. This constrained the ability of Western capitalists to devalue their domestic fixed capital stock while they were still dependent on the domestic output of sectors such as coal, steel, automobiles, aluminium and so on. They were forced to subsidise loss-making industries because there was no alternative source for their output. When production shifted to the East they could rid themselves of these sectors. This raised productivity, reduced the cost of investment and so raised the rate of profit, as Marx noted in *Capital III*:

the commodity that emerges from one branch of industry as a product enters another branch as means of production. Its cheapness or otherwise depends on the productivity of labour in the branch of production from which it emerges as a product, and is at the same time a condition not only for the cheapening of the commodities into the production of which it enters as a means of production, but also for the reduction in value of the constant capital whose element it now becomes, and therefore for an increase in the rate of profit. (1981, p.174)

Capitalists under the whip of competitive pressure continuously revolutionise production in order to reduce their costs and increase profits. In doing so they increase the proportion of dead labour (constant capital) to living labour and by investing in new machines squeeze out living labour, the very source of new value and of new profits. By cheapening the means of production of labour and capital, increased productivity raises the absolute and relative rate of surplus value and can reduce the cost of machinery, buildings and raw materials. In the major Western economies, machines have been replaced by labour, as manufacturing with a relatively low labour intensity have been replaced by services with a relatively high one. This is reflected in an upward trend in profit rates.

The most up to date figures for the US rate of profit show that this upward trend has continued after the recession of 2008.The rate of profit estimated here is the total of surplus value (non-farm proprietors income, rent, net interest and corporate profits, after the inventory valuation adjustment [IVA] and Capital Consumption Allowance [CCA]) divided by national income less profits plus the current price fixed capital stock) or $(PI + R + CP)/((NI - (PI + R + CP)) + CPFCS)$. It is based on official data from the US Bureau of Economic Analysis (BEA; 2012). This is only a proxy for the real rate of profit the real world, variable capital does not perfectly equal national income less profits as income can be transferred between periods, interest and rent charged before or after they are due, wages paid in advance through loans and so on. Similarly, the mass of constant capital does not equal the fixed-capital stock, depreciation may be shifted between periods and it includes inventories, raw materials and energy supplies, plus stocks of finished and unfinished goods. Although adjustments are made to limit profits to those generated in production, in practice total profits are influenced by windfalls, transfer pricing and interest rates, as well as unequal exchange and the repatriation of profits made abroad to the United States. Nonetheless, as it can be assumed that these factors always influence the general profit rate, and as there is a very good correlation between this rate of profit and the business cycle, it is possible to assume that it is a reasonable proxy if only that. During the Second World War the US rate of profit peaked at 22%, up from 8% during the 1930s Great Depression. It remained at high levels throughout the 1950s until it began to decline from the late 1960s onwards, falling to a nadir of just 11% in 1981, the deepest recession since the war. The onset of market liberalisation during the early 1980s saw a shallow recovery to reach 12% in 1988. But it was only with the collapse of the CPE in the early 1990s that it rose significantly, peaking at 13% in 1996. It fell briefly after the bursting of the hi-tech bubble in 2000, rose again to 14% in

2006, slumped to 12% during the credit crunch of 2008, before rising again to 15% in 2013, its highest level since 1967. The US rate of profit illustrates how the US capitalists were able to take advantage of globalisation, increasing profit rates by closing manufacturing with high organic compositions of capital, reducing the cost of reproduction of labour power by cutting wages through speed-ups and the importation of cheap consumer goods from China. To this must be added unequal exchange, buying Chinese products cheaply and selling them for higher prices on the domestic market. The transition economies have a lower organic composition of capital, much lower value of fixed capital stock and a cheaper workforce, so they will have a much higher rate of profit than the will the United States, even if that profit is appropriated by foreign multinational corporations. Half of Chinese exports are manufactured by foreign corporations, while the remaining half are often dependent on Western retail corporations for their foreign sales.

The 2008 credit crunch was caused by the combination of these factors, as was the subsequent recession and recovery. Policy makers cannot prevent crises in general but it does not mean that their mistakes did not lead to or at least exacerbate this crisis. Policy is a catalyst. While it does not create the conditions for crisis, it can make them worse. Indeed they most certainly did. The packaging of good and bad debt in mortgage-backed securities or collateralised debt obligations meant that bankers did not know the value of the debt they owned or owed. This weakened the banking system, froze credit and dramatically deepened the crisis after the decision of the Federal Reserve to allow the collapse of Lehman's in September 2008.

Rising world profits had two contradictory effects. US retail banks had the funds to invest due to recycled profits from China, and Middle Eastern oil nations and multinational corporations with bumper cash balances were able to fund investments independently of the banks. This meant that the banks needed new sources of revenue from the NINJAs (no income, no job, no assets). Mortgage Equity Withdrawal (MEW) fluctuated between 4% and 9% of US disposable income from 2003 to 2007, before falling to between –2% and –6% from 2007 to 2012 (Calculated Risk 2012). MEW represents an advance on wages, its repayment a deduction from them. This significantly affects aggregate demand and exacerbates both the boom phase of the cycle and the subsequent recession. It certainly is an important factor in the origins of this crisis.

The cycles of globalisation could therefore be summarised like this, the first cycle of globalisation can be dated from 1991 to 2001. It saw the collapse of the centrally planned economies and their transition to capitalism: the consolidation of the Thatcher/Reagan defeats of the Labour movement, the resolution or abandonment of the third-world national liberation movements such as the African National Congress and the Palestinian Liberation Organization, the privatisation of nationalised industries, a reduction in size of the welfare state, growth of foreign investment; destruction of heavy industrial capacity in the West and the onset of the Internet and Computer Technology revolution, and the consolidation of the upward trend in profit rates evident since the early 1980s. The glut of raw materials exports from the transition economies drove down the price of circulating constant capital. The Asian stock market crash of 1997 was the nadir of the restoration process. The dot-com boom from 1998 to 2001 meant the world was rapidly wired up on the back of speculative fever for the "new economy". This was combined with the wholesale transfer of manufacturing production to the East and the horizontal and vertical integration of production through computer technology. From the late 1990s profit rates began to fall. The dot-com crash of 2001 was the inevitable result, but the devalued infrastructure it had paid for was now installed. The recession was short-lived and limited to some of the Western nations.

The second cycle of globalisation from 2001 to 2010 saw a residential housing boom and bust in the West. Rising profits and cash surpluses in major multi-national corporations combined with recycled profits from the oil exporters and China drove down interest rates via the accumulation of huge quantities of US and UK foreign debt at very low rates of interest. This essentially free money provided the loans for the credit crunch boom. Rising manufacturing productivity lowered the cost of reproduction of labour power and led to wages falling as a proportion of national income as capitalists eroded the terms and conditions of Western workers.

The transformation of manufacturing technique by the application of ICT, reduction of trade costs and lowering of tariff barriers enabled much more efficient just in time working in factories, reducing inventory, while rising productivity reduced the cost of new capital even while its technical scale increased. The bursting of the credit crunch bubble after 2008 caused a serious crisis across the world economy. The financial dislocation hit trade as shipping firms could not insure their loads. This in turn exacerbated the depth of the recession.

Between April 2008 and May 2009 world trade fell by 20% and world industrial production by 11% (Ebregt & van Welzenis 2012). The US fixed-capital stock was written down by 5% for only the second time since 1929. But the reflationary measures of China with a stimulus package worth around half of national income, and the decision of Western governments to guarantee their banks' losses limited the crisis. By July 2010 world trade and industrial production had retraced their entire fall. Over the next two years profits have similarly recovered. The United States lost more jobs, more than 6 million, than in any recession since the Second World War, but through pay cuts and short-time working capitalists offloaded the cost of the crisis onto the working class. Profits quickly recovered even while wages fell as a proportion of national income. Over the next three years the labour market slowly recovered, so that by mid-2014 employment had recovered its entire fall.

The recession had accelerated the on-going trend towards the transition economies, particularly China and the Russia, and large emerging nations such as Brazil and India, also known as the BRIC countries, as they were otherwise known (O'Neill 2003). If the cause of the recession was the recycling of surplus profits to the West that drove down interest rates and enabled reckless bank loans to poor workers – the so-called subprime borrowers – then the continued availability of that money has enabled Western governments to offset some of the worst elements of the crisis. Interest rates remain low. Profit rates remain high. Firms have record levels of cash on their balance sheets.

The third phase of globalisation from 2010 onwards will see the strengthening of all of these trends, but at the same time at the cost of undermining the very basis of globalisation itself. In the now restored capitalism of China, nominal dollar national income grew from $1,317 billion in 2001 to $6,692 billion in 2011 a rise of 408%. Russia's nominal dollar national income grew faster, from $306 billion in 2001 to $1,885 by 2011, or by 515%. Brazil's national income raised from $500 billion in 1991 to $2,000 billion in 2011 a rise of 300%. India from $450 billion in 1991 to $1,750 billion in 2011, a rise of 385%. By the closing years of the first decade of the twenty-first century, these aptly named "emerging markets" accounted for more than 40% of world production at current prices and for more than half when adjusted for purchasing price parity (IMF 2012).The reorientation of the Chinese economy towards the domestic market is underway, even if exports remain very important to it. China now has 163 of the world's top 2,000 corporations. The largest of these firms are limited to its domestic banks and raw materials firms. It remains excluded from the high-tech manufacturing corporations that still dominate each sector of production. If it is to complete the transition into a real rival to the Western powers, it will need to be able to create its own rivals to the existing Western multinationals. China's state sponsorship of these nascent firms implies that it may be able to do so, although this is not certain. If it can do so, then the development of China's own multinational corporations will begin to limit the ability of Western firms to extract surplus profits, as they lose monopoly control of key technologies. As China seeks to control ever-larger areas of strategic raw materials it will impinge on Western oil and mining companies. The emerging markets now account for 40% of world GDP in money terms and more than 50% adjusted for PPP. Their growth calls into question US hegemony and financial profits dependent on the supply of legal services, patents and royalties connected to the current legal structure of the world economy.

By 2011 it was clear that the credit crunch crisis was no global slump. The world economy declined by 0.6% during 2009, but this decline is dwarfed by the growth of the world market during the transition of the central plan to capitalism. This increase, not measured by the official statistical agencies, was around 17% of world capitalist production in 2001 and 27% in 2011. This explains why these theorists could not account for the resilience of the world capitalist economy as a whole, and the ability of the former periphery to drag the former centre out of the hole it had dug itself. It was an increase in capitalist production between 28 and 45 times larger than the fall in output registered during the "Great Recession".

References

Aslund, A., 1995. *How Russia Became a Market Economy*. Washington, DC: The Brookings Institution.

Aslund, A., 2001. *The Myth of Output Collapse after Communism*. Carnegie Working Papers 18. Washington, DC: Carnegie Endowment for International Peace.

Bannister, J., 2009. China's Manufacturing Employment and Compensation Costs: 2002–06. *Monthly Labor Review*, 4(April), pp.30–38. Available at: www.bls.gov/opub/mlr/2009/04/art3full.pdf [Accessed April 1, 2012].

Becker A. C., 1994. Intelligence Fiasco or Reasoned Accounting: CIA Estimates of Soviet GNP. *Post Soviet Affairs*, vol. 10, no. 4, pp. 291–329.

Bergson, A, 1997. How Big Was the Soviet GDP? *Comparative Economic Studies*, 39(1), pp.1–14.

Boyes, R., 2007. Germany Starts Recovery from €2,000bn Union. *Times Online* (London), August 27. Available at: www.timesonline.co.uk/tol/news/world/europe/article2317382. ece [Accessed October 12, 2009].

Bureau Economic Analysis (BEA), 2012. Washington D.C.: U.S. Department of Commerce.

Bureau of Labor Statistics, 2012. International Labor Comparisons. In *International Comparisons of Annual Labor Force Statistics, Adjusted to U.S. Concepts, 16 Countries, 1970–2011*. Available at: www.bls.gov/ilc/flscomparelf.htm [Accessed October 23, 2012].

Calculated Risk, 2012. Q3 2012: Mortgage Equity Withdrawal Strongly negative *Calculated Risk Blogspot*. Available at: www.calculatedriskblog.com/2012/12/q3-2012-mortgage-equity-withdrawal.html [Accessed January 7, 2013].

Council of Economics Advisors [Sachverstandigenrat zur Begutachtung der gesamtwirtschaftlichen Entwicklung] (1999), *Wirtscheflspoltik unter Reformdruk, Annual Report 1999/2000*. Stuttgart.

Dornbusch, R., & Wolf, H., 1994. East German Economic Reconstruction. In O.J. Blanchard, K.A. Froot, & J.D. Sachs, eds. *The Transition in Eastern Europe*. Chicago: University of Chicago Press, pp.155–90.

Eberstadt, N., 1995. *The Tyranny of Numbers*. Washington, DC: American Enterprise Institute.

Ebregt, J., & van Welzenis, G., 2012. *CPB World Trade Monitor Feb 2012*. Netherlands Bureau for Economic Policy Analysis. Available at: www.cpb.nl/sites/default/files/cijfer/ CPB World Trade Monitor: December 2011/cpb-world-trade-monitor-december-2011. pdf [Accessed February 22, 2012].

Funk, M., & Rahn., J., 2002. How Efficient Is the East German Economy? An Exploration with Microdata. *Economics of Transition*, 10(1), pp. 201–23.

Gavrilenkov, E., 1997. Russian Economic Growth: Perspectives and Impediments. *Hitotsubashi Journal of Economics*, 38, pp.33–44.

Harrison, M., 1996. Stalinism in Post-Communist Perspective: Comment. *Europe-Asia Studies*, 3(1997), pp. 499–502.

Harrison, M., 2003. Post War Russian Economic Growth: Not a Riddle. *Europe Asia Studies*, 55(8), pp. 1323–29.

Harrison, M., & Markevich, A., 2008. The Soviet Market for Weapons. In *Guns and Rubles: The Defense Industry in the Stalinist State*. New Haven, CT: Yale University Press, pp. 156–79.

IMF, 2012.*World Economic Outlook Database*. IMF World Economic Outlook Database. Available at: www.imf.org/external/ns/cs.aspx?id=28 [Accessed October 25, 2012].

Johnson, S., Kaufman, D., & Shliefer A., 1997. The Unofficial Economy in Transition. *Brookings Papers on Economic Activity*, 2, pp. 159–239.

Kuboniwa, M., 1997. Economic Growth in Post War Russia: Estimating GDP. *Hitotsubashi Journal of Economics*, 38(1), pp. 21–32.

Kuboniwa, M., & Gavilenkov, Y., 1997. *Development of Capitalism in Russia: The Second Challenge*, Tokyo: Maruzen Co. Ltd.

Lavigne, M., 1999. *The Economics of Transition: From Socialist Economy to Market Economy*. Second edition. Basingstoke: Palgrave.

Marx, K., 1981. *Capital Volume III*. London: Penguin Classics.

McKinnon, R., 1991. *The Order of Economic Liberalization: Financial Control in the Transition to a Market Economy*. Baltimore: John Hopkins University Press.

Navrozov, L., 1988. Assessing the CIA's "Soviet Economic Indices". In P. Wiles, ed. *The Soviet Economy on the Brink of Reform: Essays in Honor of Alec Nove*. London: Unwin Hyman, pp.112–52.

OECD, 1997. *OECD Economic Surveys: Russian Federation 1997*. Paris: OECD.

O'Neill, J., 2003. *Dreaming with BRICs: The Path to 2050*. Global Economics Paper No: 99. London: Goldman Sachs. Available at: http://www2.goldmansachs.com/ideas/brics/book/99-dreaming.pdf [Accessed February 1, 2010].

Rosefielde, S., 1996. Stalinism in Post Communist Perspective: New Evidence on Killings, Forced Labour and Economic Growth in the 1930s. *Europe Asia Studies*, 48(6), pp. 959–87.

Rosefielde, S., 2003. The Riddle of Post-war Russian Economic Growth: Statistics Lied and Were Misconstrued. *Europe-Asia Studies*, 55(3), pp. 469–81.

Rosefielde, S., 2004. Post-war Russian economic growth: Not a Riddle – A Reply. *Europe Asia Studies*, 56(3), pp. 463–466.

Rosefielde, S., 2005. Tea Leaves and Productivity: Bergsonian Norms for Gauging the Soviet Future. *Comparative Economic Studies*, 47, pp. 259–73.

Rosefielde, S., & Pfouts, B., 1995. Neoclassical Norms and the Valuation of National Product in the Soviet Union and its Post Communist Successor States. *Journal of Comparative Economics*, 21, pp. 375–89.

UNCTAD, 2012. *Statistical Database*. FDI Statistical Database. Available at: http://unctadstat.unctad.org/ReportFolders/reportFolders.aspx [Accessed October 24, 2012].

World Bank ECA Country Department III, & Goskomstat of the R.F.S.S.C., 1995. *Russian Federation: Report on the National Accounts*. Washington, DC: World Bank.

6 Conclusion

The collapse of the Berlin wall in 1989 signalled the end of the cold war and the defeat of "Communism". By the mid-1990s capitalist globalisation embraced the world. The transition of non-capitalist central planning to market capitalism threw a searching light on statisticians responsible for the measurement of economic output. If national income is a measure of economic production within the market boundary, then the creation of market economies out of the wreckage of the central plan should have seen an increase in capitalist national income. Something is, after all, more than nothing. But every statistical survey showed the opposite. The expansion of production within the market boundary was measured as a reduction of it.

Measuring National Income explains this contradiction. It undertakes a critical history and reassessment of measures of Soviet national income from their origins in the USSR in the 1920s, to the United States in the 1930s and post-war reapplication back to the Soviet Union and other centrally planned economies. It shows that measures of Soviet national income abandoned the key material location of national income in the measurement of real value production in an actual market economy. Instead, statisticians replaced the objective fact of market prices, with various alternative measures of their own creation. The demonstration of how an essentially subjective "national income" was imputed to the centrally planned economies, in the absence of genuine national income, prepares the ground for a reassessment of the growth of the world market with the transition of the centrally planned economies to capitalism.

The early efforts of Soviet statisticians to develop measures of the economy through the application of Marx's *Capital* were summarised in the 1923/4 *Balance* that measured the output of material commodity production in the Soviet state capitalist economy of the early 1920s. This posed a novel problem from the inception of the Soviet regime in 1917: how to measure the value of output of an economy in transition from capitalism to planning. At their root, all estimates of national income aggregate the total value of production actually exchanged at market prices. Value is not a measure of the physical quantity of use values created or services produced but of their exchange value, that is how much they are sold for on a market. But how is it possible to measure the value of production in an economy in which nothing is sold – when there is no market price and when the objective foundation of national income statistics is absent/

The young Wassily Leontief (Spulber 1965) pointed out other weaknesses to the *Balance*. In contradistinction to Marx's method the *Balance* only measured material production, that is the output of commodities with a physical existence. It did not measure the value of "unproductive" sectors, where production is bought but not sold, such as health care or the military, and it did not include services, where production is consumed as it is produced, such as the opera, meals in restaurants or haircuts. Nonetheless, the *Balance* anticipated later Western national income measures and input–output tables. That is not surprising. The Western measures were developed by Leontief alongside another Soviet exile Simon Kuznets.

After the introduction of the CPE in 1928, the relative historical basis for the *Balance* was abandoned by the new Stalinist orthodoxy. Based on an unacknowledged debt to the "Mechanist" school of early Soviet political economy, the Stalinists now asserted that the law of value continued to operate in the centrally planned economy albeit in a modified form (Lapidus & Ostrovitianov 1929).

Stalinist theoreticians never could reconcile the operation of the theory with the absence of its precondition – objective abstract labour measured through the act of exchange. The 1930 *Materialy* accepted that the centrally planned economy produced use values, not value. It was no longer predicated on abstract labour time measured through exchange (Pervukhin in Davies et al. 1985). It nonetheless sought to measure value production where no value was produced. It did so by assigning a "price" to the physical aggregate of labour time expended. This had some parallels to the labour theory of value that determined the price of production in a capitalist economy, but critically it did not measure socially necessary labour time but concrete labour time. Inefficient production was "paid", through an accounting mechanism, at a higher price than efficient production. Production units had a positive incentive to hoard labour and raw materials to ensure that they met planned targets. The objective basis of these national income statistics was no longer the fact of sale, but the subjective creation of the planning agencies. This was no longer national income as defined by Marx or described in *Capital*. But the official Soviet statistics of physical quantities of output and the amounts of labour required to produce them provided the objective foundation for nearly all subsequent estimates of Soviet national income, whether from the East or the West.

The need for objective, independent or more accurately, Western estimates of Soviet output became acute during the Second World War. In 1939 Colin Clark – with the first-ever application of PPP – attempted to provide estimates of Soviet output independent from the official propaganda. Clark showed that when measured in Western prices, the growth in Soviet output was much lower than the official figures. During the war the demand for independent information was a key intelligence requirement of the US military and diplomatic authorities. They needed to assess the military capacity of the Soviet economic base, its ability to withstand the Nazi invasion, its likely strength after the war and the objective basis for any claims for reparations. Leontief drew up the first official estimate of Soviet output in 1943 under the aegis of the OSS, the wartime forerunner to the CIA. Its Soviet department was headed by the young Abram Bergson, who as a student of Leontief and Kuznets had written an early study of the Soviet wage system in 1937. The Soviet department of the OSS was transformed into the US Air Force's Project RAND after the war (Engerman 2009) as Bergson oversaw the extension the US SNA to the USSR.

Bergson's project was not uncontested. Julius Wyler (1946), in collaboration with Paul Studenski, developed an estimate of Soviet output at US prices. Naum Jasny (1960), another Russian Marxist exile based in the United States, sought to correct "distorted" Soviet planned prices. Jasny undertook a detailed examination of Soviet price statistics to show how the introduction of new machines distorted growth figures. These machines did not exist in the 1926 base year used in Soviet national accounts. Their price – an administrative price based on a subjective "value" not on the objective fact of sale – was estimated on their initial installation price attributed by the apparatus to aggregates of concrete labour time. This "price" – in fact a unit of account used to measure the physical quantity of labour required for production – was higher than the later "price", because efficiencies raised productivity with the expansion of the scale of production. The issue of how to account for the "hidden inflation" of innovation became a consistent theme of Western debates in the years to come. Alexander Gerschenkron (1951) an opponent of Jasny and colleague of Bergson at Project RAND, similarly noted how industrialisation affected the measure of national income. Because pre-industrialisation base-year prices were high, their use would show a larger increase in output than would lower post-industrialisation given-year prices. This became known as the Gerschenkron effect, and "correcting" for it, or more accurately using the lower given year prices, was the major means through which Western experts produced lower estimates of Soviet output than the official figures.

Western experts debated the accuracy of Soviet official statistics in general and the effect of central planning on prices. They concluded, albeit with different emphases, that Soviet statistics could be used to develop independent estimates (Grossman 1960). Although different layers of the apparatus had material interests in distorting statistics in their own interests, the same pressures that provided managers with incentives to lie, limited the scale of their lies. Managers would lie to meet plan targets to secure bonus payments, but as the plan targets for the next period were based on the previous period, these lies tended to shift production between periods rather than raise its absolute level. Figures moved in consistent patterns, and there was a correlation between outputs and inputs. The chimerical search for the "real" figures was never abandoned. But no such figures existed. Soviet prices were not market prices and without the objective act of sale never could be. Captured plan documents supported the view that there was no alternative set of figures used separate from the published ones. Hidebound by their adherence to a marginal utility theory that did not apply to an economy without consumer choice, none of the Western experts noticed that concrete labour times are not socially necessary labour times. Indeed, none of the Marxist experts did either. Stalin's purge of the best of Marxist theorists in the 1930s meant that no alternative theory of the Soviet economy that accounted for this was ever created.

Trotsky (1936), the leader of the anti-Stalinist Left Opposition, came closest of the Marxists, but his contribution, while acute, did not provide a systematic economic analysis of Soviet national income estimates.

There were essentially two methods or combination of methods developed. One set of experts priced physical quantities of Soviet output at Western prices, usually in US dollars but occasionally in UK pounds. They then guesstimated appropriate amounts of depreciation and of the value of services, often based on a head count of the number of workers employed in a given activity. The other set of experts sought to revalue Soviet output to remove the price "distortions" of the central plan. These distortions, it was believed, rose from two sources. Jasny and Gerschenkron had highlighted the inability of the apparatus to account for the introduction of new machines but as important was the absence of rent, interest and technical depreciation due to obsolescence, from the Soviet MPS. The MPS never measured the output of the service sector or government, this issue of coverage was resolved by using comparable Western data.

Abram Bergson (1953) developed the definitive version of Soviet National Income and Product – *The Real National Income of Soviet Russia Since 1928*. Bergson was aware that neoclassical marginalist theory was predicated on consumer sovereignty and therefore did not apply to an economy without markets. The purchase of things was the means through which consumers expressed their preferences (Bergson 1964), but bemoaning the absence of markets in the centrally planned economy, Bergson argued that some theory – even if inapplicable – was better than no theory. Bergson, in his 1930s' study of Soviet wages (Bergson 1944), argued that because there were wage differentials based on skills and output, a form of capitalist wage market existed; this encouraged Bergson to swap consumer preference for planners' preference. Planners were subject to the laws of neoclassical economics Bergson asserted, even if the prices signals necessary to influence their behaviour did not exist and could not be known.

Bergson and a large team funded by Project RAND and the CIA developed the most widely used "building-block" method for estimating Soviet national income (Marer 1985). Bergson applied an AFC that repriced Soviet output by redistributing official estimates of Soviet "value" and physical production, according to the categories of the market economy. It included estimates for interest, rent and moral depreciation, even though these were never charged in the central plan. It explicitly created a counter-factual estimate of what the value of Soviet output would have been if it were produced by the market economy that did not exist. These estimates were not real. But Bergson asserted that this counterfactual non-existent "reality" was more real than real. In fabricating an economy in the books, Bergson believed he described the "real" Soviet economy better than the real Soviet economy. Paradoxically, precisely because Bergson's estimates were a reworking of official data, they were only marginally different from the figures of the Soviet authorities themselves. G. Warren Nutter (1962) produced an alternative estimate of Soviet industrial production at the behest of the Eisenhower administration, but Nutter's insistence that it was not possible to produce a real estimate of Soviet national income and his position outside of the RAND Sovietologists meant that his criticisms of the entire project were sidelined.

After the late 1950s the spirit of enquiry, which was so obvious in the initial often bitter debate, evaporated. Bergson's theory became an almost unquestioned orthodoxy. This method, backed by the might of the CIA and official agencies, such as the World Bank, was then applied across to all of the new centrally planned economies that arose after Second World War in CEE, China, Cuba and Vietnam. The field stagnated until the unanticipated collapse of the centrally planned economies in the late 1980s.

The collapse of "communism" reopened elements of a debate around Bergson's method. Western statisticians faced a fundamental problem. By valuing centrally planned production as market production Bergson's method obliterated the distinction between central planning and capitalist commodity production. When real market production was created during the transition, Bergson's method was unable to measure the creation of real national income, because according to his counterfactual accounts, national income existed in the books, before it existed in reality.

Neoclassical economists were also confronted by the results of the big-bang privatisation of the centrally planned economies of CEE and the CIS. They had not predicted the collapse of production that resulted from the introduction of market prices. According to their orthodoxy freeing the economy to allow the operation of market forces should have led to a rapid growth in output as inefficient sectors were priced out of operation to be replaced by efficient market producers. Enabling consumers to express their preferences would increase total utility. Everyone would be better off and happy. Instead, output collapsed. Income inequality soared as elements of the apparatus and Western-sponsored capitalists seized huge quantities of assets for very low or no prices. Economists resolved this problem with a two-pronged strategy. They ignored it or they explained it away. The transition from one mode of production (central planning) to another (capitalism) was viewed as a statistical problem by the accountants of the IMF, the OECD and the World Bank. The issue was not the creation of a new market system of production, but of the transition of the accounting systems from the old MPS of the central plan to the SNA of the market economy. While celebrating the destruction wrought by the market and the creation of a capitalist economy in reality, they revised down the original size of the Soviet economy, to reduce the absolute fall in production and derived alternative estimates of the change in physical production to reduce the size of the relative fall. These alternatives disputed the quality of centrally planned production, noted the resilience of electricity output, the under reporting of new market production and changes in trade subsidies. Indeed Anders Aslund (2001), a neoconservative adviser to Yeltsin during the first phase of privatisation, concluded that the output collapse was a "myth".

These re-estimates were no more objective than the original ones. Neither of the alternative versions of "reality" could be tested against actual market prices, because real market prices did not exist before the market existed. The relatively lower fall of electricity production during the early phase of transition concealed the collapse of production of the high-value sectors in a market economy, such as machine tools, where output fell by 80%. In a market economy such a collapse in production would have affected prices because of the operation of supply and demand. This is precisely what could not have taken place during the initial years of the transition. Genuine market prices only began to determine production decisions after the 1998 East Asian crash. The decline of physical output measured during the transition to capitalism certainly occurred. The total quantity of use values produced by the central plan slumped. But whatever the scale of the decline of the physical production of use values, production within the market boundary increased. As national income is a measure of production within the market boundary, then national income – real value production realised in real market exchange – increased inversely to the fall in the total output of use values.

Simon Kuznets had overseen the application of Bergson's methods to China during the mid-1960s, but until the late 1970s Western estimates of Chinese national income had suffered due to the paucity of official statistics available there. This was partly addressed after 1978 as China improved its statistical reporting alongside the implementation of a programme of market reforms. This market reform programme was initially aimed at subsistence farmers who were permitted to market their surpluses. These reforms were then rapidly extended through the 1980s to the so-called SEZs which supplied cheap labour to foreign multinationals, culminating with the subordination of the state industrial sector to market prices in the late 1980s. The rapid growth of the market sector seemed to provide Western analysts with a straightforward application of their theory. In this instance the introduction of the market did lead to a rapid increase in output. By the end of the first decade of the twenty-first century, China was the second-largest capitalist economy in the world. But even here, by aggregating the output of capitalist and non-capitalist sectors, Western statisticians underestimated the growth of China's distinctively capitalist production and real national income.

By disaggregating the output of the centrally planned and market economies, it is possible to estimate the growth of distinctively market production and real national income during the transition to capitalism. The EBRD published estimates of the proportion of total output produced for the market during the early transition period in CEE and the CIS. In China, official statistics reported by the OECD show the growth of market production in the producer, service and agricultural sectors. By deflating aggregate figures by the proportion of market production, a much closer approximation to the real growth of national income in the transition economies can be estimated. This can be illustrated through the proportion of physical outputs produced for the market and through national income estimates. This study uses the production of electricity, a vital indicator of production across the economy; aluminium, a basic manufactured material requiring extensive infrastructure; hydraulic cement, a key input in construction; steel, a key input in construction and manufacturing; and automobiles, an advanced manufacturing product requiring high levels of technological development, to indicate the growth in the proportion of world capitalist production produced in the transition economies. It proves two things: first, that capitalist production, and therefore value production, increased significantly even in the CIS and CEE and secondly, that the growth of output in the transition economies has been offset by the decline in industrial output of the older Western G7. It deflates GDP (PPP), measured using the Geary Khamis purchasing power parity method developed by the GGDC, to show how the growth of physical capitalist production is mirrored in national income statistics.

Stephen Rosefielde was a former Bergsonian who, after the collapse of central planning, questioned key aspects of Bergson's AFC. He pointed out that this AFC was an ideal quantum with no existence in the planned economy. How could planners respond to the AFC if it did not exist? How could "planners' preference", the claimed alternative to market price, shape planning decisions when it was an unknown unknowable. Rosefielde provided mathematical proof that, if it was necessary, it could not. He added that because Soviet output could not be sold at any price during the transition, it must have been useless. If it was useless, so it must be valueless. If it was valueless, then measures of Soviet national income – a measure of value – must have been overestimated. The entire notion that the central plan developed the economy, even during the peak periods of advance such as the mid-1930s, was false. Conversely, Mark Harrison asserted that the Soviet planners did indeed develop the productive resources, that the growth in output was real. As it was real, so it was useful, if it was useful so it had a value. Each side shows the weakness of the other. The Soviet economy was a planned not a market economy. It produced nothing for sale and so nothing was sold. As price is a measure of sale, if nothing was sold, so nothing had a price. If nothing had a price, then prices did not exist, if prices did not exist, then they cannot be a measure. The production of the central plan was real, but of use values, not exchange values. The marginalist elision of use value and exchange value ends up chasing its own tail.

Globalisation aptly describes the creation of a global world market in the 1990s. The transition of the centrally planned economies to capitalism extended the rule of capital across the whole world for the first time since the Bolshevik Revolution of 1917. The transition of the centrally planned economies to the capitalist market economy meant that total capitalist production of these outputs has rapidly increased but that those originating in the transition economies have increased proportionately faster.

Profit rates can be restored, with the conditions for a new long cycle established, either through the destruction of capital accumulated during economic crises or wars or through the expansion of the proportion of living labour relative to accumulated capital by the extension of the world market. Globalisation fulfilled both conditions. The transition economies had little or no capital accumulated. They were not societies predicated on capital accumulation, but had a large, highly skilled workforce with very low wages. The growth of China meant that the one-off increase in the world labour force from capitalist restoration was supplemented by a rapid increase in urbanisation as small farmers became wage labourers. This enabled Western capitalists to consolidate the defeat of their domestic labour movements, which was launched in the 1970s–1980s neo-liberal offensive,

Table 6.1 The increase in capitalist production, decade averages

Output	Transition capitalist as a % of world capitalist, 2000	Transition capitalist as a % of world capitalist, 2010	Increase in world capitalist production as a %, 1990–99	Increase in world capitalist production as a %, 1999–2010
Electricity	16	29	45	52
Aluminium	24	52	49	86
Hydraulic cement	39	65	60	122
Steel	24	53	39	53
Automobiles	6	30	16	39
GDP PPP GK	12	26	42	61

Sources: BP (2012), GGDC (2012), OICA (1990–2011), USGS (2012), and WSA (1989–2012).

allowing the physical relocation of manufacturing production to the transition economies and particularly China. This lowered the world organic composition of capital and restored profit rates. These high profit rates were concentrated in the multinational corporations and made them less dependent on the banking system for the financing of their expanded reproduction. The banks loss of their major big business borrowers, forced them to concentrate on the retail market, mortgages, loans and credit cards. The glut of finance capital and low interest rates encouraged investment bank speculation resulting in the credit crunch of 2007–08.

Studenski observed that the practical consequence of the application of neoclassical theory to measurements of market output was logical incoherence, confusion and failure, how much more so when applied to the central plan? A subjective value theory unable even to explain the value of money, how can it explain the significance of the market boundary, when it denies it is significant? Bergson's AFC confused and obscured the distinction between central planning and market economies, such that it comprehensively failed its greatest test – the measurement of a real market economy when real markets were created with the transition of the plan to capitalism. Possibly the largest-ever one-off increase in the size of the world market and national income, was measured as its stagnation and decline. This embarrassing failure proves the limits of a *hypothetical-deductive* method that separates economics from the real world it purports to describe. Immune to empirical verification it sails off into the sunset, more real than reality, even truer than truth.

Measuring National Income shows that in the debate around the application of value measures to non-market economies, the argument made in that without the empirical fact of market exchange, then such applications have some comparative worth, but are not, and can never be, an actual measure of the real "value" or national income produced in economies which did not produce value or national income. It resolves the issue around the truth or otherwise of Soviet statistics, by pointing out that they were both true and not true: true, more or less, as a measure of physical output but not true as a measure of market output without a market. As is shown in Table 6.1, by 2001 when the process of capitalist restoration was complete, the transition economies accounted for 37% of world capitalist employ-ment, 31% of its aluminium, 44% of hydraulic cement, 24% of steel, 16% of electricity, 8.5% of cars and passenger vehicles and 17% of GDP (GK PPP). Far from the 1990s being a decade of capitalist stagnation, world capitalist aluminium production increased to 60.3%, hydraulic cement to 96%, steel to 56%, electricity to 61%, automobiles to 27% and GDP (GK PPP) to 52%. Following this one-off addition, growth in the world capitalist economy accelerated markedly over the next decade, before opening a new phase following the credit crunch of 2008, because the contradictions that shaped its advance during the period of globalisa-tion now anticipate its end.

References

Aslund, A., 2001. *The Myth of Output Collapse after Communism*. Carnegie Working Papers 18. Washington, DC: Carnegie.

Bergson, A., 1944. *The Structure of Soviet Wages: A Study in Socialist Economics*. Cam-bridge, MA: Harvard University Press.

Bergson, A., 1953. *Soviet National Income and Product in 1937*. Westport, CT: Greenwood Press.

Bergson, A., 1964. *The Economics of Soviet Planning*. New Haven, CT: Yale University Press.

BP, 2012. *BP Statistical Review of World Energy 2012*. London: BP. Available at: www.bp.com/assets/bp_internet/globalbp/globalbp_uk_english/reports_and_publications/statistical_energy_review_2011/STAGING/local_assets/pdf/statistical_review_of_world_energy_full_report_2012.pdf [Accessed April 1, 2012].

Clark, C., 1939. *A Critique of Russian Statistics*. London: R. & R. Clark.

Davies, R. et al., 1985. *Materials for a Balance of the Soviet National Ecomony 1928–30*, S.G. Wheatcroft & R.W. Davies, eds. Cambridge: Cambridge University Press.

Gerschenkron, A., 1951. *A Dollar Index of Soviet Machinery Output, 1927–28 to 1937*. Santa Monica, CA: RAND Corporation.

GGDC, 2012. *The Total Economy Database*. Available at: www.conference-board.org/retrievefile.cfm?filename=TEDI_Jan20121.xls&type=subsite [accessed May 1, 2012].

Grossman, G., 1960. *Soviet Statistics of Physical Output of Industrial Commodities*. Princeton, NJ: Princeton University Press.

Jasny, N., 1960. *Soviet Industrialization 1928–1952*. Chicago: University of Chicago Press.

Lapidus, I., & Ostrovitianov, K., 1929. *An Outline of Political Economy*. London: Martin Lawrence.

Marer, P., 1985. *Dollar GNPs of the U.S.S.R. and Eastern Europe First*, Baltimore and London: John Hopkins University Press.

Nutter, G.W., 1962. *Growth of Industrial Production in the Soviet Union*. Princeton, NJ: Princeton University Press.

Spulber, N. 1965. *Foundations of Soviet Strategy for Economic Growth: Selected Soviet Essays, 1924–1930*. Bloomington: Indiana University Press.

Trotsky, L., 1936. *The Revolution Betrayed*. New York: Dover.

WSA, 1989–2012. *Annual Crude Steel Production Archive*. Brussels: WSA. Available at: www.worldsteel.org/statistics/statistics-archive/annual-steel-archive.html [Accessed Feb-ruary 1, 2012].

Wyler, J., 1946. The National Income of Soviet Russia: A Statistical Puzzle. *Social Research*, 13, pp. 502–18.

Bibliography

Aslund, A., 2001. *The Myth of Output Collapse after Communism*. Carnegie Working Papers 18. Washington, DC: Carnegie Endowment for International Peace.

Bergson, A., 1944. *The Structure of Soviet Wages: A Study in Socialist Economics*. Cambridge, MA: Harvard University Press.

Bergson, A., 1953. *Soviet National Income and Product in 1937*. Columbia, NY: Greenwood Press.

Bergson, A., 1964. *The Economics of Soviet Planning*. New Haven, CT: Yale University Press.

Clark, C., 1939. *A Critique of Russian Statistics*. London: R. & R. Clark, Ltd.

Davies, R., et al., 1985. *Materials for a Balance of the Soviet National Economy 1928–30*, S.G. Wheatcroft & R.W. Davies, eds. Cambridge: Cambridge University Press.

Engerman, D.C., 2009. *The Rise and Fall of America's Soviet Experts*. Oxford: Oxford University Press.

Gerschenkron, A., 1951. *A Dollar Index of Soviet Machinery Output, 1927–28 to 1937*. Santa Monica, CA: RAND Corporation.

GGDC, 2012b. *The Total Economy Database*. Groningen Growth and Development Centre. Available at: www.conference-board.org/retrievefile.cfm?filename=TEDI_Jan20121.xls&type=subsite.

Grossman, G., 1960. *Soviet Statistics of Physical Output of Industrial Commodities*. Princeton, NJ: Princeton University Press.

Jasny, N., 1960. *Soviet Industrialization 1928–1952*. Chicago: University of Chicago Press.

Lapidus, I., & Ostrovitianov, K., 1929. *An Outline of Political Economy*. London: Martin Lawrence.

Nutter, G.W., 1962. *Growth of Industrial Production in the Soviet Union*. Princeton, NJ: Princeton University Press.

Spulber, N., 1965. *Foundations of Soviet Strategy for Economic Growth: Selected Soviet Essays, 1924–1930*. Bloomington: Indiana University Press.

Trotsky, L., 1936. *The Revolution Betrayed*. New York: Dover.

Wyler, J., 1946. The National Income of Soviet Russia: A Statistical Puzzle. *Social Research*, 13, pp. 502–18.

Bibliography

Index